1.95p

Fascism in Western Europe 1900–45

Titles in the General Studies Series

fascism

IN WESTERN EUROPE 1900-45

H. R. Kedward B.Phil., M.A.

Lecturer in History at the University of Sussex

Blackie

GLASGOW & LONDON

BLACKIE & SON LIMITED
Bishopbriggs · Glasgow
5 Fitzhardinge Street · London W1H 0DL

Printed in Great Britain by
Butler & Tanner Limited, Frome and London

Foreword

In his brilliant memoirs[1] the veteran anarchist and
socialist, Victor Serge, described pre-1914 Europe as a world
without escape. 'Even before I emerged from childhood', he
wrote, 'I seem to have experienced deeply at heart that
paradoxical feeling which was to dominate me all through the
first part of my life: that of living in a world without any
possible escape, in which there was nothing for it but to fight
for an impossible escape. I felt repugnance, mingled with wrath
and indignation, towards people whom I saw settled comfortably
in this world. How could they not be conscious of their
captivity . . . ?'

Something of the same fury and contempt towards the old
Europe motivated the leaders of fascism. Unlike Victor Serge,
they were drawn by their actions into new systems which
rivalled or surpassed the old in their rigidity and dogmatism,
but in their ideals they believed they had found an escape. Their
signs and symbols, their military formations, their promises and
obsessions were paraded before the credulous eyes of Europe as
a modern cult of salvation. The fervour of its propaganda and
the prophetic role of the leader made fascism one of the most
powerful movements in history. Before it plunged into self-
destruction, it raised hypnotic illusions of a new civilization,
illusions which millions found to be personally acceptable.

The aim of this book is to relate and analyse this wide and
dynamic appeal. At the outset I wish to emphasize the caution
of my approach and interpretation. The material presented here
comes from a wealth of pioneer studies, and yet the history of
fascism is still in its infancy. In many respects the documentation
is inadequate; personalities and motives are obscure and certain
major events remain impenetrable. I would also like to stress the
need for curiosity without the obstruction of pre-formed, or

[1] V. Serge, *Memoirs of a Revolutionary 1901-41*, ed. and trans. P. Sedgwick
(O.U.P., 1963).

unbending, patterns of thought. Fascism was, and remains, a profoundly divisive phenomenon: the very usage of the term in a generic sense has itself provoked rigorous academic argument. It is my intention to suggest that this and many other problems connected with fascism are by no means fully resolved, and that, within this open area of controversy, questions can be as stimulating and productive as answers.

Throughout the preparation and writing I have been grateful for the ideas and criticisms of my colleagues at Sussex and elsewhere, some of whom would wish to be firmly dissociated from my approach. For the typing and generous oversight of the manuscript I wish to thank Mrs. Pat Kirkpatrick, while to my wife and to Anthony Copley, friend and fellow historian, I owe much of my interest in, and concern for, the psychology of human behaviour. Finally, I must thank so many eminent scholars to whose research and conclusions this book is so obviously indebted.

H. R. K.
UNIVERSITY OF SUSSEX
1969

Contents

Acknowledgments

The author and publishers are grateful to the following
for permission to include in this book copyright material
as detailed below:

BOOKS

Lawrence and Wishart Ltd., for the extracts from *Art and Social
Life* by G. V. Plekhanov, translated by E. Fox.

The New American Library Inc., for the extracts from *Notes from
Underground* by F. Dostoevsky, translated by A. R. MacAndrew.

Penguin Books Ltd., for the extract from *Rimbaud* edited by
O. Bernard; and for the extract from *Thus Spake Zarathustra*
by F. Nietzsche, translated by R. J. Hollingdale.

D. Van Nostrand Company Ltd., for the extracts from
Nationalism: Its Meaning and History by H. Kohn.

Oxford University Press, for the extracts from *The Speeches of
Adolf Hitler* translated by N. H. Baynes.

Sir Oswald Mosley, for the extracts from *The Greater Britain*
and *Fascism, 100 Questions Asked and Answered* by Sir Oswald
Mosley.

Weidenfeld and Nicolson, for the extracts from *The Poet as
Superman. D'Annunzio* by Anthony Rhodes; and for the extracts
from *Three Faces of Fascism* by Ernst Nolte.

The University of Michigan Press, for the extracts from *Italy:
A Modern History* by Denis Mack Smith. Copyright © 1959 by
The University of Michigan.

Hurst and Blackett Ltd., for the extracts from *Mein Kampf* by Adolf Hitler.

Eyre and Spottiswoode (Publishers) Ltd. and E. P. S. Lewin, for the extract from *Hitler—The Missing Years* by Ernst 'Putzi' Hanfstaengel; Eyre and Spottiswoode (Publishers) Ltd. and Quadrangle Books Inc., for the extracts from *The Nazi Seizure of Power* by William Sheridan Allen, copyright © 1965 by William Sheridan Allen.

Martin Secker and Warburg Ltd. and Miss Sonia Brownell, for the extracts from *The Road to Wigan Pier* by George Orwell; Martin Secker and Warburg Ltd. and G. P. Putnam's Sons, New York, for the extract from *The Civil War in Spain* edited by R. Payne.

Barrie and Rockliff, for the extract from *The Fascists in Britain* by Colin Cross.

Stanford University Press, for the extracts from *Falange* by S. G. Payne.

Faber and Faber Ltd., for the extract from the poem 'Autumn Journal' by Louis MacNeice, from *Collected Poems of Louis MacNeice*.

Hodder and Stoughton Ltd., for the extracts from *Failure of a Mission* by Sir Nevile Henderson.

Jonathan Cape Ltd., the Executors of the John Cornford Estate, and Pat Sloan as editor, for the extract from the poem 'Full Moon at Tierz: Before the Storming of Huesca' from *John Cornford: A Memoir* edited by Pat Sloan.

The Controller of Her Majesty's Stationery Office, for the extracts from *Hansard*.

Macmillan and Company Ltd., for the extract from *All Souls and Appeasement* by A. L. Rowse; and for the extract from *Life of Neville Chamberlain* by Keith Feiling.

The Hamlyn Publishing Group, for the extract from *Hitler: A Study in Tyranny* by Alan Bullock.

The Observer, for the extract from a review by A. J. P. Taylor.

William Heinemann Ltd. and Peter Drucker, for the extract from *The End of Economic Man* by Peter Drucker.

Oxford University Press, New York, for the extract from *The Burden of Guilt* by Hannah Vogt, translated by H. Strauss.

Arthur Barker Ltd., for the extracts from *Sawdust Caesar* by George Seldes.

PHOTOGRAPHS

Radio Times Hulton Picture Library: pages 28, 29 (*top*), 41, 47, 54, 66, 89, 90, 139, 146, 183, 187, 223.

Keystone Press Agency Ltd.: pages 29 (*bottom*), 56, 60, 118, 159, 179, 186 (*both photographs*), 189, 204, 205.

Bilderdienst Süddeutscher Verlag: page 49.

Thomson Organization Picture Service (Topix): pages 67, 126.

The Wiener Library: pages 69, 170.

The Associated Press Ltd.: pages 82, 98, 124, 198, 231.

Joseph Wulf: pages 234, 235.

The Nature of Fascism

CHAPTER ONE

Introduction

On 10 June 1944 the small French town of Oradour-sur-Glane entered the history of Nazi atrocities. The German Army's 2nd S.S. division, *Das Reich*, was moving from the south-west of France to strengthen the Normandy defences against the invading Allies, and by the time it reached Oradour it had suffered heavy losses due to attacks by the French Resistance. Its morale was low and the certainty of further losses as it moved through France heightened its aggression. The killing of hostages in occupied France had been common for over two years and prisoners taken by either side in the guerrilla warfare were normally shot.

The small town of Oradour, situated in cornfields and hitherto isolated from the events of the war, had no arms store and no centre for Resistance activities. It was a slow-moving peasant and shop-keeper community. On Saturday, 10 June, the town was busier than usual due to a medical visit to the school, for which children from the whole neighbourhood were present, and a distribution of tobacco—an event of importance in wartime France. The cafés, the shops and the houses were full. At 2.15 a convoy of lorries drove into the town square and about two hundred fully-armed S.S. got out and went from house to house, forcing the inhabitants into the street and into the central square under the pretext of examining their papers. The soldiers moved quickly and brutally. The organization was thorough: the houses were completely searched. The schools were not forgotten and the children were marched to the same square 'in the interests of their own security'. Some children were promised sweets if they would come without trouble. One child alone slipped through the garden and escaped. Out in the fields the workers were rounded up or shot if they tried to run.

By 2.45 the square was full and the men were separated from the women and children. A demand was made to the acting mayor for thirty hostages. He replied that it was impossible; he could only offer himself and his family. At 3 o'clock the women and children were taken to the church, women fainting and children crying, while the men tried to call out to them. The pretext given for the operation was: 'There is a depot of arms here: while the search is proceeding all men will stay in the agricultural barns.' They were divided into groups, taken to different points of the village and imprisoned in large barns. About ten minutes later an explosion in the centre of the village seemed to be a signal. The soldiers in each barn machine-gunned their prisoners. One man who eventually escaped said later:

> *The first who were killed fell on the others and protected them for a few moments. I fell on my face and covered my head. The wounded cried, others called for their wives and children. Then the firing stopped. There was a long silence before our murderers came back with hay, wood and faggots, and covered the bodies. They then set fire to the pile, which caught rapidly and burnt through the dead and wounded.*

Another wrote:

> *After the shooting the Germans set the bodies on fire. The flames leapt up, licked round me and burnt my hair. I buried myself in the bodies to avoid the burning but my shoulder caught fire. I managed to stand up and reach the door. It was locked and I stumbled to the back of the barn. Five of us were there and we could see how others were burning alive . . .*

Only five men escaped from the barns.

In the church the women and children were massacred in the same way. Victims hurled themselves against the walls in attempts to escape. One woman alone survived. Afterwards she described her escape:

> *A fusillade of shots rang out in the church, then straw, faggots and chairs were thrown on the bodies which sprawled across the flagstones. Having escaped being killed by the*

shooting, I slipped behind the altar, taking advantage of the smoke. There were three windows with the glass broken. I don't know how, but I pushed myself up to one and leapt through, jumping about nine feet. Looking back I saw that I had been followed by a woman who handed her baby to me. The Germans, hearing the crying of the child, machine-gunned us. The woman and her baby were killed. I was injured but managed to reach a nearby garden where I hid in extreme pain until found by friends the next day.[1]

The ashes of the bodies in the church and barns were found later. Over six hundred villagers were killed. The town had been sacked after the massacre and the S.S. division had entered a neighbouring village laughing hysterically and behaving in an uncontrollable state of manic tension.

This atrocity presents in miniature the animal bestiality which destroyed six million Jews and thousands of other enemies of Nazism. More widely it illustrates a contempt for the individual and a love of violence which was common to all movements of fascism. What can the historian do in the face of such barbaric events? He will find himself irresistibly drawn towards moral condemnation. Even an historian of the post-war generation will want to respect the sufferings of so many millions. He may in fact feel more outraged than older historians and wish to dwell on Fascist horrors which he never experienced. He will certainly find it impossible to remain totally neutral.

Nevertheless, however indignant and angry he may be, the historian must fight to preserve his objectivity. His aim is to understand and explain, to describe and recount, and this aim persists even when the subject matter provokes so much emotion. But what does 'understanding fascism' mean? It means treating the phenomenon of fascism in the round, approaching it from a wide variety of angles and examining it seriously as a cultural as well as a political movement. In the end the story of Oradour-sur-Glane may appear as typical of fascism, but it should not be allowed to exclude other typical characteristics which are less well known and less dramatic. Fascists can no longer all be dismissed

---

[1] These eye-witness accounts of the Oradour massacre were translated from G. Pauchou and P. Masfrand, *Oradour-sur-Glane* (Charles-Lavauzelle, 1945), *passim.*

as psychopaths or the scum of society, and fascism cannot merely be seen as an appeal to man's animal nature. The history of fascism must be interlocked with the whole history of modern Europe—not treated on one side as an ulcerous growth or a temporary nightmare. Fascism is as much an organic part of modern Europe as liberalism or communism. It is also as complex and varied. 'We play the lyre,' said Mussolini, 'on all its strings: from violence to religion, from art to politics.'

This complexity will be one of the themes of this book and it will become evident as the different Fascist movements are described. The tempting conclusion may well be that there is no such thing as fascism, only a number of groups and parties which showed similar characteristics but were really quite distinct. There would certainly be some truth in this view, but it would tend to ignore the conviction of most Fascists that they were part of a general movement designed to change not merely their own nation but the whole of society. All the movements described in this study as Fascist were influenced by each other. Hitler retained a lasting admiration for Mussolini and he himself was a powerful influence on the lesser Fascists of the 1930s; they in their turn provided stimulus and admiration for each other. In 1936 Léon Degrelle, the Belgian leader of the Fascist movement *Rex*, said: 'There is only one man in the French Parliament who really knows the people and he is Doriot.' In the same year Jacques Doriot formed his own Fascist movement in France.

This basic pattern of interaction and co-operation makes it possible to talk guardedly about Western European fascism. There was no annual international congress of Fascists, but most Fascists had visions of a new Fascist order which they were preparing for Europe. These visions fell apart or were rudely shattered during World War II when Hitler's driving monomania swept even the dreams of fascism before it, but in origin the hopes and aims of the various movements had much in common. The nature of Western European fascism lies in this common character; and just as it looked to a Europe of the future, so its roots must be sought in the Europe of the past, deep in the 19th century and beyond.

CHAPTER TWO

A Synthesis of Ideas

Throughout history there are examples of powerful systems or régimes based on a synthesis of opposites. Napoleon I was able to merge the *ancien régime* and the Revolution and his rule was more powerful than that of either Louis XVI or Robespierre; the Church of England in the 16th century became a powerful synthesis of Catholic tradition and Protestant revolt; the modern welfare state has grown on a combination of two apparent opposites, freedom and control; the régime of Stalin brought together ancient Russian autocracy and revolutionary communism. In both origin and rule fascism follows this pattern. Its power rested on one of the most intricate syntheses of modern history.

Synthesis is not a mere addition of two or more units, nor is it a middle course or a compromise between them. Friedrich Hegel and Karl Marx, whose theories on history established the idea of synthesis firmly in the modern mind, both emphasized that it is the merging of several contradictory elements into a new and unique whole. Fascism had just this character. It took ideas, methods and attitudes from conflicting sides and presented the world with a unity so full of contradictions that an early collapse was widely expected. In these very contradictions, however, lay its strength.

The origin of its ideas must therefore be sought on both sides of 19th-century conflicts. There is no simple, direct ancestry of ideas which can be labelled 'potentially Fascist', nor was its background purely political. Its ideas contained elements taken and twisted from philosophy, art, psychology and religion, as well as a wide range of politics. In the following sections, therefore, the conflicts described will often be illustrated from spheres of thought which were detached from political history. It is in this way that the full ideological appeal of fascism can best be displayed.

There is one great danger in this approach. It would be easy to confuse fascism with this whole world of energetic and vigorous ideas from which it grew. For decades the philosophy of Nietzsche was abused in this way. The Nazis used him only by the most unscrupulous selection of extracts, but one still hears reference to 'Nietzsche, the father of Nazism'. It is essential to see that the ferment of ideas presented here was the basis not only for fascism but also for modern art and music, modern science and technology, the growth of psychology and a new theology. Fascist ideology was one particular synthesis made up of ideas which had a variety of influence. When it is analysed and broken down into its component parts it is found to contain much that in a different setting would be exciting and acceptable. For this reason the label 'Fascist' must be carefully used and 'potential Fascist' not at all, for may not a 'potential Fascist' turn his violence into art, his rhetoric into the pulpit or his wish to control people into advertising? Fascism is full of ideas but it is the synthesis which gives it its character. The following sections first describe the background of conflicting ideas and then hint at the synthesis. The full nature of the latter will emerge in other chapters.

1 SOCIALISM AND CAPITALISM

This conflict is perhaps the most familiar one. Much of it still continues and the arguments for both theories are well known. It needs to be mentioned first, because Fascists were generally more aware of this conflict than any others. In the early 20th century the two giant systems of thought, socialism and capitalism, were disputing for control of industrialized Europe. On the one hand, capitalism had the advantage of being the prevailing system, controlling the politics, economics and social values of all western countries. At best, its ideals were those of an efficient, productive and contented society in which all men

would achieve happiness in their own particular way according
to their ability and their place in the social structure. At worst, it
allowed unscrupulous exploitation of the poor and under-
privileged by the rich and powerful. In most countries this worst
side of capitalism was beginning to be balanced by growing social
services. Bismarck's Germany had begun to give concessions to
the workers in the form of insurance and unemployment benefits.
This was followed by France and Britain and eventually Italy. In
addition, the growing strength of trade unions was beginning to
give the worker a bargaining force against his employer. In
general, however, power and privilege were still monopolized by
the traditional ruling classes. Money was all-important, closely
followed by the prestige of rank and birth. Education was
opening the channels of success, but as yet the mass of the
working proletariat was barely affected. The capitalist system had
brought a civilization which was the wealthiest and most
advanced that the world had ever known. To those who were
its leaders and rulers any attempt to change it seemed madness
or treason. Capitalism was convinced of its own value, a value
which, it believed, would become obvious to everyone, even its
most bitter opponents.

Socialism on the other hand was equally convinced that the
capitalist system was in decline and would eventually collapse.
Furthermore, because all Socialists saw capitalism as both unjust
and immoral, this collapse had to be accelerated by undermining
the system. Socialism was therefore linked with revolution or, at
the very least, with radical change. The values which it opposed
to capitalism were mainly those derived from a long revolutionary
tradition: justice, equality, the rights of all men, fair distribution
of wealth and privilege, and an end to all oppression. To these
had been added the ideals and theories of Marxism. Marx and
Engels were responsible for putting revolutionary hopes on a
scientific basis. Other Socialists had inspired followers with
utopian dreams of a new world: Marxism gave them historical
certainty. The system of capitalism, it was held, would become so
unbearable for more and more people that a revolution would be
inevitable. The result would be the victory of the proletariat and
the emergence of a classless society in which the guiding principle
would be 'From each according to his ability, to each according

to his needs'. Marxism forecast this future with such strength of
political and economic argument that Marxists adhered to it with
a conviction bordering on religious belief. At the beginning of
the 20th century, however, a revisionist movement developed
within socialism, pointing out that Marx had exaggerated the
position and that the workers would do better to forget revolution and concentrate on gaining reforms one by one. This
revision of Marxism is equivalent on the Socialist side to the
welfare concessions made by capitalism on the other. But despite
this gradual closing of the gap, the conflict was as intense as ever.
It finally became the dominant issue in politics as Socialist parties
everywhere began to win seats in the national parliaments.
Particularly in Germany, where, by 1910, their success was
considerable, Socialists appeared to threaten the entire achievements of capitalism. By 1914 the history of Europe appeared
poised between the two systems.

The war acted as a diversion from this conflict. Despite the
internationalism of Socialist theory, which had emphasized class
solidarity rather than national interests, the Socialist parties of
Germany, France and Britain contributed to the national war
effort. In Italy the party remained more true to its theory and as
a result lost those of its members who were excited by the war
and who wished to follow the national fortunes of their country.
Among these was Mussolini.

For two to three years the war occupied the centre of the
stage, but by the end of 1916 disillusionment was widespread
and Socialist ideals began to re-emerge. When, in 1917, the
Russian Socialists under Lenin and Trotsky carried through their
successful revolution, the old conflict regained its importance.
The end of international war in 1918 left the field clear for the
warfare of classes. Socialism and capitalism confronted each
other, with the shadow of the Russian Revolution encouraging
one and terrifying the other.

But the future presented another alternative. In the years that
followed the war, it became apparent that the conflicting systems
had not enlisted the support of the entire public. Thinkers and
politicians who were looking for a 'Third Way' between or
beyond socialism and capitalism, found their ideas widely
received. Fascism was born. Large numbers of all classes who

felt excluded or threatened by the two dominating systems saw in this new ideology a decisive answer to the conflict which promised to engulf Europe in social chaos and ruin. Fascist leaders varied considerably in the presentation of their ideas, but they mostly exploited this middle position in which they found themselves. Adopting elements from Socialist theory and practice, they yet contrived to attract the strongest supporters of capitalism. Fascist theory and power were built on this dual nature. In the details which come later it will be seen that some fascisms were more Socialist or more capitalist than others. What they had in common was their claim to resolve a great European conflict in terms which were attractive to both sides but which were uniquely their own.

2 RATIONALISM AND IRRATIONALISM

The belief that man was a rational being, capable of discovering his own interests and following them for the good of himself and society, was the dominant philosophy of industrialized Europe. This was the triumphant philosophy of the Enlightenment, and every step in the development of science and technology seemed to prove that order and reason were indeed natural to man's history. Steeped in this confidence were thinkers like the Utilitarian Jeremy Bentham in England and the Positivist Auguste Comte in France. Comte sums up their optimism with his emphatic statement that there is 'an unvarying advance in human development'. He, like Bentham, represented the interests of the middle or upper classes, whose wealth and power were rooted in the industrial progress of the time and for whom civil order was vital if this progress were to be maintained. Their confidence in man's rationality would seem to be a part of their own social stability. But rationalism was not the god of the ruling classes alone. The early Socialists of the century were just as influenced by the Enlightenment and although they called for change and revolution they did so in the name of rational progress. Karl Marx shares with many of his bourgeois opponents the belief in man's good sense and intelligence. Like them he talked of the evolution of history towards a more perfect society The disagreements came over the nature of that society: and such discord was fundamental. Nevertheless, the traditional view of the 19th century as one in which progress and reason were the main values of society can be accepted.

The result was a uniformity and orthodoxy which was true for both bourgeois and Socialist. Bourgeois ideals of art and manners, of social and political customs and economic behaviour were rigid and self-assured. Socialist ideals appeared more flexible and colourful because socialism was geared to revolution, but the average Marxist was as dogmatic and confident about his values as the typical bourgeois. G. V. Plekhanov, one of the great Marxian theorists of the late 19th century, wrote a tough and unyielding study of art called *Art and Social Life*. Attitudes to art have always been a revealing reflection of a thinker's general philosophy and Plekhanov, in demanding that art serve society, showed clearly his central dogma. He quoted with approval the judgment of the Russian intellectual Chernyshevski: 'All human activities should serve a useful purpose for man if they are not to be empty, frivolous occupations . . . Art must serve some essential purpose and not be an idle amusement.' This was his theme and his conclusion was in the same vein: 'He who is blind to the lessons of social life . . . will not find anything new, search as he may, except new rubbish.' [1] The 19th century was full of such self-confidence. Whether the subject was sex or religion, politics or art, the temptation to believe that one's ideas were eternally valid, buttressed by the strength of reason, was immense. Hegel's Introduction to his *Philosophy of History* (1832) is a clear summary of this whole attitude. In it he affirms:

> . . . *Reason is the Sovereign of the world . . . the history of the world, therefore, presents us with a rational process . . . this Reason is the* True, *the* Eternal, *the absolutely* powerful *essence . . . it reveals itself in the world and in that world nothing else is revealed but this and its honour and glory.* [2]

The attack on this fortress of reason had first been mounted by many of the Romantic writers and artists who stressed the

---

[1] G. V. Plekhanov, *Art and Social Life*, trans. E. Fox (Lawrence and Wishart, 1953), pp. 166, 218.

[2] G. W. F. Hegel, *Philosophy of History*, trans. J. Sibree (Dover, New York, 1956), p. 9.

unpredictability of the individual. The Romantic interest in self-expression later became, in the course of the century, a preoccupation with the irrational. There never was a school or movement of irrationalism, but certain individuals in all countries found the complacency of reason an obstacle to artistic and individual development. They reacted vigorously against it. At times the impact was only slight. For example, Théophile Gautier, the French poet, rejected the ideas, later repeated by Plekhanov, about the social value of art:

> No, you idiots, no, you cretins, you can't make soup out of a book or a pair of boots out of a novel . . . I swear by the guts of all past, present and future Popes—no, a thousand times no! I am one of those who consider the superfluous essential: my love for things and people is in inverse proportion to their utility.[1]

It was a colourful reaction and he and his colleagues defended art for art's sake with a show of social eccentricity. Gautier himself led a small alligator on a string round the streets, but the ripples of his revolt barely spread beyond artistic circles.

Far more significant was the attack by the Russian novelist, Fyodor Dostoevsky. His *Notes from Underground* (1864) begins with a shattering confession of irrationalism by the central character:

> I'm a sick man . . . a mean man. There's nothing attractive about me. I think there's something wrong with my liver. But actually I don't understand a damn thing about my sickness: I'm not even too sure what it is that's ailing me. I'm not under treatment and never have been, although I have great respect for medicine and doctors. Moreover, I'm morbidly superstitious—enough, at least, to respect medicine. With my education I shouldn't be superstitious but I am just the same. No, I'd say I refuse medical help simply out of contrariness. I don't expect you to understand that but it's so. Of course I can't explain whom I'm trying to fool this way. I'm fully aware that I can't spite the doctors by refusing their help. I know very well that I'm harming myself and

[1] Quoted in G. V. Plekhanov, *Art and Social Life*, trans. E. Fox (Lawrence and Wishart, 1953), p. 172.

*no one else. But still it's out of spite that I refuse to ask for
the doctor's help. So my liver hurts? Good, let it hurt even
more.*[1]

This man lives an underground life, alien to the ordinary world
which he finds stupid and shallow. He refuses to surrender his
total freedom of thought and constantly injures himself to prove
he is unpredictable. When he ventures into the streets he looks
for conflict and argument; he seeks friendship then immediately
abuses it. He first pities then insults a prostitute and when she
comes to his house he drives her away even though he had
needed and wanted her love. Irrationalism is at the centre of this
man's character: he will neither be a piano key nor a number;
he stands for individuality against any system. In this book
Dostoevsky anticipated many of the discoveries of modern
psychology: people are indeed capable of living like the underground man, acting against their own interests and denying the
ideas of progress and rationalism on which so much 19th-century
thought was based. This understanding made Dostoevsky into a
leading spokesman for the alternative view of man and society.
In his own situation it led him to justify religious belief: the
security of religion would enable man to live with his weaknesses.

Contemporary with Dostoevsky was the artistic and moral
revolt of the poets Baudelaire, Verlaine and Rimbaud in France.
Their lives and poetry were a rejection of orthodox morality and
bourgeois society. The individual, they claimed, should follow
his desires since no other guide had ever brought happiness or
peace. They despised the dogmatism and hypocrisy which they
found in the Church; they flouted the sensibilities of the ordinary
man and they experimented with the forms of art. Rimbaud
welcomed the Paris revolution of the Commune in 1871, but he
was no political thinker. His influence was in the realm of art
and individual action. He was prepared to destroy himself as a
poet in an irrational wish to be someone entirely different. At
eighteen he wrote in *A Season in Hell*:

*My day is done. I am leaving Europe. The sea air will scorch
my lungs: lost climates will tan my skin. I shall swim, stamp*

[1] F. Dostoevsky, *Notes from Underground*, trans. A. R. MacAndrew (New
American Library of World Literature, New York, 1961), pp. 90–1.

*down the grass, hunt, above all smoke. I shall drink liquors
as strong as boiling metal—as my dear ancestors did round
their fires.*

*I shall return with limbs of iron, dark skin, a furious eye:
from my mask I shall be judged as belonging to a mighty
race. I shall have gold: I shall be idle and brutal. Women
take care of these ferocious invalids returned from hot
countries. I shall be involved in politics. Saved. At present
I am damned. I loathe the fatherland. The best thing of all
is a good drunken sleep on the beach.*[1]

Succeeding poets and artists looked on Rimbaud as a personal
liberator. He had had the courage and ability to break away from
all conventions. His very destructiveness was something on which
to build.

In the writings of Friedrich Nietzsche one sees the perception
of Dostoevsky and the revolt of the French poets carried into a
complete reassessment of man. Nietzsche was both philosopher
and prophet, poet and psychologist. He had no respect for the
achievements of man and society in the 19th century: he disliked
both the moral values of Christianity and the political values of
capitalism and socialism. In *The Genealogy of Morals* (1887) he
launched an outspoken attack on the state of man in his age:
he saw in him the triumph of jealousy, resentment and rancour.
Modern Christian man, he declared, was a product of a slave
morality: he had risen against the high values of nobility and
creativity and imposed a sickly civilization which denied life and
suppressed all true feelings and emotions.

*The levelling and diminution of European man is our
greatest danger, because the sight of him makes us despond.
We no longer see anything these days which aspires to grow
greater: instead we have a suspicion that things will continue
to go downhill, becoming ever thinner, more placid, smarter,
cosier, more ordinary, more indifferent . . . Without doubt
man is getting 'better' all the time . . . This is Europe's true
predicament: together with the fear of man we have also lost
the love of man, reverence for man, confidence in man,
indeed the will to man . . .*[2]

[1] *Rimbaud*, ed. O. Bernard (Penguin, 1962), pp. 304–5.
[2] F. Nietzsche, *Genealogy of Morals*, trans. F. Golffing (Doubleday, New York,
1956), p. 177.

Nietzsche's answer to this was to say that man must live with
the passion of the Greek god Dionysus, the god of festivity, song,
wine, frenzy and dance; and with the control of the god Apollo,
the symbol of order and self-discipline. Both Dionysian and
Apollonian, the new man would be a superman because he
fulfilled and controlled himself. Nietzsche's superman was no
more political than Rimbaud's artistic revolt had been; he was
to replace the old Christian ideas which Nietzsche believed to
have enslaved man. The superman would liberate the very depths
of passion and feeling and give them strong creative direction. 'I
unmasked Christian morality,' said Nietzsche, and he went on to
proclaim, 'God is Dead.' No longer would man have to look to
an ideal outside himself: he could turn inwards and become a
full, complete person. The will to achieve this fulfilment he called
'the will to power': it was not a sexual or a political drive but a
striving towards the whole personality. Those who reached this
supreme point of creativity would probably be those who had
conquered suffering, for Nietzsche shared a common view of the
artist at the end of the century: 'The artist must be sick to
create.' This was the core of Nietzsche's irrationalism: 'The
sublime,' he said, 'is the artistic conquest of the horrible.' Unless
man faced the sick, the horrible, the violent in his character he
would never be able to overcome himself and turn these passions
to greatness.

The influence of Nietzsche has been inestimable. At the time
he was seen as providing the most outrageous attack on the
values which the 19th century took for granted. Because he went
mad soon after his most prophetic book (*Thus Spake Zarathustra*),
many people discounted his works as lunacy, but among intellectuals and artists Nietzsche set in motion a flood of ideas which
could not be diverted. They became the mainstream of the early
20th century. Between 1880 and 1914, orthodoxy in art,
religion and morality became associated with the past. Experiment in style and freedom of expression dominated the cultural
scene. The breakthrough in art was perhaps the most sensational:
colours and shapes took on not the dimensions of everyday
reality but the form of the artist's imagination. Expressionist
artists used bold, startling colours and distorted lines to convey
their inner feelings. 'Who wishes to be creative', Nietzsche had

said, 'must first destroy and smash accepted values'; and Emil
Nolde, the German Expressionist, wrote of his paintings in a
Dionysian form: 'colours with a life of their own, laughing and
crying, happy and dreamy, burning and holy, like love songs and
eroticism, like melodies and magnificent chorales! Colours that
vibrate like silver and bronze bells, heralding happiness, passion,
love, spirit, blood and death.' Fundamental emotions became
sacred. Edvard Munch, the Norwegian artist, who was both a
neurotic and the painter of neurotic states of mind, wrote: 'I
want to show men who breathe, feel, love and suffer. I want to
bring home to the spectator the sacred elements in these things
so that he takes his hat off just as he would in church.' The
single-minded stress on the human, and the expression of the
human in all its lurid and violent details, overturned the position
of art in society. Despite the fact that Expressionists portrayed
the beautiful as well as the unpleasant, public opinion was
outraged. Man was *not* like this, was the reaction; but the revolt
against rationalism continued, unchecked by this hostility.

It was not all Dionysian. Parallel to Expressionism ran the
Apollonian stream. Painters such as those in the Cubist school,
Picasso, Braque and Gris, concentrated on form rather than
expression. In their paintings, landscape and figures were broken
up and reassembled with new dimensions and the painting itself
became more important than the objects from which it had
started. Soon the objects were unrecognizable and the way to
abstract painting was open. 'The Cubists', said the poet
Apollinaire, 'have raised the question of what is beautiful in
itself.' This was not the art of frenzy: it seemed too calculated to
be irrational, but the public were unable to appreciate its
experimental value. If anything, Cubism was reviled as more
irrational than Expressionism. The logic and pattern of everyday
things had been rejected. 'Rubbish cubed,' said Plekhanov, and he
could not have spoken more accurately for most public opinion.

Combining Expressionism and Cubism, the movement of
Futurism was perhaps the most violent pre-war art group to
shock the public. It began with literary and art manifestoes in
1908–9 and was led by an Italian writer and critic, F. T.
Marinetti. It declared war on all orthodox art and taste. The past
was dead; only the future was important. Art should therefore

seize the things of the future: machines, speed, dynamism, noise and force. The Futurist painter Boccioni said of past art, 'Dante, Beethoven, Michelangelo make us sick', and he endeavoured to represent pure dynamism and movement in his paintings. Carra went even further and claimed to paint sounds, noises and smells. The group of artists in the Futurist school organized public 'entertainments' of their art, with the freely avowed aim of outraging the audience. Glue was put on the seats, several seats of the same number were sold twice to provoke a fight and noted eccentrics were given free entry. Marinetti, a skilful showman, would calmly peel and eat the fruit that was thrown at him. Such actions amused and delighted many other artists who were not of the Futurist school. The breakthrough in art was generally an aggressive one. In forcing the gates of 19th-century order and rationalism, it took on a militant character. When Paul Klee, one of the great innovators in painting, first heard the revolutionary music of Schönberg, he threw out a challenge to conventional society: 'Burst you stuffed shirt, your knell is ringing.'

The irrationalist revolt was endorsed by the philosophy of Henri-Louis Bergson. In the decade before World War I his lectures at the Collège de France in Paris stimulated the search for dynamic, vigorous values which would give life to the spirit as well as the body of man. He found in evolution an impulse of vitality which kept creatures from stagnation or extinction, and he taught that both intelligence and instinct were forms of this impulse. They alone, however, would not enable man to discover his highest reality or the ultimate reality in life. What was needed was intuition. This was Bergson's contribution to irrationalism. Against the god of reason he balanced three faculties—instinct, intelligence and intuition—only one of which was rational. This new balance favoured the aspects of human expression which the modern artists were excitedly exploring. Bergson's influence in this period was almost as great as that of Nietzsche. For those with religious interests like the Russian painter Kandinsky and the French poet Charles Péguy, Bergson was more important. He gave revived hope to religion, for religious belief, freed from the orthodoxy of the 19th century, could appeal to intuition in the same dynamic way as art. It is not a mere coincidence that the

pre-war period saw a resurgence of youthful religion as well as
an explosion of irrational art and politics.

The inclusion of politics in the irrationalist upheaval does not
mean that all dynamic thinkers or artists were dynamic politicians. Most irrationalist art was a repudiation of all politics.
The Expressionist artists in Germany were, in many ways,
anarchic, denying the value of all restrictions and control.
Similarly in Paris the Cubist revolution was carried through in
the non-political, cosmopolitan atmosphere of the Montmartre
studios. But the movement of Futurism was an exception and in
its political statements one can see the potential danger of politics
based on irrationalist fervour. At Trieste in 1909 Marinetti
announced:

> We are as far removed from international and antipatriotic
> socialism . . . that ignoble exaltation of the rights of the belly
> . . . as we are from timid clerical conservatism, symbolized
> by the bedroom slippers and the hot water bottle. We sing of
> war, the only cure for the world . . .[1]

War involved noise, dynamism, destruction and mechanical
movement—all the treasured objects of Futurist art. For
Marinetti World War I was to be grasped as an aesthetic
experience. Boccioni agreed and was killed in the very war he had
welcomed, but Marinetti lived on and became a considerable
influence on Mussolini.

In this way aesthetic irrationalism made its closest historical
link with fascism, a link which will be apparent in the description
of Mussolini's rise to power. Mussolini and his party used many
of the dynamic ideas and methods that Marinetti had proclaimed
and made the same appeal to youth, but this was not the whole
secret of their success. To irrationalism they added a calculated,
rational appeal to the frightened middle classes. They were the
party of both energy and control, violence and order. The
synthesis was Mussolini's greatest achievement and strength.

Thus rationalism and irrationalism were combined into a new
totality. The revolt and anarchism of the irrationalists in the
19th and early 20th centuries was the background to Fascist

[1] Quoted in James Joll, *Intellectuals in Politics* (Weidenfeld and Nicolson,
1960), p. 177.

freedom of expression and uninhibited love of aggression and emotional action. Few of these irrationalists would have recognized their ideas in fascism, for the rationalist side was equally pronounced. Using the rationalist love of order and authority, its self-confidence and dogmatism and its great appeal to the settled classes of society, fascism incorporated into its theory and practice the very attitudes which the irrationalists had rejected.

Mussolini was not the only one to achieve this synthesis. The Nazi movement in Germany showed a similar character. 'Irrational violence' and the 'cult of the superman' were among the many Nazi concepts derived from the revolt against reason, but had there been no more to Nazism than this it would have remained on the fringe of politics, like anarchism in the 19th century. Its rapid and astonishing ascent to power between 1929 and 1933 was due also to its tactical opportunism and shrewd sense of political compromise, 'virtues' which were well known to the rational world of hard politics in the 19th century. Thus the two major variants of fascism contrived both to assault and defend society. The Third Way lay as seductively between rationalism and irrationalism as it did between socialism and capitalism.

3 THE CIVILIZED AND THE PRIMITIVE

The confident society of the 18th century despised the uncivilized past and found little of value between the Roman Empire and the Renaissance. 'The Dark Ages' was a phrase used to describe this period in history—a period held to have been dominated by superstition and ignorance. Equally rejected was the primitive world which had preceded the ancient civilizations of Greece and Rome. Most 18th-century philosophers believed that pre-civilized society was one of warfare and destruction, a state of nature in which anarchy prevailed. Thus there was little interest in uncivilized countries, in native tribes or primitive man. The focus was on 18th-century Europe and the triumph of the Renaissance spirit of reason and inquiry. History seemed firmly directed towards progress and light.

In the 19th century this attitude was strengthened by industrial and scientific development. Technology in particular moved man to admire his own skill and achievements. The invention of the steam engine and the extensive use of iron for ship, rail and bridge building enabled him to dominate distances; canals, constructed with a variety of lifts, locks and inclines, overcame differences of levels; electricity harnessed in power stations by the end of the 1870s produced man-made light, and, finally, the internal combustion engine motorized the roads and the air. Less dramatic but equally important were the invention of the flush lavatory, tools and machines for the mass production of all consumer goods and systems of construction for rapid housing development. In medical science the stethoscope, anaesthetics, vaccination and the X-ray were among the many inventions and discoveries which controlled the natural world of disease. In chemistry, physics and natural science the direction was the same. Civilization was being created and extended wherever 19th-century man cared to look, and, identified with it, whatever anti-clericals and atheists claimed, stood Christianity. When overseas discoveries and exploration began to excite the European countries and the imperialists began to stake their claim to remote parts of the world, it was in the name of civilization and Christianity that they supported their actions. Between 1870 and 1900 it was taken for granted that Europe had a responsibility to convert and enlighten those lands which had not had the fortune to develop with the West. The Age of Empire was the climax of the Idea of Progress. What had been learnt from European history was now to be transmitted to the world at large. Whatever the original motivations of imperialism, this cloak of responsibility and enlightenment was now thrown grandiosely over the whole enterprise.

Alongside this 19th-century worship of the civilized, however, there ran a seemingly contrary interest in the uncivilized, the natural and the primitive. The Romantics again provide a starting point. Sir Walter Scott's novels in Britain, Chateaubriand's emotional Christianity in France, and the writings of Goethe, Novalis and Schlegel in Germany were among the many intellectual influences which made the medieval and folk world the object of investigation and adulation. A pride in nationality was stirred by stories of ancient heroes; folk songs and myths were written down and distributed to inspire national music and poetry, and the roots of language carefully investigated for signs of cultural origins. Passages like this one by the German Romantic, Herder, became the emotional basis of nationalism. It is full of evocative names:

> *We pass now to the family of peoples which more than all others have contributed to the health and woe of this continent—be it by reason of their tallness and bodily strength, their bold, enterprising hardiness and valour, their heroic sense of duty that moved them to march after their chiefs wherever they might lead and to divide conquered countries as spoils of war, or also by reason of their far-flung conquests and the constitution laid down everywhere after the German model. From the Black Sea throughout Europe German arms have spread terror: from the Volga to the Baltic there extended once a Gothic Empire: in Thrace, Moesia, Pannonia, Italy, Gaul, Spain, even in Africa diverse German peoples had their seats and founded Empires at various times.*[1]

Throughout the 19th century, Germans were in the forefront of this romantic nationalism, but they were far from alone. Mazzini, the Italian revolutionary and nationalist, introduced one of his works in a way which echoes Herder:

> *Having proved, by the testimony of our ancient records, and the vestiges of past religions, the absolute independence of our primitive civilization from the Hellenic, the writer will then proceed to trace the origin of our nationality from those Sabellian tribes, dwelling as I have said, round the ancient Amiternus, who along with the Osques, Siculians and Umbrians first assumed the sacred name Italy . . .*[2]

Similar passages could be found extolling the Anglo-Saxons, the Franks, the Magyars and the Slavs. Flamboyant histories of these European peoples provided an outlet for the civilized society of the 19th century. Through the deeds of primitive heroes, through

[1] Quoted in H. Kohn, *Nationalism: Its Meaning and History* (Van Nostrand, 1955), p. 104.
[2] *Ibid.*, p. 119.

their violence and romantic nobility, the urbanized, industrialized West could live vicariously: if actual heroism were impossible the next best thing was a full-blooded account of it. Richard Wagner's great operatic cycle, *The Ring*, played just this role in Bismarckian Germany. Both the welter of sound and the size of production submerged the Bayreuth audience in a flood of emotion and took them away from business, local politics and finance into the twilight world of Siegfried, the Nordic Gods and the Rhinegold. As long as they could return from this twilight world to a life and society which gave satisfaction, then the romance of mythology could stay in its artistic place, but the suggestion that this world of heroes and gods ought to become the real world was always close to the surface.

Wagner's work belongs essentially to the Romantic tradition of Herder. At the same time the discoveries of natural science had introduced new perspectives in the search for the primitive. The Darwinian theory of evolution shattered the complacency of the civilized world. Although it was yet another indication of man's ability to probe even further into the natural world, it had some disquieting lessons for 19th-century Europe. Not only did it completely upset Christianity's trust in the story of Genesis, but it also suggested that animal nature and human nature were unexpectedly close and related. Man, who had been 'little lower than the angels', was now 'little above the animals'. The way was open to discover animal and instinctual drives within civilized man; as a result psychology and anthropology developed rapidly in the last decades of the century. At first, however, it was another side of Darwinism which most stimulated popular interest in the primitive. Darwin himself took no part in this development and dissociated *The Origin of Species* from its ideas, but he could not prevent his discoveries from being put to the most dubious uses.

The aspect so spuriously adapted was Darwin's account of survival among plant and animal life. He had talked of a struggle for survival out of which only the strongest and most adaptable species emerged. This concept of 'survival of the fittest' could easily be applied to human history. In a century of national rivalry, class struggle and economic competition, the Darwinian formula seemed to be a self-evident truth. Only the strong survived. The most popular aspect of this bastardized Darwinism was its application to race history. In their fascination with primitive European peoples the early nationalists had confused culture with race. Race is in fact transmitted by heredity, culture by tradition, but this distinction was entirely blurred in this period. The most outstanding example of this confusion was a four-volume work entitled *Essay on the Inequality of Human Races* (1838–55) by the Frenchman Arthur de Gobineau. It appeared before Darwin's major discoveries but it was strongly affected by the current interest in biological science. Races, Gobineau said, were permanently unequal: some were superior, others were inferior. Those that were strong owed their position to the purity of their blood: they had not become weak through intermarriage. Only one race, he maintained, was capable of creating a true civilization and that was the Aryan race from which the Germans were descended. They were the purest, strongest and most creative race. Gobineau was intensely serious and was convinced of the truth of his findings. He was himself an aristocrat, increasingly isolated in a post-revolutionary France which had discarded the aristocratic traditions of the *ancien régime*. Frenchmen therefore took little notice of his work. Germans on the other hand found much to admire. In 1894 a disciple of Gobineau, Professor Ludwig Schemann, said:

> *All good Germans regard Gobineau as one of the most extraordinary men of the 19th century, one of the greatest God-inspired heroes, saviours and liberators sent by Him across the ages.*[1]

When Darwinism was added to the ideas of Gobineau the mixture was powerful, and the Germans' fascination for their remote Aryan ancestors became a cult of Germanic virtues and strength. For this reason the growth of Aryan racialism must be seen as a primitivist movement. Like Wagner's *Ring*, the cult of Germanism evoked the myths and heroism of a past shrouded in mist, of lands which were indeterminate and of peoples who were unknown to history. There is, in fact, no such thing as an Aryan race: Aryan was a language of one of the ancient Indian cultures. In the 19th century, however, popular stories about Aryan deeds

[1] Quoted in L. L. Snyder, *The Idea of Racialism* (Van Nostrand, 1963), p. 49.

and virtues gave flesh and blood to the so-called race. The Aryan myth became well established in the German consciousness. Only a minority of German writers took it seriously but they were influential in education and society. Most young Germans had probably read one or more of their novels. One of the most popular, written by Hermann Burte, appeared in 1912. Called *Wiltfeber, the Eternal German*, it was a direct appeal to the illusions of fanatical Germanists, but it had excitement and the lure of the distant past to attract the ordinary person. Still more primitive and extreme was the growth of paganism in secret German circles at the end of the century. Here the interest was in the rituals and ceremonies of pre-Christian Aryanism as handed down in popular ancient sagas. In particular, the sun was an object of worship and was used as a symbol of rebirth. With paganism went occultism, a science concerned with the super-natural, and in Vienna the German Austrian Guido von List led an occult circle in regular visitations to the past. His science was a secret one: his appeal was primitive.

Germans were by no means alone in primitive racialism, paganism or occultism. The same emotions thrived in other countries to differing degrees. In particular, the effect of imperialist expansion was to give the white man an arrogant sense of superiority over his coloured subjects, while at the same time luring him into the primitive world of native life. In Britain many public schools would have endorsed the motto of Abbotsholme, 'Education means Empire', and one of the most popular youth magazines, *The Boy's Own Paper*, filled its pages with stories of uncivilized tribes, lion-hunts and dangerous explorations in jungle regions. These subjects were also the content of Rudyard Kipling's novels; they entertained, thrilled and flattered the reader, who could not avoid identifying himself with the hero. In France the adventure stories of Pierre Loti had a similar romantic appeal: man was pictured in the sensuous grip of far-away places or battling against the elements of nature.

As in literature, so in painting. The discovery of Japanese art, tribal masks and negro sculpture had an influence on European painting which cannot be overestimated. The French painter Paul Gauguin went to Tahiti in search of bright colours and primitive simplicity. He settled on the island, took a thirteen-year-old native girl for his mistress, and by the letters and paintings he sent back to France created a myth of the romantic primitivist surrounded by flowers, fruit and beautiful women. The reality was not so picturesque: racked with disease, he was eventually spurned by even the older native women, and died embittered and alone. Less romantic but just as significant was Picasso's enthusiastic discovery of negro art in a Paris museum, a find which led him to give mask-like, primitive heads to the women in his first breakthrough paintings. Primitive art became a recognized form, pulling art history away from the civilized Renaissance tradition and exploring the naïve, the magical and the demented.

Just as the irrational received the support of Bergson's philosophy, so the primitive appeared to be endorsed by the findings of psychology. In a late work, *Civilization and its Discontents* (1929), Sigmund Freud showed how man's instinctual desires, especially his desire for sexual pleasure, had been repressed and driven underground by the inhibitions of civilized society. The frequent result was psychological sickness in the individual. Freud himself lived an eminently respectable life with his family and he had no intention of encouraging sexual orgies or a return to primitive values, but, like Darwin and Nietzsche, he could not prevent the abuse of his theories, which began to be known just before World War I. His main concern was to describe psychological processes and to heal the mentally ill, but his statement that man was naturally aggressive and pleasure-seeking was easily turned into a justification of primitive actions.

Thus in the half-century before 1914, the primitive challenged the civilized as the object of man's interest and excitement. They could, of course, inspire each other, as in Aryan racialism and imperialist expansion, for here the attraction of remote or uncivilized races went hand in hand with supreme confidence in the present. In general, however, the enticing world of the primitive undermined the values of civilization. The contrast showed modern Europe to be dull, mechanical and lifeless: it was seen to be without colour or romance; its lack of violent exaltation was deplored; its religion was too safe and conventional. Primitivism and irrationalism joined forces in this attack on civilization. They were not necessarily the same, for primitivism, especially in German racialism and European imperialism, was authoritarian with a strong sense of physical and mental discipline. Irrationalism always tended to be anarchic and it stemmed more from the revolt of the individual than from a love of the primitive. In combination, however, they could mount a formidable attack on civilized society. In reply, society could point to its technical achievements and its material security. The pull in both directions was powerful.

In fascism elements of the two were brought together. The primitive was enthroned in party rituals, the use of ancient symbols and above all in racialism. In Nazism the barbarity of anti-Semitism reduced European history to a level of bestiality far beyond even the wildest dreams of 19th-century primitivists. Other racialism was not so animal but all fascisms used 'Darwinian' notions of struggle and survival, which involved to some degree the ideas of racial superiority. Brutality in political action was the most consistent element in fascism. In itself this was the most blatant rejection of civilized values. Brute force allowed Fascists to act out their fantasies of being all-powerful, heroic and superhuman. In this way the gods and heroes of 19th-century stories emerged from books and operas and occupied reality. There is a vital difference between thinking force and acting force, and the youth who read the sagas of primitive warfare should not be confused with the Nazi who butchered his fellow men, but so many years of primitive tales and hero-worship must surely be significant in the history of fascism. One has only to note the continuation of this kind of literature under the Fascist régimes: it was an important stimulus.

Such strong, primitive strains in fascism appealed to large numbers of people who would never have murdered or fought with the ferocity of actual Fascist members. Primitivism in small doses was an acceptable commodity throughout much of inter-war Europe, but there is every sign that fascism did not depend on this alone. It balanced its primitivism with a cogent display of civilization. The benefits of a modern society, its technological wonders and its material progress, were both exploited and continued by Fascist rule. By merging evolutionary ideas with supreme self-confidence, Fascists claimed to be at the very pinnacle of western civilization. History, they believed, had

justified them—a belief similar to that of the Marxists, their
principal political enemies, and not unlike that of the 19th-
century liberals who had also claimed the support of history.
Even more telling was the Fascist manipulation of propaganda:
the public was shown what it wanted to know. If it wanted to
believe Hitler was a kind, humane man it could look at numerous
photographs of the Führer patting the heads of children.

By these methods fascism's split identity, both primitive and
civilized, was presented to the public as an organic unity. In
some cases this was unsuccessful. Few people took the French
Faisceau movement seriously; during World War II Quisling in
Norway and Doriot in France were upheld by the German
occupation, not by the power of their synthesis, despite the fact
that they too combined the primitive and the civilized. There
was no uniformity of either appeal or success in fascism, and the
balance between primitive and civilized was different for each
movement. The Spanish *Falange*, in particular, is not encompassed
by the background described in this section. In general, however,
this synthesis of the primitive and the civilized was an essential
part of the complex nature of fascism. With each conflicting
ingredient its complexity grew but its strength was not
diminished.

4 THE MASS AND THE ÉLITE

> At Hamburg on 20 March 1936, Hitler declared:
>
> *In Germany bayonets do not terrorize a people . . . here a
> government is supported by the confidence of the entire
> people. I come from the people. In fifteen years I have slowly
> worked my way up together with this Movement. I have not
> been imposed by anyone upon this people. From the people I
> have grown up, in the people I have remained, to the people
> I return. My pride is that I know no statesman in the
> world who, with greater right than I, can say that he is the
> representative of the people.*[1]

But in May 1930 he had said:

> *What we want is a picked number from the new ruling
> classes: who . . . are not troubled by humanitarian feelings,*

---

[1] *The Speeches of Adolf Hitler*, vol. ii, ed. N. H. Baynes (O.U.P., 1942),
pp. 1, 312–13.

Mass support . . .
Berlin crowd welcomes Hitler back from the Munich conference, September 1938

> *but who are convinced that they have the right to rule as being a superior race, and who will secure and maintain their rule ruthlessly over the broad masses.*[1]

The contradiction is glaring: an appeal to the people and a confession of tyranny side by side, mass politics and rule by an élite. The two sides of this final synthesis have roots as long as any of the others: in fact the argument about who should rule in society is as old as politics itself.

In the 19th century the debate over the French Revolution was the basis for all subsequent theories on this emotional question. The revolutionaries, supported mainly by the writings of Tom Paine, had demanded political equality: all men should have a say in the choice of rulers; government should be responsible to the people. In eloquent opposition to these theories stood Edmund Burke and, later, the French arch-conservative Joseph de Maistre. Burke's main interest was to preserve traditional values and liberties from any threat, be it from tyrannical king or tyrannical mob. The latter term he applied to the revolutionaries. In his eyes they threatened to swamp quality with quantity; the sheer numbers of the mob would crush the best life from France, and it would be Britain's turn next. Against this rule of quantity

[1] Quoted in R. A. Brady, *The Spirit and Structure of German Fascism* (Gollancz, 1937), p. 152.

. and new élite.

1. Hitler, with stormtroopers mounting a guard of honour, at a Nazi Party rally

2. A group of the new leaders, Hess, Göring, Streicher and Goebbels (*l. to r.*)

and numbers he placed the natural ruling qualities of the court
and aristocracy. De Maistre went further by restating the ancient
view that the king ruled by divine right: even if the king were
cruel, his subjects should still love and obey him. In this way the
case against democracy was firmly founded. It prospered at first,
due to the terror and extremism into which the Revolution
stumbled. The supporters of Burke could point to the Paris
massacres as evidence of the tyranny of democracy. Democrats
on the other hand had only their hopes and intentions as
argument.

The issue, in very similar terms, is still vigorously alive. The
Burke–Paine debate is restaged in every developing country. In
Europe it echoed throughout the last century in varying forms
but by 1900 most European nations had made considerable
concessions to democracy: the franchise had widened and
education was designed to teach people to use their vote wisely.
There was still a ruling élite but its base was broader and the
doors of entry were opening. The long struggle waged in the
cause of democracy appeared to be effective. Parliamentary
government seemed to hold the key to the future and the age
of party politics had arrived. All parties began to campaign by
electioneering and propaganda, and the people were no longer
seen as a mob or even a mass but as individuals who had votes.
The 19th century was as much the age of parliamentary
democracy as of capitalism, reason and progress.

Nevertheless, democracy was far less secure than it appeared:
Burke and de Maistre continued to have their followers, and the
conservative theory of natural, traditional rulers died hard. The
real danger, however, came from elsewhere. In the latter half of
the century a new form of nationalism swept over Europe and
one of its main enemies was parliamentary democracy. Earlier
nationalism had been a liberal, democratic and revolutionary
phenomenon and the revolutions of 1848 were its greatest
monument. After 1848, revolutionary fire was diverted into
socialism and anarchism, neither of which believed in the value
of the nation state. Marxism prophesied that the state would
wither away: the nation would no longer determine history; it
would be the international working class who would inherit the
earth. This clarion call to the workers of the world threatened

the entire traditions of Europe, which, since the Middle Ages, had been geared to the nation state. Under this threat it was understandable that conservatives began to close their ranks to protect their nations from destruction. Nationalism became a conservative movement.

This change in nationalism is perhaps one of the great turning points of modern history. Nationalist parties, groups, circles and leaders sprang up all over Europe with similar methods and aims. In general their aim was to protect the nation from external attack and internal disintegration, and their methods were to build up national pride and emotion against all ideas and parties which threatened to weaken the state. The ideas of Friedrich Hegel were a source of inspiration: in his writings on history he had proclaimed that 'The State is the Divine Idea as it exists on Earth': nothing could be higher or more exalted than the State; it was the finest stage of human development. As such, he continued, its interests were everybody's interests. The individual would find through the State his complete freedom and spiritual fulfilment. Duty to the State was the highest moral command. These sentiments of Hegel formed the emotion of nationalism. In any dispute between the nation and the individual, the national interest was supreme. In this way the nation became an object of religious veneration and much of the primitivism discussed in the last section was put at its service. Folk tales, racial histories, past heroisms and all forms of art were laid round the plinth on which the nation stood, proud in its historical achievements. The theorists of such nationalism included Lagarde in Germany, Barrès and Maurras in France and Corradini in Italy. Without exception they all found democracy and parliamentary government an obstacle to national greatness. Democracy, they claimed, protected the individual and involved the nation in interminable party wrangling. What was needed was strong government by those with the national interest truly at heart, that is, by a national élite. In this way the Burkean theory was rephrased and given a new setting. The call for natural rulers was heard again, not in Burke's traditional terms, but in vigorous, dynamic phrases which inflamed the patriotism of all classes.

The pressure of this nationalism on the forces of democracy was intense. Germany, in particular, allowed her politics and foreign policy to be strongly affected by it. No country was able to subdue its appeal. In 1914 the rival policies of nation states threw Europe into war. The nationalist movements embraced it with delirium. Warfare and violence were fully acceptable to the nationalist creed.

To this extent pre-war nationalism appears as the direct ancestor of fascism. Fascist ideals of strong leadership and ruthless rule by a national élite are foreshadowed by these earlier movements. What keeps them distinct from each other is fascism's use of mass politics, which seems totally contradictory to élitism and was frequently scorned by the conservatives as vulgar and dangerous. But it was fascism's ability to attract and use the masses which made it in the end more powerful than conservative nationalism.

What is meant by 'mass politics' in this context? Certainly not democracy in its parliamentary sense. Although Fascists used parliaments to some extent, they were as hostile to parliamentary democracy and party politics as were the nationalists. But democracy in another sense, yes; in the revolutionary and Socialist tradition which looked for the rising of the people and the overthrow of the old order. The French revolutionaries had called on the people of Europe to rise and throw off the yoke of despotism; Karl Marx had prophesied that the proletariat would inevitably carry a revolution against the bourgeoisie, and revolts had been staged throughout the 19th century in the name of the masses. The vision of the people taking over society and creating a new world was by 1900 even more widespread than it had been during the French Revolution.

In the decade before World War I this prospect was announced with renewed vigour by the doctrines of Georges Sorel. A French intellectual who was a Socialist but belonged to no creed or party, Sorel published in 1906 a series of articles later called *Reflections on Violence*. In these highly influential writings he attacked parliamentary democracy and insisted that all great social changes came when a mass movement rose up against its enemies, inspired by a dominating ideal of the future. This ideal he called a 'myth' and a past example of such a myth was the second coming of Christ:

The first Christians expected the return of Christ and the

> *total ruin of the pagan world, with the inauguration of the*
> *kingdom of saints at the end of the first generation. The*
> *catastrophe did not come to pass, but Christian thought*
> *profited so greatly from the apocalyptic myth that certain*
> *contemporary scholars maintain that the whole preaching of*
> *Christ referred solely to this one point.*[1]

In just such a way, Sorel continued, the Socialists of the 20th century could be inspired by the myth of the General Strike, a moment in the future when all workers would stop work and the capitalist world would collapse. The new society would then be born out of the destruction of the old. All violence would be linked to this myth and would show how inspired the workers were.

When the Sorelian myth is added to Marxist prophecies, one can see what potential power lay in the idea of mass politics. If the masses could be roused to action in pursuit of some great cause, the earth could be moved. Such a hope was considerably removed from the moderate democratic pressures which were affecting European politics. It was much more emotional and appealed to the irrational side of man. It was much vaguer too: a vote or a seat in parliament was something concrete but a myth or an ideal was intangible. In this, of course, lay its appeal, as Sorel well knew. Each man would have a different version and would feel he was following his own interests.

Here then was the tradition of mass politics which fascism adopted. It was a left-wing tradition whose spokesmen had included Marx and Sorel, but in fascism it was merged with the right-wing theory of rule by an élite, and twisted to tyrannical ends. The mass who rose in support of fascism was not the proletariat, the traditional heirs of revolution, but a mass of people from all classes who were inspired by Fascist ideals of strength, national power and authority. The Fascist myth was put over with a maximum of physical and propaganda force but it was not without its gentler, seductive side. Mussolini wrote in 1932:

> *The Fascist accepts and loves life: he rejects and despises*
> *suicide as cowardly. Life as he understands it means duty,*
> *elevation, conquest: life must be lofty and full; it must be*
> *lived for oneself but above all for others, both near and far*
> *off, present and future.*[2]

[1] G. Sorel, *Reflections on Violence*, trans. T. E. Hulme and J. Roth (Allen and Unwin, 1950), p. 113.

[2] B. Mussolini, *Fascism. Political and Social Doctrine* (Ardita, Rome, 1935), p. 19.

Such a portrait may be unrecognizable when Fascist violence is remembered, but it was seriously used to inspire followers and pacify doubters. Fascism was not based merely on the brutal magnetism of violence: its myths were more complex and its mass politics more subtle. Its ruling élites understood as clearly as any other modern government the power of widely based public support. This is what made them vulgar in the eyes of more traditional élites: but vulgar or not, the synthesis worked, and Fascists worshipped few things more than success.

One of the leading Fascists of Occupied France, Joseph Darnand, said at his trial in 1945: 'I was profoundly revolutionary in my ideas: a complete revolutionary on the social plane. I had become a real Socialist.' The statement was greeted with derision: he had been a man of violent action, not of ideas, and no Socialist would have recognized him. Yet such claims from Fascists are frequent: they are full of contradictions and defy political science, but they point to a reality of history—the paradox that was fascism. Its nature was by no means constant and the web of ideas presented in this chapter stretched unevenly over the various national movements, but whatever their precise character they shared this central quality of paradox. The Fascist synthesis was a 'Third Way' between several alternatives and it contained elements of all sides. The novelty of such a combination was stressed by the English Fascist, Sir Oswald Mosley, and with novelty went freedom of action:

> It is thus that every Fascist movement has arrived at power —not by combinations of men drawn from the old political system but by the discovery of new men who come from nowhere and by the creation of a new force which is free from the trammels of the past . . . A great man of action once observed 'No man goes very far who knows exactly where he is going', and the same observation applies with some force to modern movements of reality in the changing situations of today.[1]

[1] Sir O. Mosley, *The Greater Britain* (B.U.F., 1932), pp. 151, 160.

PART TWO

A History of Fascism

CHAPTER THREE

Italy: The Triumph of the *Fasci*

On 23 May 1915 Victor Emmanuel III, King of Italy, signed a declaration bringing his country into the war against Austria–Hungary. For almost a year Italy had debated the question of neutrality or intervention: politicians and public opinion, the press and parliament had become deeply divided, and the declaration and reality of war did not heal their divisions. In the next three years 564,000 Italians were killed and over a million were wounded: the country suffered a disastrous defeat by the Austrians and Germans at the battle of Caporetto in 1917, and despite a small compensatory victory at Vittorio Veneto in 1918 emerged from the war and the peace negotiations with few gains and no increase of international prestige. Judged by results, the decision to enter the war appeared to have been a mistaken one, and the four years which followed did nothing to divert Italians from the harshness of failure. Between 1918 and 1922 the economy slumped, politics were anarchic, labour and industry were locked in conflict and the public was both led and confused by street-corner rhetoric, rival party programmes and outbreaks of social and political violence.

Yet throughout this time of failure and confusion one consistent emotion was evident. The vigour with which conservative nationalist groups had advocated war, and activist groups had welcomed it, became a permanent feature of Italian society. No defeat, military or diplomatic, sapped the enthusiasm of those who accepted war as a liberation, an opportunity for heroism and a call to historic Italian virtues. The spokesman of this belligerent patriotism was the middle-aged poet Gabriele d'Annunzio. Before 1915 his flamboyant verses had been geared to Italian art, the history and character of the nation and the role

of Italy in Mediterranean culture. After 1915 his words and
actions were completely identified with the war. At a party called
to celebrate the King's declaration of war in 1915, he cere-
moniously announced the birth of a new age:

> *Companions, here is the dawn. Our vigil is over. Our gaiety*
> *begins. The frontier is passed. The cannons fire. The earth*
> *gives forth its fumes and the Adriatic is grey, at this hour,*
> *like the torpedo boats that cut through it. Companions, can*
> *it be true? After so much wavering the incredible has*
> *happened. We shall now fight our war, and blood will flow*
> *from the veins of Italy. We are the last to enter the struggle*
> *but will be among the first to find glory. Here, companions,*
> *is the dawn. Here is the knell. Let us kiss one another and*
> *take leave. What is done is done. Now we must separate—to*
> *find one another again. God will surely allow us to meet*
> *again, dead or alive, in a place surrounded by light . . .*[1]

Despite his fifty-two years d'Annunzio became a hardened, heroic
and brutal fighter, distinguishing himself as a pilot by exploits
which gained him an international reputation. By 1918 he was
covered in service medals and was the idol of the new generation.
World War I has often been called 'the first war of the masses':
it was also the first war of the young. This fact tends to be
obscured by the use of the term 'veterans' to signify those who
fought and survived. War veterans in Italy were frequently young
men in their early twenties who had savoured the situations of
death and violence and had become addicted. Their heroes, if
they were not among them, were the *Arditi* troops, the mobile
shock units which were thrown into the front of all battles and
emerged from the war as almost mythical figures of daring and
courage. For d'Annunzio, for the *Arditi*, for the young who
admired and emulated them, the peace changed nothing. War
and patriotism remained the ideal, and mundane, everyday life
was repellent. The future, they determined, should be theirs.
D'Annunzio in 1918 said:

> *Whatever happens, one thing is certain after the war. The*
> *future will bring something quite new to us, such as we have*

[1] Quoted in A. Rhodes, *The Poet as Superman. D'Annunzio* (Weidenfeld and
Nicolson, 1959), p. 149.

never seen before. Something stronger, more beautiful, will be born from all this blood and sacrifice. All forms of art and politics will be overthrown: the new ones will be healthier. I believe that we are entering a new era, whose transformation will surpass that of the Renaissance and the French Revolution. Happy are they who shall see this new world; happy too those who, like us, have announced it, foreseen it, prepared it . . .[1]

This future was to be fascism. Profiting from the divisions and confusion of post-war Italy and developing the activist and nationalist sentiments into a political system, Benito Mussolini became the ruler of Italy, and *Il Duce* of the Italian people.

The fact that it was Mussolini rather than d'Annunzio who achieved this position, was due to the former's greater sense of pragmatism and expediency in the crucial years 1919–21. Mussolini was by background an extreme Socialist who, before 1919, had vehemently denounced bourgeois Italian society, liberal Italian politics and conservative Italian nationalism, but he had never been a narrow dogmatist and his allegiance lay more with the concepts of revolution and action than with the details of Marxist doctrine. He was an adventurer, a *condottiere*, and, retrospectively, it does not seem inconsistent that he changed in 1914 from denunciation of the war to an outspoken campaign for intervention. As a Socialist and editor of *Avanti!*, the main Socialist newspaper, he was bound by doctrine to see World War I as an internecine struggle between bourgeois imperialist nations, a struggle irrelevant to the class conflict on which socialism was based: as such, the war was to be opposed, even ignored. As a revolutionary man of action, on the other hand, he was susceptible to the excitement and potential of the war. It was this side of Mussolini which changed the course of his career and carried him away from the Socialist Party, away from *Avanti!* and into a kind of nationalism which was both reactionary, looking back to the past glories of Italy, and revolutionary, looking forward to the triumph of a new and dynamic vision of society. Above all, as a professional journalist

[1] Quoted in A. Rhodes, *The Poet as Superman. D'Annunzio* (Weidenfeld and Nicolson, 1959), p. 163.

he had a sense of occasion: his last words in *Avanti!* read:

> *We have had the unique privilege of living in the most*
> *tragic hour of the world's history. Do we wish to be—as*
> *men and as Socialists—passive spectators of this grandiose*
> *drama? Or do we wish to be . . . its protagonists? Let us not*
> *salvage the letter of the party if this means killing the spirit*
> *of socialism.*[1]

The growing affinity with d'Annunzio is already clear, but throughout the war Mussolini's career was only a shadow of the poet's and in 1918 the eyes of Italy's youth were not on the ex-Socialist. Despite this, by 1921 Mussolini had captured the stage and d'Annunzio had been forced to retire to a country villa, an eccentric, disillusioned and fallen hero. If the activism and patriotism which d'Annunzio embodied were the emotions of fascism, the means whereby Mussolini outmanœuvred him were its politics.

The future, Mussolini had stated in 1914, was inevitably geared to the war. In 1918 it seemed just as inevitably geared to revolution. The success of the Russian Bolsheviks in 1917 was a model for all Socialist revolutionary movements in the instability of post-war Europe. Italy was no exception, and the wide public support given to the Socialists in the elections of 1919 threatened the bourgeois values and liberal politics under which Italy had lived since unification in the mid-19th century. The reaction of the threatened classes was one of confusion and fear. The industrialists of Northern Italy faced the possibility of losing their capital and means of production: the landowners throughout Italy faced expropriation. At first Mussolini, still influenced by his Socialist youth, did nothing to allay these fears. Backed by his own paper *Il Popolo d'Italia*, and a scattered following (mainly in the large towns), he too called for a revolution. At a meeting in Milan on 23 March 1919, the new movement of fascism was founded to pursue this goal. Its symbols were the black shirt and the *fascio*, a bundle of rods with an axe, the token of State power carried by the lictors ahead of the consuls in Ancient Rome. The emphasis was therefore

[1] Quoted in E. Nolte, *Three Faces of Fascism* (Weidenfeld and Nicolson, 1965), p. 169.

both on revolution and authority, and most of the early Fascists were men of revolutionary sympathies, but, like Mussolini, disillusioned with the Socialists for their failure to accept the recent war. With this dual character, revolutionary but not Socialist, nationalist but hostile to the nationalism of the conservatives, fascism appealed to those who wanted action without the limitations of doctrine. Branches of the movement, *Fasci*, began to generate almost spontaneously all over Italy and in most cases organized themselves into semi-armed groups, *squadre*, for quick action against political opponents. The example of the *Arditi* served equally well for peacetime activity. In October 1919 at the First National Congress of Fascism the number of *Fasci* was given as 100 and the total number of Black Shirts as 40,000. It was not a large number by national standing, and the policy of outbidding the Socialists for the leadership of the revolution was of little success. No Fascist was elected to Parliament in 1919. The movement looked little more than a loosely organized band of dissident Socialists and unemployed war veterans attempting to impress and scare the bourgeoisie with extreme speeches and occasional street riots. It was this impotence which forced Mussolini in 1919 to reconsider his position, and, as in 1914, he followed events.

In September 1919 d'Annunzio had revived his wartime image with the dramatic seizure of the Adriatic port of Fiume, in the name of Italian rights and history. Fiume lay between Italy and the new state of Yugoslavia, and, although promised to Italy in 1915, had not been given to her at the peace negotiations at the end of the war. Collecting together an army of war veterans and personal followers, d'Annunzio occupied the town after the Italian government had repeatedly refused to do so. He had preceded his campaign with a barrage of insults levelled at the 'treacherous' government and with a ritualistic appeal to the hearts and traditions of all 'true Italians'. The town, temporarily occupied by international forces, surrendered to him without a fight and he became its ruler for over a year in defiance of his own government and much of world opinion. The exploit, d'Annunzio proclaimed, was in the great tradition of Garibaldi's Thousand who had conquered Sicily in 1860. Its inspiration, he continued, was even older, and he taught his legionaries the

chant *Eja, Eja, Eja Alala!* with which Achilles was said to have
spurred his chariot horses. The chant and the claim that he and
his followers were the inheritors of epic military virtues were
only part of d'Annunzio's histrionic role. He instituted the
dialogue with the crowd, beginning with his question from the
palace balcony 'Whose is Fiume?' and ending with the roar of
the crowd 'Ours! Ours!'; he painted the slogan 'Italy or Death'
over the walls of the square and he passed a constitution which
gave equal rights to women, provided a high level of social
welfare and made music a religious and social institution. During
1920, as supplies became more difficult, as discipline disintegrated,
as the society of Fiume became more disorganized, it was clear
to most of Italy that d'Annunzio was neither a politician nor a
ruler. His own response to declining fortune was to become more
revolutionary, more anarchic and more individualistic. Stories of
mass orgies, sexual abandon and endless political intrigue
replaced the accounts of dedicated patriotism, and when Italy's
Prime Minister, the old Liberal Giolitti, ordered the recapture
of Fiume and its return to the international authorities, there
were many Italians, once fervent supporters of d'Annunzio,

who now saw little reason to
protest.

Among these was Mussolini.
He had responded with
rhetorical alacrity to the possi-
bilities of the event, had placed
the Fascist movement firmly
behind the nationalist claims of
the poet, but had then seen with
perception the waning influence
of d'Annunzio's anarchism. By
the end of the Fiume incident
Mussolini had cleverly gauged
the growing demand in Italy for
stability and order.

This demand had become
more vocal in response to other
events within Italy. In September
1920 the Socialist revolution

looked imminent: workers of the great metallurgical industries occupied their factories as a gesture of revolutionary defiance. Had the Socialist Party decided to lead the workers to political power there could have been little effective opposition—but the Socialists hesitated. Disrupted by doctrinal differences over the problem of whether or not to join the new Communist International, they failed to seize their moment of maximum political power. In 1921 their strength in Italy declined rapidly. The revolution had not arrived: many who had wanted it were bitterly disillusioned, those who had feared it began to move from the defensive to the attack. The situation was one which favoured an appeal to order and recovery.

By intuition and political ruthlessness Mussolini and the local *Fasci* provided this appeal. Capitalizing on the fears of the middle classes, utilizing the nationalism of d'Annunzio without repeating his mistakes, fascism sold itself to the Italian people in 1921 as the patriotic answer to the Red Socialist danger and the political chaos of ineffective Liberalism. In this way the original revolutionary aims of 1919 were shelved and a renewed emphasis placed on Fascist order, reliability and power.

Mussolini in his own account of the history of fascism stresses three things about this period. Firstly, his own leadership:

> I led a life of intense activity. I managed the Popolo d'Italia *and every morning I was able to give the political text for the day, not only in Milan, but to the principal cities of Italy where the political life of the Nation found its sources. I led the Fascist Party with a firm hand. I must say that I gave some very strict orders . . . I watched the activity of our enemies. I maintained for the Fascists a clear, clean stream of purpose. I maintained the freedom necessary for our elasticity of movement . . .*[1]

Secondly, he maintains that violence was necessary but was always used with care and subtlety:

> I restrained our own violence within the strict limit of necessity. I enforced that viewpoint with lieutenants and with the rank and file. At times they obeyed me with regret and

[1] B. Mussolini, *My Autobiography*, trans. R. W. Child (Hurst and Blackett, 1936), p. 313.

> *pain. They were thinking of companions treacherously*
> *murdered.*[1]

Thirdly, he stresses the Fascists' claim that it was the Socialists who were the disturbers of civil order, the enemies of Italy, the betrayers of the nation, and that the Fascists alone maintained the true values of Italian life:

> *The Fascist action squads turned their activity into the*
> *suburbs firmly held by both communists and socialists. The*
> *swift decisive work of the Fascists served to drive from their*
> *nests and put to flight the subverters of civil order. The*
> *political authority was powerless: it could not control the*
> *disorders and disturbances . . . At last over the horizon I*
> *had brought defenders of civil life, protectors of order and*
> *citizenship. There had come a spirit of revival for all good*
> *works . . . A whole people might now be united in the name*
> *of the Roman Littorio, under the direction of Italian youth—*
> *a youth which had won the War and now would again*
> *attain a serene peace of the spirit and the rewards of the*
> *fruitful virtues of discipline, work and fraternity.*[2]

Ever since the defeat of fascism in World War II it has appeared necessary for historians to ridicule and correct these boastful vaunts of Mussolini, but this is where the historian can do a disservice to history. If he is too concerned to explode the myths of fascism, to reduce it to its proper size and to point out its lies and inaccuracies, he may miss the essential historical point—for whatever the truth or falsity of Mussolini's claims, there were enough Italians who believed him to bring fascism to a position of supreme power.

Any account of European fascism in the 20th century must begin by saying that its strength lay in the willingness and enthusiasm with which large numbers of ordinary people welcomed its ideals, believed in its claims and endorsed its methods. In Italy in 1921 this was historical reality. In Germany in 1933 it was even more true. The wide appeal and attraction of fascism is something which must first be admitted before any understanding of it can emerge.

[1] B. Mussolini, *op. cit.*, p. 124.   [2] *Ibid.*, p. 130.

For this reason Mussolini's account of Italian fascism in the extracts above must be approached as both falsity and truth. He was by no means the strong leader of disciplined, obedient troops that he made himself out to be. Frequently he was both surprised and alarmed at the actions of local Fascists who acted independently and with more violence than he either wanted or thought necessary. Yet the legend and image of Mussolini as the strong commanding general of an organized political movement took root in these very circumstances of *dis*order and *dis*obedience. Similarly Socialist violence, though frequently of spontaneous cruelty and revolutionary fervour, was no more destructive of civil order than Fascist retaliation, involving as it did calculated attacks on Socialist buildings, organized murder, and provocative demonstrations leading to street fighting and local civil war. Fascist squads were usually more mobile than the Socialists: they used the most modern methods of transport and communication, particularly the telephone. Unlike the Socialists, who were a large parliamentary party with responsibilities to workers with regular jobs, the Fascists had nothing to lose until they too entered parliament in the elections of 1921. Their seats then numbered only thirty-five, but they were won with the approval of Giolitti's government, who gave a lead to the middle and upper classes in the toleration of Fascist methods. Once in parliament, Mussolini tried to moderate the violence of the Fascist squads and at one point resigned his leadership, but this was a gesture inconsistent with his vanity and ambition and he ended by following the extremists rather than curbing them. The objective conclusion therefore on Socialist and Fascist violence would be that Mussolini was quite wrong when he accused the Socialists of being the main cause of civil disorder, but that his accusations rang true not only to his followers but also to Giolitti's government and the public who had most to fear from the Socialist threat.

Examples of this situation—Fascist violence tolerated in the interests of order and bourgeois security—can be found in the history of most Italian towns in 1921–2. One incident is sufficient to fix and define the atmosphere:

One of Italy's most famous squadrists, Sandro Carosi,

*entered a workmen's café with some companions, drew his
pistol and with a broad smile forced one of the men present
to stand against the wall with a cup on his head: he was
going to prove his marksmanship. But the bullet entered the
man's head and killed him—in mock despair the marksman
bewailed his unsteady hand. The newspaper reported the
occurrence under the headline* Uno sfortunato Guglielmo
Tell *and justice saw no reason to intervene.*[1]

The word *sfortunato* ('unfortunate') is illuminating. It was
possible in the chaos of these two years to regard fascism as
basically a responsible, orderly movement and to pass over its
brutal character as 'unfortunate'. Those who were not Fascists
but wished to use Mussolini to bring a return of strong government mostly thought in this way. They included not only the
conservative nationalists and several of the older conservative and
liberal politicians like Salandra, Orlando, Giolitti and Albertini,
but also Pope Pius XI, many of the army leaders like the old
General Diaz, and a considerable percentage of civil servants,
policemen, industrialists and landowners. It was with the
approval, sometimes enthusiastic, sometimes reluctant, of these
people and groups that Mussolini became Prime Minister of Italy
in 1922.

He did so, the Fascist histories maintain, as a direct result of
the 'march on Rome'. This event, like Mussolini's leadership, is
one of the sacred myths of Italian fascism and it too is part truth
and part falsity. In the 1860s Garibaldi had dreamed of declaring
a united Italy from the Capitoline Hill in Rome after marching
on the city, but his dream was never fulfilled. In Fiume in 1920
d'Annunzio held the vision of Rome before the eyes of his
faithful legionaries. The 'march on Rome' became a concept to
inspire heroism and sacrifice. The Fascists appropriated this goal
and ideal, and in 1922, after three years of preparation, skirmish-
ing and minor battles, the time appeared favourable for the
supreme assertion of power. 'Now', Mussolini wrote, 'we were
on the eve of the historic march on the Eternal City.' Faced with
such language, the temptation is again to ridicule and thereby to
underestimate the significance of the event.

[1] E. Nolte, *Three Faces of Fascism* (Weidenfeld and Nicolson, 1965), p. 201.

On 26 October 1922, the Fascists, acting on central party orders, began to occupy public buildings in Northern Italy. Encountering little resistance, Fascist confidence grew and the idea of a great spontaneous rising of the true Italian people began to take hold of the Fascist imagination. There also sprang up a belief in the organization and courage of the Fascist squads, who formed into columns of marchers and began to advance from the north and east on the capital. Neither idea was correct. The occupation of strategic points was in most cases achieved by compromise with the public officials and there was no widespread uprising or even excitement. Nor did the marchers qualify as epic heroes: they were poorly equipped and grew irritable at the delays, the short rations and the constant outbreaks of rain. They halted thirty miles from Rome and there learnt the news that Mussolini, who had travelled to the city in an overnight sleeping-car, had been asked to form a government. Rome had not been conquered by fascism: it had first been undermined by the failures of democratic Italy to provide a coherent and stable alternative, and had then turned to the only political force which possessed a semblance of authority. Mussolini promised an end to civil war and political chaos, a return to economic stability and a revival of national glory, and in the circumstances this was widely acceptable even at the price of political freedom. For what had freedom brought?—almost a Socialist revolution and four post-war years of disturbance and division. Many Italians reasoned in this way, and such reasoning came to take on the force of irresistible logic.

Thus the march on Rome, legally rewarded by success, could assume the proportions of great drama. Those who had marched became the honoured veterans of fascism, the élite of the party and the future models for all aspiring Fascists. The march was not a revolution but it soon became one in retrospect, and its new and inflated image was as true for Fascist Italy as its real nature is for modern historians.

At the head of government Mussolini had the choice of adapting fascism to fit the democratic traditions of parliamentary rule, or altering the whole political structure to suit the demands of his followers. At least, he appeared to have the choice. In fact the more determined and extreme of the Fascist leaders had not

A march of Fascist women in 1923

been fighting merely to see Mussolini invested by the king as a legal prime minister. This would be to accept only the formality of power. Rather they looked for a total transformation of society, an elimination of their enemies and the emergence of the dynamic, forceful Italy which Mussolini had always promised— and, despite some initial concessions to moderation, this was the attitude Mussolini was forced to adopt. As criticisms of Fascist methods became more intense, and as the Socialist, Liberal and Catholic parties began to form the common front which had eluded them before 1922, so Mussolini found the pressure of his extremists more attractive. In 1924 he was compelled to decide. On 10 June a popular Socialist deputy, Giacomo Matteotti, disappeared. He had, a short time before, launched the most telling of his regular attacks on Mussolini's rule and the whole Fascist system. In August his murdered body was found in a ditch. In answer to the wave of public indignation Mussolini proclaimed his own sense of horror. Morale in the Fascist Party fell and the opposition in parliament and outside strengthened. Two leading Fascists, Rossi and Marinelli, were arrested and accused of the crime. The whole Fascist movement appeared to be threatened and the extremists to have lost ground, but their pressure on Mussolini mounted: he was called on to solve the crisis in true Fascist style. On 3 January 1925, he made his decision. Speaking to the whole country he personally accepted responsibility for the Matteotti murder and reaffirmed his belief in Fascist government. The extremists had won, and in 1925 the institutions of totalitarian rule were developed, opposition was crushed and an amnesty passed for all those implicated in the Matteotti affair. Mussolini said in his speech:

> . . . *If fascism has turned out to be only castor oil and rubber truncheons instead of being a superb passion inspiring the best youth of Italy, I am responsible . . . Italy wants peace and quiet and to get on with its work. I shall give it all these, if possible in love, but if necessary by force. In the forty-eight hours after my speech the whole situation will be changed.*[1]

The change brought Italian fascism to its third major stage. It had begun as an activist, nationalist emotion, it had then become organized as a movement of semi-military units. It was now transformed into a régime. As such it lasted until 1943.

---

[1] Quoted in D. Mack Smith, *Italy: A Modern History* (University of Michigan, 1959), p. 385.

CHAPTER FOUR

Germany: The Power of Nazism

While d'Annunzio was gaining his world reputation as a pilot, an obscure Austrian corporal in the German armies made his public début. For his courageous activities as a despatch carrier at the front, Adolf Hitler, aged twenty-nine, was awarded the Iron Cross First Class in the closing months of World War I. He fully expected this tribute to be one of the many marks of German victory. He was a fervent nationalist who had welcomed the war as a chance for German greatness and an end to his own aimless, impoverished youth. In the war he found a spirit and excitement which inspired him to harangue his fellow soldiers on the military future of Germany, the need to drive the Jews and all other aliens out of national life, and the promise of a new Germany rising over Europe. He talked with an ob-sessive, dynamic fury which both frightened and amused his audience; he then retired into himself and refused to com-municate. Identified as he was with the whole German war effort, he could never tolerate the thought of defeat, and when the German armies were forced by imminent collapse to sur-render to the Western Allies he attributed the entire disaster to treason within Germany. He was not at the front when, in

Adolf Hitler (*on right*)
during World War I

October 1918, the German position became hopeless—a fact which enabled him to create his own fantasy of events. Instead he was suffering from temporary gas poisoning of the eyes and loss of memory. He later wrote about his experience:

> *During the night of October 13–14 the British began to throw gas-shells onto the southern front before Ypres. We were still on a hill south of Werwick on the evening of October 13 when we came under a drum-fire lasting several hours, which continued throughout the night with more or less violence. About midnight a number of us dropped out— some for ever. Towards morning I felt a pain which got worse with every quarter hour that passed, and at about seven o'clock I tottered rearwards with scorching eyes reporting myself for the last time in that war. A few hours later my eyes had turned into burning coals and it was all dark around me. I was sent to hospital at Pasewalk in Pomerania and whilst there I was destined to see the Revolution.*[1]

In Italy the Socialist revolution had never materialized. In Germany it broke out in the same month, November 1918, as the collapse of the German armies. The relation between these two events was not one of cause and effect except for Hitler, the Nazis and bitter anti-Socialists, who insisted that Germany had been 'stabbed in the back' by the 'November criminals'. As Hitler himself relates, he did not see the end of the war: he saw only the Revolution. And he hated what he saw. The world in which he had found a sense of purpose and a measure of achievement had gone, and the heirs were not the military or the heroes of whom he had talked at the front, but the Socialist politicians who stood for everything he despised.

The German Revolution overthrew the Kaiser William II and his imperial régime, and set up a Republic in which the government was to be responsible to parliament as in the régimes of Britain and France. Its head was to be a president and its ideals those of the revolutionary Left, stemming from the traditions of 1848 and the doctrines of Marxism. Its existence was declared and defined in the town of Weimar, and in 1919 the so-called

[1] A. Hitler, *Mein Kampf (My Struggle)* (Hurst and Blackett, 1935), p. 90.

Weimar Republic began to tackle the desperate problems of peace with the Allies and peace within Germany.

The Allies had refused to negotiate with any representative of the defeated imperial régime. The new Republic therefore was saddled with the responsibility of dealing both with the accusations and peace terms of the victorious powers. Germany was accused of causing the war, and the harsh Peace of Versailles was designed to make her pay for this international crime. President Ebert and his government were astounded at this treatment. The Republican politicians in Germany saw themselves not as the guilty but as victims of the Kaiser's régime and his belligerent foreign policy. Their reaction, therefore, was to reject the peace if any alternative could be found. None was available: the army was exhausted; the country faced starvation if the Allied blockade was not lifted, and the government had neither the strength nor the inclination to restart the war. Submission was the only course. As a result Germany lost her colonies, her eastern provinces in Poland, and temporarily the coal-producing area of the Saar: her army was dwarfed to a mere 100,000, her air force was disbanded and her economy faced with crippling reparations in money and goods for an unspecified period of years. The Republic, responsible in the eyes of its political enemies for Germany's defeat, was now made responsible for accepting a humiliating peace. Hitler was foremost among those who felt themselves totally and insidiously betrayed.

Within Germany the difficulties were acute. The Revolution had not been a unified movement with one aim and doctrine. Although in the end it was known as a Socialist victory, it was won not only against the old monarchist interests but also against a dedicated minority of Socialists who adopted an extreme position similar to that of the Bolsheviks in Russia. The attempt of this group, the Spartacists, to wrest control of the Revolution from the moderates led to the most bitter fighting of the revolutionary period. They were defeated, and their leaders, Karl Liebknecht and Rosa Luxemburg, murdered, due to an alliance between the moderate government and the military. From that moment German Communists, looking to Russia for leadership, were as hostile to the Republic as were the Nationalists. The Weimar régime became 'a candle burning at both ends'.

That it survived for as long as it did was due to its increasing economic and diplomatic success in the years 1924–9. It was never in the full sense a Socialist republic. It relied on a coalition of parties ranging from Socialist to Liberal–Conservative, and was forced to tolerate both the continued power of capitalist industry and the large estates of the old imperial aristocrats, the Prussian Junkers. Not least, it had to rely, not only in 1918 but also in the years of riots and revolution (1920–3), on the support of the army. The break with Germany's imperial past was, therefore, far from complete. Attitudes and ideas which had grown and crystallized in the years before 1914 were still vocal and attractive under Weimar. Nationalism, anti-Semitism and militarism were three of the most significant. They had their prophets and their institutions, and the Weimar period saw not their eclipse but their intensification. Their appeal grew, and leaders of influence and ability emerged. Until 1933, when he became all-powerful, Hitler was only one among many.

It might seem incredible that he became a nationalist leader at all. He was of lower middle-class origin: his father had been a minor customs official in provincial Austria. He had little formal education and no social prestige. Contrary to the idealized Aryan image he was black-haired and dark-eyed and even his Iron Cross could not elevate his military standing: he remained merely a corporal. In the 1920s he was seen by most conservative nationalists as a vulgar street orator.

Nationalism was widely diffused throughout German politics and after 1918 no group could claim a monopoly of nationalist ideas. They came from the old conservative forces of the Empire, from the middle-class business and industrial circles which had clamoured for expansion before 1914, as well as the Social Democrats, and at street level a combination of Socialist and nationalist demands was not unusual. There was thus no accepted definition of a German nationalist. One would hardly have picked Adolf Hitler in 1918 to head German nationalism, but such a statement is misleading. For whatever his apparent disadvantages there was room within the broad compass of nationalism for him to create his own following. This he did, and however many of his ideas were secondhand Hitler's nationalism in the form of

Nazism was a new movement, revolutionary in scope, ideals and method.

Hitler had been in Munich when war was declared in 1914, and he returned to the Bavarian capital after his hospital cure in November 1918. The Wittelsbach King of Bavaria had already been overthrown by the Revolution which had begun in Munich before it began in Berlin, and Hitler found himself confronted by the successful Socialist revolutionaries. He saw them all as members of a Jewish plot to undermine Germany, and wrote of his repulsion to the whole situation. But the politics in Munich were far from stable and between early 1919 and March 1920 power passed from the Socialists to a Communist soviet, and then, after violent fighting and waves of repression, it moved into the hands of a right-wing military government. Munich became a centre of political reaction and determined anti-Socialism. It remained as part of the new Republic only with hostility and reluctance. The Bavarians had always been suspicious of central control from Berlin and this was yet another feature of pre-war Germany which was perpetuated after defeat. In the years 1920–3 Munich was the natural home of those wanting separation from Berlin, those looking for a new régime, and those war veterans now unemployed who regretted the passing of war and rejected the Republican peace. Munich and Hitler were therefore closely identified. He had seen the brief triumph of the Bavarian soviet and he retained a lifelong hatred of communism. He had also seen the violent, ruthless destruction of the soviet, and of this he approved. The agents of this destruction had been not only the regular troops but also young volunteers belonging to the *Freikorps* movement. The *Freikorps*, not unlike the Italian Black Shirts, were war veterans who continued the war into peacetime. They volunteered for service against Communist Russia and joined any repressive military measure within Germany. Their ideals were nationalist ones but they were soldiers above everything. 'Our job is to attack, not to govern' was one of their slogans; another read 'Moderation is a crime against one's *Volk* and one's State'. The idea of the *Volk*, the German people, was the central one in German nationalism and active service for the *Volk* was deemed the highest achievement among these young fighters. Their brutality and exaltation of

Hitler's rhetoric: 1. H. O. Hoyer's painting of Hitler addressing a meeting of the German Workers' Party

power was no less an influence on Hitler than their successful destruction of the soviet.

Against this background Hitler's ideals and hatreds grew into politics. Apart from greater subtlety and political skill, the Hitler of the Third Reich was little different from the Hitler of 1920. He was not slow to reveal both his ambition and his ideas. In Munich a small group of ex-soldiers and workers under the leadership of Anton Drexler had created a 'German Workers' Party' (*Deutsche Arbeiterpartei*). Its aim was to combine the nationalist sentiments of the war years with the interests of the working classes. Hitler first joined the party and then, using his skill as an orator and his personal dynamism as a leader, took control and shaped it to his own will. The party was renamed the National Socialist German Workers' Party and National

Socialism was born. Hitler's first post under Drexler had been to organize the propaganda of the party and this continued to be his preoccupation. The masses had to be attracted if a wider and stronger German nationalism was to be created, and the history of Nazism in its early years is almost entirely the history of its propaganda.

In December 1920 the party bought its first newspaper, the *Völkischer Beobachter*.[1] Only 800 copies of its first edition were printed, but the new editors, Dietrich Eckart, a talented literary figure with ingrained anti-Semitism, and Alfred Rosenberg, who became the ideologist of Nazism, improved the circulation rapidly. The writing was aggressively aimed against Jews, Marxists and the Weimar Republic, and news was almost entirely about the party. When it became a daily paper in August 1923 its sales were nearly 25,000. Those who read it could be in no doubt of Hitler's intentions.

The leader himself at this period has been described by an aristocratic patron who found Hitler's movement forceful and persuasive. 'Putzi' Hanfstaengel wrote:

> *Hitler lived a shadowy existence and it was very difficult to keep track of his movements. He had the Bohemian habits of a man who had grown up with no real roots. He was hopelessly unpunctual and incapable of keeping to any sort of schedule. He walked around leading a fierce alsatian named Wolf and always carried a whip with a loaded handle . . . In fact he was not vain about his appearance. He was always decently, soberly and unostentatiously dressed and did not expect to impress on his exterior alone. His appeal lay in his power as an orator and this he knew and played on for all he was worth. He . . . believed in the power of the spoken word to overcome all obstacles.*[2]

This ability as a speaker was Hitler's main weapon of propaganda. Speaking in beer halls, concert halls and outdoor

[1] Variously translated as *People's* or *Racial Observer*. There is no English equivalent of the German *Völkischer* which comes from *Volk*, meaning 'race' or 'people'.

[2] Ernst 'Putzi' Hanfstaengel, *Hitler: The Missing Years* (Eyre and Spottiswoode, 1957), pp. 44–67.

Hitler's rhetoric: 2. Hitler speaking at an open-air meeting in Munich, 1923

meeting places, he had to rely on his own voice, unamplified, and the driving repetition and rhythm of his words. A historian of Nazi propaganda, Z. A. B. Zeman, has quoted the estimate that the frequency of Hitler's voice in a normal sentence was 228 vibrations per second, whereas 200 vibrations is the usual frequency of a voice in anger. He concludes that, 'The onslaught on the eardrums of the audience was tremendous.'[1]

By 1922 these meetings at which Hitler spoke were doubly impressive. To Hitler's display of oratorical force was added the physical force of S.A. units. The S.A. (*Sturmabteilungen:* 'Storm-troopers') were formed, like the Italian *squadre*, to provide a permanent military framework for political decisions. Power would not only be the aim of the movement: it was to be the basic formula of action. The Italians wore a distinctive black

[1] Z. A. B. Zeman, *Nazi Propaganda* (O.U.P., 1964), p. 11.

uniform; the S.A. adopted an equally assertive brown one with red armbands on which the swastika was displayed. Like the *fascio*, the swastika was a reference to remote history. It was a symbol of rebirth belonging to ancient cultures and it became the sign of a new Germany.[1]

After the S.A. came the S.S. (*Schutzstaffeln*: 'Protection squads'), composed of hand-picked men set aside to be Hitler's bodyguard and later becoming the élite corps of the Nazi movement and State. Both formations gave the Nazi meetings an appeal which the war veteran, the unemployed worker and the young nationalist found to be magnetic and inspiring. Those in the Weimar Republic who were nationalists but resisted this appeal did so because of its mass, vulgar quality. Nazism did not grow initially by gathering the old nationalism under its wing, but rather by attracting a new audience who responded emotionally to the fervour and power of the mass displays. For this audience the element of socialism in Nazi doctrine was welcome. Hitler spent much time in contrasting his social ideas with those of 'the Jew Marx'. He left his exact programme vague and encouraged people to expect from Nazism what they wanted. His socialism stressed the importance of the community: individuals, especially Jewish individuals, were to be sacrificed for the good of the whole. The message taken away from his speeches by the under-privileged in society was simple: in Nazism their needs would be met at the expense of traitors and Jews. Its skill lay in its very avoidance of detail.

In 1923 Hitler made his first bid for power. Building on the sympathy in Munich for anti-Weimar sentiments, and using the forces of discontent and reaction in the city, he attempted to take over the Munich government as the first stage of a march on Berlin. The 'march' of Mussolini in the previous year was well known to the Bavarian Nazis and their illusions of power fed on this recent model of Fascist success. But whereas Italian fascism had been widely developed throughout Italy, the Nazis were a small provincial movement with resources far short of their ambitions. The *Putsch* (revolt) failed. Despite the support of General Ludendorff, one of the retired wartime leaders of the

[1] See Chapter Twelve, p. 223.

German armies, the Nazi attempt disintegrated in the main street of Munich. Faced by a local army garrison which refused to go over to Hitler, the S.A. and marching ranks of Nazis crumpled at the first sign of fire. Hitler was leading, arm-in-arm with two colleagues. The man on the right was shot dead and fell, dislocating Hitler's shoulder. It was the end of all resistance. Hitler fled by car. Only Ludendorff, defiantly proud, walked on through the respectful soldiers.

The Munich *Putsch* appeared to the rest of Germany as merely one in a series of disturbances which marked the disastrous economic year of 1923. Thousands of people had lost their savings as the mark crashed to a fraction of its previous value. The year of inflation was more dangerous to the Republic than any previous political threat. It alienated a large number of the population and increased the appeal of anti-Weimar movements. Hitler had chosen his moment with care. But the army, in spite of considerable anti-Republican sympathy among its officers, stood by the government. The Republic survived and the economy, under the guidance of Dr. Hjalmar Schacht, recovered.

As it did so the future of Nazism appeared bleak. Hitler was in prison, serving a short sentence delivered by a well-disposed Bavarian court, and the S.A. was banned and dispersed. Like most politicians out of power, Hitler used the unexpected period of leisure to write his life story and political testament: 'The Landsberg prison was my college education at State expense,' he said later. He had already made the maximum propaganda value of his trial, and his book, *Mein Kampf* ('My Struggle'), was to be the blueprint of a future Nazi State. To this extent the years of eclipse (1923–5) were as fundamental to Nazi development as the initial years of growth. *Mein Kampf* should be seen as an integral part of Nazi history. Many people throughout Europe who later had to confront the power of Hitler as Führer of the Third Reich knew of the book's existence but failed to read it. Even some historians have brushed it aside and emphasized Hitler's opportunism rather than his underlying purpose. In the same way people dismissed Mussolini as a mere journalist. In both cases the result was to underestimate the depth of belief and conviction which lay at the base of fascism. Without an irrational, fanatical belief in Nazi ideals the thousands who

joined the movement before 1923 would have had little reason
to continue their support.

It was both to strengthen and clarify these Nazi ideals that
Hitler wrote *Mein Kampf*. Its core is a sustained attack on all
things Jewish. After describing his discovery of the Jewish society
in pre-war Vienna and his disgust at its activities in the press, in
art, literature and drama, he wrote: 'One thing now became clear
to me . . . to my inward satisfaction I knew finally that the Jew
was no German. It was only now that I thoroughly understood
the corrupter of our nation.' The details of Hitler's anti-
Semitism will be dealt with later, but in the context of Nazi
history in the 1920s it must be said here that Hitler's views were
not unique. He was preaching to a large audience which needed
no persuasion. Anti-Semites throughout Europe had seized on an
infamous Russian forgery, *The Protocols of the Learned Elders of
Zion*, and believed implicitly in its 'revelations' of a Jewish world
conspiracy. The forgery, dating from the early 1900s, set out
Jewish plans for corrupting and dominating the world. It had
been translated into all languages and despite the fact that its
fraudulent nature had been exposed it had lost none of its
insidious power. Throughout the Nazi period it was used as
fact, and the Jew was seen as the arch-enemy of the human race.

Such 'historically based' anti-Semitism provided Nazism with a
sham revolutionary cause and made up for all the deficiencies in
the party's social and political doctrine. On one thing Nazis
agreed: the Jew must be destroyed. Once this was fully stated
in *Mein Kampf* Hitler went on to advocate for the Nazis all the
things of which he accused the Jews. In short, he claimed that
the Jews were seeking world domination with political and
economic mastery; that the Jews believed they were the chosen
race, and that they would stop at nothing to achieve their ends.
These 'facts' filled Hitler with hatred, but when the tables were
turned and these aims attributed to the Nazis, he was full of self-
admiration and approval. For in *Mein Kampf* he too sought
mastery of the world and the triumph of a chosen race, the
Aryans, and he too would concede nothing in the pursuit of this
ambition. To a logician or a psychologist Hitler's position was
indefensible, riddled with inconsistency and sickness, but to the
Nazis the book appeared historically true and prophetic. It was

in fact a document of emotion and pretentious culture, but on such bases Nazism was built.

In all essential points Hitler did not deviate from *Mein Kampf*. Retrospectively his international enemies remembered that he had envisaged a European war to create a vast German Empire and destroy Russia in the East. But in 1925 these dreams were seen as the preposterous ravings of a fanatical politician, posing as a martyr for the true Germany. Twenty years later the world had seen almost every detail put into effect.

On 20 December 1924 Hitler emerged from prison. On 27 February 1925 four thousand Nazis crowded into a meeting in the Munich beer hall from which the unsuccessful *Putsch* had been launched. The campaign for power was once more under way. The *Putsch* was by now a coveted memory. Time and skilful twisting of events had made it into something approaching a success. As with Italian fascism, one sees again the tenacity with which belief held on to its own reading of history. Nazism could neither be wrong nor fail.

Hitler at Landsberg after serving his prison sentence

The renewed offensive met fluctuating opposition. Hitler was at first forbidden to speak in Bavaria and other states, but the ban was later lifted. The S.A. were forbidden to wear their uniforms, so they appeared in their underclothes—the prohibition was removed. The most effective opposition came from events, for Hitler found himself hindered by the growing stability of the Republic. He did everything to keep the defeat of 1918 before the people, but support for Weimar increased as the economy strengthened and the Foreign Minister, Stresemann, began to put Germany back on the diplomatic map. There has been a tendency to pass over the years 1925–9 as a period of Nazi stagnation. The figures of attendance at meetings do not, however, substantiate this. In 1927 at the annual congress some 100,000 Nazis were said to have come to Nuremberg in special trains. This was a considerable increase on other years. In 1928 the party polled over 800,000 votes in the general elections and could count on twelve deputies to parliament. Local branches of the party had increased in number and Nazism was established in Berlin, not with any strength but with hard, ruthless discipline under the authority of Dr. Goebbels. Goebbels was unquestioningly loyal to Hitler.

This is not to conclude that Nazism was nationally powerful before 1929. In parliament it faced eight parties which were numerically stronger. More alarming for the Nazis was the increase of Socialist popularity. The 'November criminals' polled over nine million votes in 1928, an increase of more than a million. The new Socialist premier was optimistic and a German *Who's Who* of 1929 mentioned Hitler only to say that he was of no significance. When all this has been said, however, the facts of continued Nazi expansion in the most stable years of the twenties demand attention. Italian fascism never had to face the challenge of social security and political calm. Nazism met both and continued to win converts. It may have been a fringe movement before 1929 but in its own soil its roots ran deep.

In 1929 German security disintegrated. In reaction to a crisis of confidence in the American money market, the economy of Europe collapsed within a year. No country could halt the tumbling prices which forced industry and business to cut employment by millions. Nobody would risk money, and the withdrawal of funds from investments hit Germany harder than any other country. Weimar prosperity had been built on foreign capital: money had poured into German industry from America and other creditor nations. It was now stopped or withdrawn. The wheels of German production ceased to turn and workers were out in the streets picking up a totally inadequate dole and menacing the rest of society by their helpless, grim, impoverished faces as they shambled through the towns to the labour exchanges or sat at the corners bitterly resenting any sign of wealth or comfort. By 1933 there were six million unemployed and the people badly affected must have numbered almost half of Germany's population. A recent study by W. S. Allen of one German town in this period has placed its central emphasis on the fear and anxiety caused in all classes by this continued unemployment.[1] Workers would do anything for money or bread. Middle-class employers would do anything to protect themselves from what threatened to be a revolutionary situation. The desperate needs of a whole community favoured the most desperate political parties. The Nazis and Communists both gained. Hitler was no economist but he recognized the many different opportunities which the depression created, not only among the unemployed, which was where the Communists also prospered, but, more crucially, among the authority-seeking middle classes. This joint appeal was Hitler's strength. His programme had always been flexible. This might have been a weakness in a long period of security. In three years of confusion and anxiety it was brilliantly successful. 'We are the result', Hitler admitted, 'of the distress for which the others were responsible.'

The extent of the depression was not fully obvious until 1931, but well before then the Nazis had finally arrived on the national political scene. In 1929 they had made a tactical alliance with the conservative Nationalists in order to fight the government's foreign policy. The government had agreed to continue to pay reparations to the Allies for a further fifty-nine years. This period of time and the amount to be paid had been worked out by a

[1] W. S. Allen, *The Nazi Seizure of Power* (Eyre and Spottiswoode, 1966).

committee under the American banker, Owen Young. The total sum demanded was far less than the original Allied claims, and Stresemann, the Foreign Minister, was prepared to accept this settlement. Both the Nazis and the Nationalists had from the beginning opposed the Versailles peace and reparations. The Young Plan seemed to them yet another act of treason by Weimar. They therefore aimed to defeat it by stirring the whole country into opposition. To achieve this the two parties needed each other. The Nationalists were a conservative, middle- and upper-class party which looked back to the glory of the Empire and drew its strength from the Junkers, from the large old-established industrial firms and from those individuals who feared the growth of communism and its threat to the established order. Nazism, on the other hand, was directed at the masses and could give to the Nationalist politicians a platform in the streets. The two leaders, Alfred Hugenberg and Adolf Hitler, came together.

Their alliance is perhaps the most instructive event of the Weimar period. The difference between the typical conservative Nationalist and Hitler has already been stressed. The career and position of Hugenberg accentuated this. In the early years of the century he had become a director of Krupp's iron and steel empire; he had made a fortune out of the 1923 inflation and had bought his way into mass communications. He was one of the largest publishers, had a controlling interest in U.F.A., the large film company, and in 1928 became the leader of the Nationalist Party (D.N.V.P.). He shared all the Nationalist ideals except anti-Semitism, which was curiously missing from his propaganda. In its place he preached a fanatical anti-communism. This was his driving concern. Hitler could not begin to match either Hugenberg's influence or his social status. His party had only twelve deputies where the D.N.V.P. had seventy-eight. The Nazi S.A. was regarded as brash and vulgar by its Nationalist equivalent, the *Stahlhelm*. Nationalist youth movements looked on Hitler's organizations with superior scorn. Yet Hugenberg felt sufficient sympathy with Nazism to solicit its help and Hitler was sufficient of an opportunist to agree. When hostility to Weimar was the common denominator there was no need to dwell on differences of belief or method. The fact of this alliance is a guide to an explanation of the Nazi rise to power. Although it was an uneasy partnership and although it collapsed when Hitler became more confident of his position, it points an answer to the difficult question 'Why did Hitler win so much support?' The short reply is this: the extension of Nazi influence through the Hugenberg alliance and the opportunities afforded by the depression allowed Nazism to appear both revolutionary *and* safe; the same two qualities that had recommended Mussolini to Italy in 1922. Fascism could be called 'the Safe Revolution'. W. S. Allen says of the town of 'Thalburg':

> *Though the D.N.V.P. had a small following in Thalburg they had two assets which benefited the Nazis. One was money. In Thalburg most of the members of the D.N.V.P. were either high-ranking civil servants, entrepreneurs or noblemen. The other asset was respectability. Not only were the 'best' people members: the party bore the tradition of having firmly supported the monarchy in the golden days of Germany's greatness. Finally, it seemed to have an intimate connection with the Army through the* Stahlhelm *whose honorary national commander was von Hindenburg. By giving enthusiastic support to the Nazis and by limiting its opposition (in the periods when the parties were at odds) to Nazi social goals, the D.N.V.P. helped pave the way for Hitler. To Thalburgers it was clear that the best people were for the Nazis except where it might affect their moneybags.*[1]

Until we have more individual studies like Allen's, we cannot be sure that his findings are typical of Germany as a whole, but where he would appear to be invulnerable is in his descriptions of Nazi propaganda. His portrait of the opportunism, skilful organization and immense variety of approach used by the Nazis in their propaganda rings true for the total history of Nazism in the period 1930–3. This particular passage contains the quintessence of Nazi success:

> *The Nazis began the final electioneering [of 1932] with a mass meeting featuring the League of German Girls. A speech by a Thalburg leader stressed 'love of Fatherland,*

---

[1] W. S. Allen, *The Nazi Seizure of Power* (Eyre and Spottiswoode, 1966), p. 134. Thalburg is a fictitious name for a real German town.

Folkish community, Germanic consciousness and German morals'. Three days later a dual meeting was held appealing to 'Rentiers, Pensioners and War Invalids' and to 'German Artisans and Businessmen'. Prices were cut to 20 pfennig, the lowest amount ever charged for a Nazi meeting. In the morning the S.A., S.S. and Hitler Youth went to church en masse and at noon the S.A. band gave a concert. Two days later a Lutheran minister spoke for the Nazis. Again the price was cut, though the Nazis were in financial trouble, for they made a public appeal for funds. The minister attacked the von Papen government, though as usual he stressed religion and nationalism. 'There is only one God in heaven whom we serve and only one Fatherland that we love.' There was a big enthusiastic crowd. Finally on election eve, the Hitler Youth and League of German Girls joined to sponsor an 'evening of entertainment' with songs and a dance as well as speeches by local leaders.[1]

The entertainment side of Nazi appeal has been often overlooked in the concern to describe its brutality. We should fail to understand anything of fascism if we had only an image of terrorism and torture. In the case of 'Thalburg', Nazism was particularly skilful not only in exerting pressure but in providing the necessities of everyday life for its supporters: soup to the underfed; uniforms for the down-and-out; warmth and entertainment for those in the streets; and a sense of community and purpose for the aimless and disoriented. In each case the aim was to strengthen Nazism, but the amenities were provided none the less.

The cold facts of Nazi growth must be set against this human situation. Despite the failure of Nazi–Nationalist agitation against the Young Plan, the elections of 1930 brought astounding results. The Nazis gained 107 seats in the Reichstag, instead of their previous twelve, and their public support leapt from under a million votes to 6,409,600. The Communists too had increased the number of their seats to seventy-seven (in 1928 they had fifty-four), but the Nazi success overshadowed everything. They were now the second-largest party in the Republic, and since

[1] W. S. Allen, *op. cit.*, p. 128.

the Nationalists suffered a severe reduction to only forty-one, it appeared as if Hitler was capturing the right-wing Nationalist vote. His position altered overnight: journalists from all over Europe printed his declarations of principle and good will: society was open to him, and a legal accession to power was within sight. Thanks to his alliance with Hugenberg in 1929, he had vastly expanded his propaganda methods. He could now reach every section of the population by relayed speeches and efficiently motorized campaigns. In 1932 he added to this the use of the aeroplane. Flying from one town to another he used the catch-phrase 'Hitler over Germany'. It was a potent slogan.

Nazi institutions increased. To the S.A. and S.S. were added Youth Movements enrolling thousands of young men and women in the name of the Fatherland and the *Volk*. A Nazi Motor Corps gave to the S.A. a flying squad for rapid action, and Dr. Goebbels perfected his department of propaganda. An intelligent, hard man, who could be charming in society and whose clubfoot induced nervousness in those who first met him,

Nazis campaigning at Frankfurt in 1932

Joseph Goebbels in 1934

Goebbels gave the Nazi movement that touch of intellect which the rantings of Hitler lacked. Hermann Göring was another asset: his record as an air fighter in the war had been excellent; he came from a landed family with aristocratic pretensions and served Nazism as a channel to wealthy and respectable society in Berlin. His flamboyance and vanity gave high colour to the drab uniformity of Nazi personnel.

With the depression unabated and a succession of governments unable to maintain either a consistent policy or civil order, the Nazis tightened their hold on public opinion. They offered a future of authority, decision, German recovery and revenge on all public enemies. Their support grew. In July 1932 they gained 13,745,000 votes which brought them 230 seats. In January of the same year Hitler made what has become one of his most famous speeches. Addressing the élite of German industrialists at Düsseldorf, he played on their fears of communism and assured them that National Socialism would do nothing to weaken German capitalism. Rather, German industry, he claimed, badly needed the security Nazism could provide: 'There is only one fundamental solution—the realization that there can be no flourishing economic life which has not before it and behind it a flourishing, powerful State as its protection . . .' These claims and assurances were followed by an openly emotional appeal:

> *Remember that it means sacrifice when many hundreds of thousands of S.A. and S.S. men every day have to mount on their lorries, protect meetings, undertake marches, sacrifice*

themselves night after night to workshop and factory, or as
unemployed to take the pittance of the dole: it means sacrifice
when, from the little they possess, they have to buy their
uniforms, their shirts, their badges, yes and even pay their
own fares. But there is already in all this the force of an
ideal—a great ideal! And if the whole German nation today
had the same faith in its vocation as these hundred thousands,
if the whole nation possessed this idealism, Germany would
stand in the eyes of the world otherwise than she stands
now! [1]

Hitler was greeted with cheers and enthusiasm. The industrialists
withdrew their caution. Hitler was assured of continued financial
support. He was equally successful with the army, who needed
considerable reassurance about the S.A. He gave it to them, yet
again changing his approach to suit the situation.

In the summer of 1932 Hitler was the obvious candidate for
government, but it would be wrong to suggest that this was the
majority opinion. Nazism never obtained a majority of public
support in a free national election. There was plenty of opposition
both to his ideals and his methods. This opposition was entirely
diffuse, ranging from Communists to conservatives, and as such
was totally ineffective as a political balance, but its existence
never ceased to irritate Hitler. He could not claim indisputable
mastery of Germany. In fact, Nazi support dropped by two
millions in the second elections of 1932. This development has
tantalized historians ever since. Public opinion appeared to be
recovering its sense of values: the economy was looking brighter
and Brüning, the Chancellor, was providing more political
authority than his predecessors. Was Germany nearly out of the
depression? Could another few months have undermined the
Nazi position?

The questions are interesting if only to heighten the drama of
the last act. This has been told with care and great clarity by
Alan Bullock.[2] By unravelling the world of intrigue round the
figure of the ageing President von Hindenburg, he has charted
Hitler's arrival at power and shown how leading politicians
hoped to use Nazism for their own ends. This was particularly

---

[1] *The Speeches of Adolf Hitler*, vol. i, ed. N. H. Baynes (O.U.P., 1942), p. 829.
[2] Alan Bullock, *Hitler: A Study in Tyranny* (Odhams, 1952).

true of von Papen, who finally secured Hitler's appointment as Chancellor. Von Hindenburg, with a lifetime of military pomp and glory behind him, had little respect and no liking for Hitler, the ranting corporal, but he gave his agreement to the appointment, and on 30 January 1933, Adolf Hitler, leader of the largest political party Germany had ever known, became head of the government. Weimar now had as its Chancellor a man whose political career was dedicated to the destruction of the Republic.

Von Papen's illusion that Hitler would act in accordance with his orders was just one of the many fatal errors of judgment which brought Hitler to power. He should not be singled out for recriminations. Just as misled and abused were the millions whose votes had swollen Nazi prestige. Hitler was the superior of all his calculating supporters. They expected him to act in their interests as he had so convincingly told them he would. Twelve years of the darkest despotism showed them how tragically mistaken they were. The Revolution of Nazism, all things to all men, became something stark and simple when in power: the Revolution of Destruction.

Hitler greeting President von Hindenburg at the opening session of the Reichstag in Potsdam, 21 March 1933

CHAPTER FIVE

France: *Action française* and its Rivals

In 1899 a small group of intellectuals began to meet regularly at the Café de Flore in Paris. The meetings were organized at first by a young writer, Maurice Pujo, and a philosophy teacher, Henri Vaugeois; later in the year Charles Maurras, critic, journalist and political writer, began to assume leadership. The background to their discussions was the crisis which had divided France for over two years, the Dreyfus Affair. Superficially it was a nation-wide argument over whether or not Alfred Dreyfus, a Jewish army officer, had sold military secrets to Germany. More fundamentally it became a question of who should rule France and with what values.

The history of France was still overshadowed by the great Revolution, and since 1789 it had proved impossible to unite all Frenchmen behind one form of government, whether empire, monarchy or republic. In 1899 the régime was republican and it had survived for twenty-nine years since it succeeded the Second Empire of Louis Napoleon. The Dreyfus Affair was its most severe crisis. Its political enemies used the conflict of opinion to point out the weakness of republican rule: a strong authoritarian government, they claimed, would never have allowed the country to be torn by such dissension and humiliated before the whole of Europe. Those who met at the Café de Flore were among the most outspoken representatives of this opinion.

Maurras was the most notable of the group. Since the age of fourteen he had been deaf, a handicap which largely explains the tenacious way in which he clung to his ideas. These had become fixed during the Affair when he felt strongly the need for a return to monarchical rule, the only régime, he stated, which had made France truly great and given it consistent order and authority.

In 1896 at the Olympic Games in Athens he had 'suffered for France' when he saw how superior were the athletes from monarchist countries such as Britain and Germany. He also became aware of the extent of the patriotic fervour with which these nations supported their teams. By comparison he saw France as an inferior country with no unity or pride, and his sense of national shame increased with the events of the Affair. He became convinced that France without a king was France without honour, stability, power or glory. Monarchism and nationalism were for Maurras inseparable.

Neither Vaugeois (who was descended from a regicide) nor Pujo showed any sign of monarchist ideas until Maurras joined them. It was the measure of the latter's brilliant, persuasive argument that within two years they had totally accepted his position. Over other nationalist values they had no need to argue. They agreed that France was corrupted and fatally divided by republican democracy, that the nation suffered from the presence of Jews, Protestants, Freemasons and other internal 'aliens' and that the true France must be re-established, if necessary by force. On this understanding the movement of *Action française* was launched. In 1905 it became fully established as an activist league and in 1908 its newspaper of the same name, *Action française*, began its daily editions to stir up violent and vociferous nationalism throughout France. An educational establishment was founded to train young nationalists, and action squads called *Camelots du Roi* (The King's Agents) moved into the streets. All who joined the *Action française* swore an oath of loyalty to the royalist pretender, the Duke of Orleans: 'The monarchy alone can assure public safety and overthrow the evils of society which we as anti-Semites and nationalists denounce . . . I therefore apply myself to the work of royalist restoration. I swear to serve it with all my power.' A cause which seemed to have died in the 1870s was now capable of inspiring dedicated young Frenchmen of all classes. The *Action française* shared the ability of later Fascist movements to appeal to a wide cross-section of the public.

Maurras was proud of the wide appeal of the *Action française* and stressed it continually, as, for instance, when he reminisced over the *Camelots du Roi*:

> *One can say that six years (1908–1914) of street battles,*
> *six years of prison and triumph, restored the national*
> *morale of all classes in the country. Young working men*
> *and young employees were as numerous in their ranks as*
> *young bourgeois.*[1]

The claims of the movement to be classless were strongly repudiated by the left-wing political parties. The Socialists in particular denounced the *Action française* as a capitalist organization. It was true that Maurras appealed more to the conservative Right than to the Left, since his avowed hatred was for the Republic, but his doctrine did entertain a strange sort of socialism, although this took the form of an ideal of community rather than a programme of economic change. In his *Political and Critical Dictionary* he wrote: 'Socialism, purged of its democratic element, is a natural part of nationalist monarchism.' Above all, it was a socialism of sentiment:

> *We have always rejected the republican slogans of liberty*
> *and equality because they are doctrines of hatred. But we*
> *have always kept the slogan of fraternity and all classes, I*
> *repeat, were represented among us: workmen, peasants,*
> *bourgeois and aristocrats. This is French Unity.*[2]

Under this fraternal banner of national unity the *Action française* engaged battle on two fronts: against Germany abroad and against 'the enemies of the true France' at home. Germany could be easily identified but the internal enemies were not so obvious. It was the object of the *Camelots du Roi* to draw attention to them. They destroyed statues of prominent republicans: they started brawls in lectures by Socialists or pacifists, and they waged a ceaseless campaign against the supporters of Dreyfus, who was finally acquitted and restored to his rank in 1906. In this way they kept the Dreyfus divisions alive right down to the eve of war. It is therefore ironic that one of their main judgments on the Affair was that it had mortally divided France. This judgment Maurras maintained throughout the years of war. He welcomed the outbreak of the war and he threw his whole movement into the fight against the traditional enemy,

---

[1] *Le Procès de Charles Maurras* (Michel, Paris, 1946), p. 149.
[2] *Ibid.*, p. 150.

Germany. To this extent he was partially reconciled with the Republic which was waging the war, but he attributed every loss of life and every reverse to traitors at home, and it was clear that none of his hatreds had diminished. After the war the struggle continued: his nationalist challenge to republican France had lost none of its violence. The internal enemies remained.

Nevertheless the detested Republic won the war, and the national hero was not Maurras but the Premier, Georges Clemenceau, one of the great opponents of Maurras during the Affair. The *Action française* looked even farther from power in 1919 than it had in 1914. It was never a movement on the scale of Mussolini's fascism and was always on the outside of national politics: an extremist pressure group full of threats and grandiose ideas, led by a hard, cold theoretician who could write with colour and brilliance, but had few other qualities with which to lead a popular movement. Maurras was no revolutionary and this fact became abundantly clear when the *Action française* was compared to Italian fascism and, later, to German Nazism. The movement itself invited comparisons by its admiration for Mussolini's 'march' on Rome in 1922 and his Fascist solution of the Matteotti affair in 1924. An election declaration from the *Action française* in 1924 stated:

> France must be given a leader who can see things clearly, plan, know, give orders, act, endure. Events and men call for the leader who is independent of the caprices of Parliament . . . For parliamentary intrigue . . . we must substitute method, authority, continuity, all that dictatorship alone can bring about, all that Italy has found in Mussolini, all that our France is still lacking.[1]

Admiration was not unqualified, however. Maurras always emphasized that the *Action française* looked for a monarch of royal descent not an upstart dictator, and to this he added a demand for a decentralized state which would restore the power of the old French provinces as they had existed before the Revolution. With these two items of policy, monarchism and decentralization, Maurras showed that he was nearer to

[1] Quoted in H. Tint, *The Decline of French Patriotism* (Weidenfeld and Nicolson, 1964), p. 176.

conservative nationalism than to fascism. Despite the *Camelots du Roi* and despite the movement's anti-Semitism and violence, the *Action française* belonged in the 1920s to the world of reaction and conservatism. It remained the great 'father figure' of French Fascists and it influenced many of them, but it failed to attract the new generation on which the power of Mussolini and Hitler was built.

This did not prevent the political Left from calling the *Action française* both Fascist and dangerous. In particular the Communists were emphatic on this point: Maurras was seen as a French Mussolini and he was to be closely watched. One sees here the beginning of that great simplification of politics which dominated the 1930s: the conviction that there were two sides battling for Europe, Fascists and Communists. The reality was far more complex, but in France it was particularly easy to fall for this simplification. Since the Revolution there had been a tendency to talk of left-wing and right-wing politics, or of France being split between Left and Right. Now in the 1920s it seemed that the old division was replaced by a new dualism: fascism on the Right, and communism on the Left. The fact that the vast majority of Frenchmen were neither Fascist nor Communist seemed to be overlooked. This simplification had one significant result: those who were passionately anti-Communist were drawn irresistibly into the Fascist camp as if there was no alternative, and the same pull operated in the other direction. In Fascist history this meant that a rash of small movements broke out, all of them of a semi-Fascist nature, in order to contain the growing number of anti-Communists. If the *Action française* had been more adaptable and more revolutionary it might have become a powerful party, but as it was, the smaller movements became its rivals.

Few of these movements were as revolutionary as Mussolini's Fascists and none had the totalitarian authority of Nazism. They fit more closely into a tradition particularly French: the tradition of leagues, which reaches back to the Revolution. The league was an organization to apply political pressure at moments of crisis: it normally took to the streets and ran meetings and demonstrations which were noisy and sometimes violent. When the crisis was over, the league tended to disappear. During the Dreyfus Affair leagues were numerous: some brutal like the Anti-Semitic

League, some dashing and flamboyant like the League of Patriots, and others almost passive like the League of the Rights of Man.

Was there a crisis in the 1920s to justify a reappearance of league activity? In a comparative sense there was nothing like the Dreyfus Affair: the Republic was never threatened in the same way. But those who were critical of republican politics could find ample reason for demonstration. In the first place, as the *Action française* repeated constantly, France had won the war but had not gained control of the peace. Maurras and his colleague Léon Daudet both called for the partition of Germany in order to leave it permanently weak. This would have been a fatal blow against Germany's position. Their 'advice' was not followed and throughout the twenties Germany recovered its European strength. When France took steps to extract back-payments from Germany in 1923 and occupied the German Ruhr, Maurras was delighted, but the French withdrawal after an ill-fated operation doubly increased his anger against the Republic. For the rest of the decade the weakness of French foreign policy was a reason given for nationalist and semi-Fascist demonstrations. Secondly, the French economy was bedevilled by the fluctuating value of the franc, and industrial progress was slow. There seemed to be a permanent financial crisis. Thirdly, French population growth was little more than nil at a time when Germany was rapidly expanding. Fourthly, the appearance of a Communist Party under directions from Russia, and the fact that the Socialists were led by an intellectual Jew, Léon Blum, increased the belief of nationalists and anti-Semites that France was corrupted by aliens.

For all these reasons the Republic was exposed to criticism and attack in the name of nationalism. The *Action française* had shown how to proceed with its action squads of *Camelots*, and its path was followed with even more vigour by its rivals. The first of these stemmed from the old League of Patriots and took the name *Jeunesses Patriotes* (Patriotic Youth). It was led by the Paris deputy, Pierre Taittinger, and was formed expressly to fight the political Left. It had a strong student contingent, and in its idealization of youth it was not unlike Italian Futurism. The National Revolution, it proclaimed, would be one of youth: it would be a revolution not of the Right nor the Left, not of any class, but of a generation. To achieve this revolution it divided into groups of fifty and put itself at the disposal of anti-Communist parties. Its mission was 'to defend the nation against internal disruption' and to this end it fought a number of street battles, one of which Taittinger reported with cryptic passion:

> *May 1925. Rue Damrémont. Baptism by fire.*
> *Our centurions fell at Montmartre into a communist*
> *ambush. Fifty of our young men were wounded; four of*
> *their comrades were killed. They died maintaining order;*
> *protecting with their breasts the peaceful citizens whom they*
> *had sworn to defend.*[1]

The number recruited by *Jeunesses Patriotes* was always exaggerated by Taittinger, who claimed over 240,000 by 1934. The police stated about 90,000, which would seem more accurate. It was never a powerful movement, and although it looked purely Fascist to its enemies, it lacked the resolve to bring about a change on the Italian scale.

The first movement to copy the Italian Black Shirts and break away from the league tradition was *Le Faisceau* (The Fasces). In name, style and policy it proved at first a close imitation of Mussolini's party. Its founder, Georges Valois, had been the economic expert of the *Action française*, which he had joined as early as 1906. He had brought to the movement the noble ideal of combining royalists with trade unionists in a new formation of national strength. His Proudhon Circle was an organization designed to achieve this end by allowing the followers of Maurras to meet ordinary working men and discuss the future of France. Proudhon, the 19th-century Socialist, had clashed with Marx in suggesting that socialism could be organized in independent groups of producers. Marx had wanted a much broader base to the Socialist society and had rejected Proudhon's ideas as utopian. Valois, however, was strongly influenced by Proudhon, whom he saw as a truly French Socialist. In a similar way he was impressed by the writings of Georges Sorel, who had envisaged the triumph of the workers through the General Strike. Sorel's doctrines had become the inspiration of French syndicalism, an extreme form of trade unionism, and Valois used many of the syndicalist hopes in his own economic doctrines. Combining Proudhon, Sorel and Maurras, he put forward in the pages of the *Action française*

[1] *La Liberté*, 3 January 1926.

a kind of national socialism which would unify the nation and end the competitive individualism of capitalist society. It was an ideal similar to Mussolini's 'Corporate State', which also set out to achieve a unity of employers and workers in national productivity.

His Socialist influences and his nationalist convictions being as they were, it was not surprising that Valois saw in Mussolini his own reflection. He was highly impressed by the victory of the Italian *Fasci* in 1922 and in November 1923 he paid a personal visit to *Il Duce*. From that moment he grew increasingly critical of Maurras and the *Action française* and in February 1925 he launched his own weekly paper *Le Nouveau Siècle* ('The New Century'). Its debt to Mussolini was clear in its appeal to the French war veterans to stand firm by the nationalist achievements of the recent war:

> As in August 1914 we desire only one party: the party of France. We desire only one policy, that of Victory.
>
> We desire these conditions: a national leader, French fraternity, a nation organized in its families, professions and provinces . . .
>
> We found neither a party nor a league. We work in order to form or reform the legions of victory, legions of soldiers, of heads of families, of producers and citizens . . .[1]

In October of the same year Valois left the *Action française* and proceeded to start a movement nearer to the image of Italian fascism. Significantly he founded *Le Faisceau* on 11 November 1925, the anniversary of the 1918 Armistice: he saw the war and his movement as one continuing process, with the war veterans providing the link. As he stressed this aspect he drew close to the pattern of both fascism in Italy and Nazism in Germany, but this was the only real point of contact. For a year it looked permanent: members of *Le Faisceau* wore blue shirts and were divided into four sections—soldiers, producers, youth and other civilians. 'We are Fascists', proclaimed their propaganda, thus openly confessing what *Action française* always denied. The split between the two movements became increasingly bitter. In December 1925 the *Action française* sabotaged a meeting of Fascist veterans and by 1927 there was almost open

[1] *Le Nouveau Siècle*, 26 February 1925.

war between them when a group of *Le Faisceau* militants tried to sack the offices of *Action française*, exchanging revolver fire in the process.

Despite these Fascist activities and the early hopes of Valois to bring nationalism and socialism together, *Le Faisceau* moved steadily away from its Italian model. Valois began to seek the support of Communists against the capitalist financiers and his Socialist influences became more and more pronounced. In 1927 the movement was sufficiently left-wing to denounce Mussolini as a reactionary, and in 1928 it was reconstituted as a national syndicalist movement owing far more to Sorel than Maurras, far more to Proudhon than Mussolini. The label of fascism was rejected and Valois renounced the use of force. He had started the first real Fascist party in France and he himself destroyed it. His own end underlined the complete change of direction: he died in a Nazi concentration camp.

The importance of *Le Faisceau* lay in the lead it gave to nationalist war veterans. Since the war, as in Germany and Italy, the 'fellowship of the trenches' had been recreated in numerous veteran groups and societies. Valois had turned several of these groups towards fascism. He was not the last to do so, but was followed by François Coty and Marcel Bucard. Coty's movement *Solidarité Française* (French Solidarity), dating from 1933, would be totally insignificant had it not been for the notorious ambitions of Coty himself. He stands in French history as a comic-opera version of the German nationalist Hugenberg. Like Hugenberg he had made his money in industry and had used it to buy newspapers. He owned two dailies and in 1928 had started a third with the overt aim of spreading semi-Fascist nationalism in politics and business. Coty, who had financed Valois until *Le Faisceau* turned away from fascism, saw himself as the uncrowned leader of Gallic nationalism. He seemed to have a nose for lost causes and no amount of posturing could increase his political influence, which was negligible. In the end he formed his own stormtroopers, called his movement *Solidarité Française*, and sent them into the streets to do battle against communism. It was the year of Hitler's triumph in Germany, but Coty's veterans, numbering under 2,000 and including North African mercenaries as well as unemployed volunteers, were little more than a parody of the S.S. When Coty died in 1934 his movement had done nothing more than irritate areas of Paris and provoke the first round of police fire on the celebrated night of 6 February.

This date in 1934 signifies in French history one of the peaks of Fascist agitation. Historians tend to disagree over its importance, but there is little doubt that French republicanism felt itself severely threatened at the time. The background was a European one: firstly, the general economic depression which affected France later than Germany but which was causing serious unemployment after 1932; and secondly, the growth and victory of Nazism. Under the pressure of the economic crisis, the international ideals of the Versailles Peace crumbled as national governments turned in on themselves and raised tariff barriers to protect their own industries. The mood of Europe was one of introspection and anxiety. In France the nationalist propaganda of the *Action française* and its rivals pounced on every sign of government weakness, ready to see the treason of Jew or Communist at any turn. In the winter of 1933–4 they were given an opportunity which seemed exactly tailored to their needs: the Stavisky scandal. A Russian émigré, Stavisky, had gained control of a municipally owned pawnshop in Bayonne and had been making a fortune in bonds bought and sold against the non-existent credit of his business. When the bubble burst and the facts of his dealings came into the open it was found that he had escaped prosecution due to connections with influential politicians. His sudden suspicious death turned the scandal into a national crisis and gave to the nationalist groups a new slogan, 'Death to the Thieves'. The *Action française* was the first to exploit the situation by publishing letters condemning one of the ministers: it refused to accept the verdict of suicide on Stavisky, believing he had been politically silenced. On 6 February 1934, the Premier, Daladier, was due to meet Parliament to present measures to settle the crisis. In the morning orders were issued to *Jeunesses Patriotes*, *Action française*, *Solidarité Française* and various veteran groups to demonstrate against Daladier outside the parliament building. By evening the assembled rioters, with some Communists among them, had turned to violence in an attempt to terrify the government into flight. But the cordons of guards held, and although burning cars lit up the Place de la Concorde the *coup d'état* was seen to be unplanned and leaderless. Fifteen were killed and over a thousand were injured before the agitators dispersed. February 6 was a failure in the hard facts of power but its reverberations shook the whole of France and the threat of Fascist rule appeared to hang over the Republic.

The rioters had acted for only a minority of Frenchmen but it was not known whether it was part of a more organized revolution or not. In retrospect it seems that the various right-wing groups had not seriously planned anything on the scale of a political revolution. Anyone wanting to bring about a real *coup d'état*, argued the historian Goguel, would hardly have concentrated so exclusively on parliamentary buildings: 'the ministries, the telephone and telegraph exchanges, the radio stations, gas and electricity works, stations and airports . . . these are the principal objectives in our times of anyone attempting a *coup d'état*.'[1]

His verdict appears just. It would almost have been out of character for the French right-wing groups to plan in such rigorous detail. Their image was more spontaneous, emotional and rhetorical: they were poorly disciplined and lacking in unity. This is not only a judgment from hindsight. It was also the opinion of Marcel Bucard, the second heir of Georges Valois and founder in 1933 of the movement *Le Francisme*. The rioters, he alleged, were not interested in overthrowing the government: they acted merely on an upsurge of emotion. The *Francistes*, he was proud to say, did not participate: *they* were interested in real power.

Francisme certainly aimed to be the most systematic of all French fascisms. Bucard had broken first with Valois, then with Coty, and in November 1933 he founded his own party. The English historian Denis Brogan treats it lightly: 'Then there were the *Francistes*, who dressed in a uniform rather like that of Hitler's stormtroopers and who took their name from the two-headed axe of the ancient Franks, but although French politics are highly historical, they were not historical enough

[1] F. Goguel, *La politique des partis sous la IIIe République* (Éditions du Seuil, 1958), p. 488.

for a party of ancient Franks to get very far.'[1] The *Francistes* encouraged this kind of satire by their theatrical pomposity: with blue uniforms went vacuous slogans and idolatry of the leader, Bucard. Nevertheless, in their self-conscious rituals they embodied much of the appeal which had brought Italy to Mussolini and Germany to Hitler. They stood between right- and left-wing politics: they chanted hymns to the sun: they praised order and progress, worshipped modern civilization and the ancient past and called for a revolution of authority. These were marks of serious Fascist intent and they were taken to their extreme. In January 1934 a prominent *Franciste*, Grégoire Lefranc, wrote: 'We aspire with all our hearts towards an entente with the Germany of National Socialism.' This was a complete departure from the nationalist orthodoxy of *Action française*. For the first time in France the idea of universal fascism, going beyond the interests of individual nations, was announced as open policy. The way to active collaboration with Hitler was open and Bucard himself was to follow it with conviction and self-assurance.

His movement, for all its calculated Fascist appeal, attracted no more than a few thousand supporters. They chanted their slogans through the streets:

> *Groaning is nothing,*
> *Speaking is little,*
> *Acting is everything.*
> *To act, join*
> *Francism!*

but there were too many other groups and parties also claiming the monopoly of action, and Bucard was not an outstanding leader. As success eluded him his ideas grew more extreme and he became an anti-Semite, expressing vicious hatred of Jewish 'internationalism'. Through his extremism his movement became a satellite of Nazism and throughout the next decade he contributed nothing new to French fascism. His challenge to society had the colour of other more successful fascisms, but he had no sense of power or political strategy. In the end his own scorn of 6 February could be turned against himself. But he had taken a

[1] D. W. Brogan, *Development of Modern France* (Hamish Hamilton, 1940), p. 655.

Jacques Doriot speaking
at a meeting of
the *Parti Populaire Français*

significant step away from
conservative nationalism, and
the workers and unemployed
who joined his Blue Shirts
showed that communism did
not have an exclusive control of
the proletariat. This was a vital
lesson for French politics; and
the man who learned most from
it was Jacques Doriot. Out of
the workers of Paris, Doriot
created the largest and most
dynamic Fascist Party which
France produced, the P.P.F.
(*Parti Populaire Français*).

In 1934 Doriot was a leading
Communist. He was mayor of
St. Denis, a populous working-class suburb of Paris, and a man
with a dedicated personal following. A proletarian himself by
background, he had risen to the top in the Communist Party by
skilful use of his limited education, a strong organizing ability
and a flair for demagogic public speaking. Above all he was, like
Mussolini, alive to the challenge of events and could never allow
political doctrine alone to determine action. It was soon
abundantly clear that his major quality was opportunism.

Only four days after the 'Fascist *coup*' of 6 February, Doriot,
the Communist, sensed the opportunity which lay in the event:

> *Those who lived through the demonstration will long
> remember the extraordinary dynamism of that crowd, its
> hunger for action. What a lesson for revolutionary
> organizations.*

He had already shown disdain for his Communist superiors,
treating them with curt indifference, and now in the crisis
caused by the right-wing threat he began to see himself as leader
of a united workers' party, a Communist Mussolini or Hitler.
He began to attack Moscow and the party in France for their

slowness in seizing the initiative. He advised a non-doctrinaire
unity of all workers, whether members of the Communist,
Socialist or Radical parties, and then decisive action against the
Right. But Moscow would take no orders from below: its policy
at that time was firmly dogmatic; even the Socialists were seen
as Social-Fascists and there was no sympathy for a broad movement such as Doriot suggested. His resistance became more open
and in June 1934 he was expelled from the party as a traitor.
It was small comfort to him that a year later the Communists
veered right round to his point of view and contributed to a
Popular Front alliance of all left-wing parties against the
Fascist menace.

Doriot took no part in this development. He was dangerously
embittered by the treatment of his party but he retained his
hold over many of the workers in St. Denis: he was a leader
without a cause. Between 1934 and 1936 he found and formulated his own. As it developed it became increasingly Fascist,
until during World War II Doriot's men were known as French
Nazis.

The movement he founded in 1936 was called *Le Parti
Populaire Français* (P.P.F.) and its first object was to preserve
European peace by bringing France to an understanding with
Hitler's Germany. 'Peace at any price' was a common slogan
in the 1930s: it had no supporter more fervent than Doriot. He
had been impressed with Hitler's conquest of power and noted
that many of his votes came from working-class areas. In particular he admired the way that Nazism had used the slump and
social crisis as a means to extend its popular appeal. The P.P.F.
denied at first that it was Fascist, but Doriot's whole activity
betrayed a strong sympathy for Nazi achievements.

By 1937 the P.P.F. showed every sign of the Fascist synthesis.
It was hostile to both communism and capitalism; it claimed to
be based on wide popular support, yet Doriot himself headed an
élite who controlled every action; it used the heroism of Joan of
Arc as a religious myth to symbolize ancient French virtues and
at the same time placed technological progress at the head of its
social programme; it was proud of its proletarian support, claiming over 70,000 workers among its members, and yet emphasized
the classless nature of its nationalism. At the head stood Doriot

as a leader in the full Fascist sense of Führer or *Duce*, embodying the spirit and will of the people he commanded.   More than one writer called Doriot 'the saviour of France', and he was the object of intellectual veneration as well as proletarian loyalty. In particular the brilliant young writer Drieu La Rochelle sang his praises in lyrical terms. Drieu La Rochelle wanted to unite all experience and all passions within himself: he looked for the Dionysian life urged by Nietzsche, and in Doriot he sensed the arrival of a superman figure. 'Doriot', he said, 'is our champion against Death: Doriot will purify the French race.' It was an irrational, primitivist sentiment which La Rochelle turned into politics. He was one of many in the thirties who expected fascism to create a totally new world: his illusions fastened on Doriot, and the P.P.F. was seen as the advance guard of the great international revolution to come.

No other French Fascist could rival the leadership of Jacques Doriot. Through his newspaper *L'Émancipation Nationale* he projected himself as the answer to communism, weak French republicanism and Jewish capitalism. He was not a natural anti-Semite, but Hitler's propaganda was infectious and it was a nationalist tradition to list the Jews among the internal enemies. By 1938 he had adopted most of the anti-Jewish ideas which were useful to his cause. Restlessly opportunistic, he also exploited every international event in his fierce street-corner speeches, but at the peak of his popularity in 1938 he could count only 250,000 supporters and this figure may well be a generous one. What he lacked in numbers he made up in display and aggression, and he attracted a good deal of sympathy from anti-Communists of most parties: but, although Doriot seemed to carry out the Fascist recipe with precision, he was never more than a minor threat to the Republic. His career during World War II when the Germans occupied France will be dealt with later, along with that of yet another Fascist leader, Marcel Déat. It is worthy of note that inter-war France was stable enough to resist all its Fascist movements, even that of the 'saviour Doriot'.

This resilience of France against fascism was in some measure aided by the very strength of the old school nationalists. One movement, *Croix de Feu*, headed by the war veteran Colonel de la Rocque, is an excellent example of a group which the left-wing parties unquestioningly called Fascist but which was really an extremely active conservatism. The same could be said of *Jeunesses Patriotes* and to a large extent of the *Action française*. None of these groups was sufficiently revolutionary to throw itself behind a Fascist *coup d'état*. They threatened and sabotaged the Republic but they stopped short of open revolution. Compared with Hitler's opposition to Weimar, their opposition to the Republic appears almost moderate. As such they kept a considerable number of nationalists away from the rival and less conservative movements of *Le Faisceau, Le Francisme* and the *P.P.F.* The multiplicity of parties was thus both a reason for and a symptom of Fascist weakness in France.

Finally there was a continuing belief among the majority of Frenchmen that the old Revolutionary and democratic tradition was the real France. Despite parliamentary weakness and periodic crises, they were not to be converted to the 'true France' of Maurras or the 'future France' of Doriot and Drieu La Rochelle. Fascism never reached the centre of French politics in peacetime. It owed its moment of triumph to the arms of Nazi Germany.

CHAPTER SIX

Britain, Belgium and Spain

1 MOSLEY AND THE BRITISH UNION OF FASCISTS

In 1937 George Orwell wrote:

We have reached a stage when the very word Socialism calls up on the one hand a picture of aeroplanes, tractors and huge glittering factories of glass and concrete: on the other a picture of vegetarians with wilting beards, of Bolshevik commissars (half gangster, half gramophone), of earnest ladies in sandals, shock-headed Marxists chewing polysyllables, escaped Quakers, birth-control fanatics and Labour Party backstairs-crawlers. Socialism, at least in this island, does not smell any longer of revolution and the overthrow of tyrants; it smells of crankishness, machine worship and the stupid cult of Russia. Unless you can remove that smell and very rapidly, Fascism may win.[1]

This self-critical appraisal of his own creed was Orwell's reaction to the failures of socialism in the 1930s, but his honesty was backed by a deep humanitarianism and sense of justice which kept his radicalism alive and his protests sensitive and constructive. He saw that fascism was a possible intellectual alternative to socialism and he was prepared, unlike many of his left-wing colleagues, to concede that fascism was not entirely evil. But, he maintained, if socialism was in danger of losing support, the answer was to rekindle its great humanitarian fire, not to leap to a Fascist alternative.

[1] G. Orwell, *The Road to Wigan Pier* (Gollancz, 1937), p. 248.

Sir Oswald Mosley, a wealthy baronet, educated at Winchester and Sandhurst, first a Conservative and then a Labour M.P., was also critical of socialism in the thirties: in fact he became its fanatical opponent. He too started from the belief that socialism must be rejuvenated, but unlike Orwell he had no radical sense of liberty. His criticisms became bitter, his anger became violent and he moved restlessly on the fringe of politics until he found the ideology of fascism and created his own Union of Fascists. He was not, however, the kind of Fascist Orwell expected to emerge in England. 'When I speak of fascism in England', Orwell wrote, 'I am not necessarily thinking of Mosley and his pimpled followers. English fascism, when it arrives, is likely to be of a sedate and subtle kind . . . and it is doubtful whether a Gilbert and Sullivan heavy dragoon of Mosley's stamp would ever be much more than a joke to the majority of English people.'[1]

Here, Orwell was only half correct. In retrospect, Mosley has indeed become something of a joke or at best an irritation, but he and his followers were the most significant Fascists to emerge in Britain between the wars, and at their height they formed an outspoken, active minority group which had little of Gilbert and Sullivan's blustering charm.

The British Union of Fascists was founded in 1932 and its pre-history is almost entirely that of the slump and depression which had gripped the British and world economy since 1929. Hitler owed his incredible mass support to the chaos and despair of these years in Germany. Mosley tried to exploit a similar economic situation in Britain. At first his ideas and actions had none of the cynical power obsession which marked the rise of the German Führer. In 1930 he was a junior minister in Ramsay MacDonald's Labour Cabinet and was assistant to J. H. Thomas, the Lord Privy Seal, who was responsible for employment. While he held this office he confronted the growing problem of unemployment with imagination and vigour. His proposals went far beyond the orthodoxy not only of British conservatism but also of his own Labour government. He envisaged a programme of action which would cut through his country's economic traditions, linked since the early 19th century to the dominant

[1] G. Orwell, *op. cit.*, p. 244.

principle of free trade. In his memorandum submitted to the Cabinet in February 1930 he argued for greater protection of British industry, a large decrease in imports and increased pensions and allowances to give the average citizen more purchasing power. He believed that if Britain concentrated on its own economy and gave priority to everything British the wheels of industry would turn more productively and the standard of living would rise.

Thus in Mosley's adventurous economic ideas there was the strong outline of an assertive nationalism. The memorandum was rejected—more because it was unorthodox and expensive than because of its nationalist pretensions. Mosley fought hard for its survival, forcing debates and divisions among Labour M.P.s and within the Labour Party itself. He was not without influential support and some of his ideas have since become a new form of economic orthodoxy. But when his case was refuted and defeated in 1930 he became convinced that the political system in general and Labour policies in particular were corrupt, useless and opposed to all qualities of leadership: action to save the country was being thwarted by blind and stupid politicians. Armed with this angry sense of rejection and frustration, Mosley left the government, the party and his respectable political career.

Between 1930 and 1932 he tried various formulas of political expression, believing all the time that he was both a talented leader and a man with a vast national cause. His vanity increased, his opportunism developed and his choice of colleagues and followers grew more reckless and indiscriminate. After total failure in the elections of 1931 and his rejection by working-class voters, he was finally convinced that the disease eating at the heart of British life and politics was the party system and the liberal tradition of British parliamentary government. With this conviction he created the British Union of Fascists (B.U.F.) with the explicit purpose of destroying the parties and factors which had repudiated his ideas. It was a movement of resentment clothed in an ideology which at first expressed Mosley's own driving ideals but was later heavily influenced by German National Socialism. Like Doriot in France, Mosley came to submerge his own national movement in an imitation of the Nazi model, and as he did so his support dwindled to insignificance.

Sir Oswald Mosley, leader of the British Union of Fascists, holding the top of a park railing thrown at him during one of his meetings

In 1932, however, the B.U.F. was aggressively British. Its bible was Mosley's book, *The Greater Britain*, in which the leader displayed fascism as the 'modern movement': 'The essence of fascism is the power of adaptation to fresh facts. Above all it is a realist creed.' Fascism alone, Mosley claimed, could understand the true nature of Britain's problems and act on them. It alone could build a Britain which was strong and viable and whose power lay not in the hands of aliens and Jews but in the native hands of Britons at home and in the Empire. 'We have in unison in our cause the economic facts and the spiritual tendencies of our age.'

With claims such as these the B.U.F. stood in the mainstream of European fascism. It looked back to all the great moments of Britain's past and called itself the only valid heir to past greatness. To give colour and form to this historical boast it adopted the *fasces* as one of its symbols. 'The *fasces*', wrote Mosley, 'are the emblem which founded the power, authority and unity of Imperial Rome. From the Rome of the past was derived the tradition of civilization and progress during the past two thousand years, of which the British Empire is now the chief custodian.'[1] In addition, the movement had its own symbol, a flash of lightning within a circle. It was held to portray the flash of action within the circle of unity.

Throughout the formative period of the B.U.F., Mosley was closely in touch with the leading Fascist movements on the

[1] Sir O. Mosley, *Fascism. 100 Questions Asked and Answered* (B.U.F., 1936), Preface.

The canteen at the headquarters of the British Union of Fascists in Chelsea

Continent. After returning from a meeting with Mussolini he wrote a description of Italian fascism which combined illusion with perception:

> *It is as remote from stand-pat Conservatism as it is from woolly-headed Socialism or the destructive Communism which it overthrew. It brings to post-war politics a new creed and a new philosophy which cannot be tucked away in any of the old pigeon-holes of thought . . . This Fascism challenges alike the 'Right' and the 'Left' of old world politics. It has produced not only a new system of government but also a new type of man, who differs from politicians of the old world as men from another planet.*[1]

This sympathy with Mussolini's party and ideology was explicitly demonstrated by the black shirts of the B.U.F. followers and their extended arm salute. Both had precedents in the smaller English Fascist groups of the 1920s––the 'British

[1] Sir O. Mosley, from *Saturday Review*. Quoted in Colin Cross, *The Fascists in Britain* (Barrie and Rockliff, 1961), p. 57.

Fascists' formed in 1923 by Miss Rotha Lintorn-Orman, a field-marshal's granddaughter with a penchant for the masculine life, and 'The Imperial Fascist League' started by Arnold Leese, a retired veterinary surgeon and a fanatical patriot—but neither of these two groups had an influence on Mosley comparable to that exerted by the European dictators.

Like a latter-day medieval knight, Mosley kept his Black Shirts as personal retainers, housing them in a Chelsea barracks, called 'The Black House', and loosing them for marches and demonstrations in the large towns. Violence became a norm and the element of thuggery within the B.U.F. grew steadily. Trained, ironically, by a Jewish boxing champion Kid Lewis, the Black Shirts specialized in smashing Jewish windows and shops in London's East End and in beating up those who heckled during the large propaganda meetings at Olympia and the Albert Hall. Clashes with left-wing groups in the streets were relatively few compared with the latent civil war of Italy in 1920–2 or Germany between 1930 and 1933, but they were just sufficient to give the false impression that Britain also was caught in the European struggle between communism and fascism.

In fact, for all its noise and violence, the B.U.F. barely touched the core of British life and politics. Even when it numbered about 20,000 members and its activities made head-lines in the national press, its influence was never more than marginal and its doctrines seemed nothing more than a sequence of eccentricities. Typical of its much-publicized statements were the following: 'The press will not be free to tell lies'; 'The Fascist movement represents Leadership not Tyranny'; 'Chain stores owned by Jewish and foreign capital will be eliminated'; 'Fascism alone can preserve the Peace, because it alone removes the causes of war'; and 'All immigration will be stopped'. Alongside these desperate illusions were visions of a policy which made good sense to a wide spectrum of voters. There were promises of increased pensions, which were calculated to impress the workers; ideas for ending the class war, designed for the ears of industrialists; a plan to replace the House of Lords with a Second Chamber based on merit and function, which would appeal to young intellectuals; and above all the grandiose dream of a Corporate State. This was the showpiece of Mosley's ideology. It owed much to the theories of Italian and French Fascists and was couched in similar terms. In place of an unrestricted private economy, fascism would create an economy geared to the national interest, in which workers and employers would work together in corporations for the benefit of the nation.

The ideology of the B.U.F. was thus a patchwork of irresponsible claims on the one hand and serious political thinking on the other. Such a combination in Italy and Germany had brought power to Mussolini and Hitler, but to Mosley it brought nothing but hostility from press, public and, eventually, police. British political life was too well categorized: there were not the large numbers of unrepresented, frustrated and floating voters that there were in Italy and Germany. Mosley found that his ideas appealed only to a minority simply because the vast majority had fairly stable allegiances to existing parties or unions. There was no crisis of democracy in Britain: there was complacency, blindness and self-satisfaction among many, and misery and hopelessness among others, but the hold of the party system remained firm, and men looked to traditional politics for political action, not to minorities like the B.U.F. or the equally powerless Communist Party.

The history of Mosley and the B.U.F. is therefore one of dwindling importance. In 1934 it had moments of Fascist glory, especially at its huge Olympia meeting on 7 June when Mosley in his black shirt was the hero of 15,000 cheering supporters. The hecklers were brutally handled and the enthusiasm of the Fascists was passionate and revolutionary. Olympia 1934 became one of their few great landmarks. But the violence which was attractive to the audience was more than distasteful to the wider public, and when Hitler's Röhm Purge followed on 30 June the British Fascists bore the brunt of a wave of revulsion. Legislation began to curb their power and in 1936 all political uniforms were banned. Raids against East End Jews continued and Mosley drew closer to Hitler's ideology and foreign policy, but as a movement the B.U.F. was impotent.

What sort of people joined this fringe political pressure group? Colin Cross, the most objective historian of Mosley's movement, wrote:

> *The typical long-service Black Shirt was a man of the lower middle class, not particularly clever but capable of loyalty and sacrifice. Fascism had an appeal because it attacked both the capitalism he resented and the socialism he feared. Without sacrificing his social rank, which was a grade above the manual worker, he could take part in a revolutionary movement. For his work he received little reward. He bought his shirt for five shillings and paid a subscription of one shilling a month if in work or fourpence a month if unemployed—the same rates as those in the Communist Party. If he travelled a long distance to a meeting he would have free transport in van or hired bus and, perhaps, a free meal. Devoted Black Shirts would stand night after night on street corners in the lonely task of selling the Fascist publications.[1]*

There were others who, with private incomes or expensive education, do not fit this picture, and there were the intellectual recruits, such as A. R. Thomson, William Joyce, A. K. Chesterton (second cousin to G. K. Chesterton), who brought to the party individual ideas about civilization and patriotism, but no common social grievance. In fact, whether drawn from young public-school men, the unemployed, the resentful small traders or disillusioned Socialists and Communists, they were not representative of their groups or class.

Once war was declared in 1939, British fascism was finally broken and dispersed. A. K. Chesterton followed his patriotic feelings and joined the army, whereas William Joyce went to Germany and offered himself to Hitler, and as 'Lord Haw-Haw' during World War II became notorious for his broadcasts in English of German propaganda. Mosley moved more cautiously and advised the B.U.F. to 'do nothing to injure our country or to help any other power' but nevertheless increased his demands for a peaceful understanding with Hitler. In May 1940 he was arrested along with other leading members of the movement and by autumn of the same year hundreds of ex-Black Shirts were detained in prison under emergency regulations. Many were soon released, but Mosley remained until November 1943

[1] Colin Cross, *The Fascists in Britain* (Barrie and Rockliff, 1961), p. 70.

when he was allowed to return to his home in London.

Most Fascists were silenced by the wave of anti-Germanism which swept the country after the Battle of Britain and by the intensification of war propaganda, but after the war some drifted back onto the fringe of politics. Mosley was one of these. In the 1960s he was still writing letters to the press, justifying his record and denying that he was either a Nazi or a man of violence. In these letters he stressed his particular brand of socialism which had been rejected in 1930, but the historian must point out that this was not the practical essence of his fascism. The allegiance of those who joined the B.U.F. was to the ideals of action, violence and nationalism and their only tangible policy was anti-Semitism.

In theory, however, Mosley produced a strongly argued example of the Fascist synthesis. Dissatisfied with all alternatives in the Britain of 1930 he created a new fusion of ideas. For Mosley such a fusion was a great personal solution to his own predicament. The same was true of both Hitler and Mussolini, but in their case they persuaded their countrymen that the solution was also a national one. This, Mosley was unable to do.

2   LÉON DEGRELLE AND THE BELGIAN *REX*

Of all the Fascist leaders to emerge in the inter-war period, Léon Degrelle comes nearest to the modern idea of the popular idol. Men fell in love with him, women became hysterical in his presence: he was young, charming and good-looking and spoke with a passionate verve which packed huge stadiums night after night. He was steeped in provincial life and spoke nostalgically of his rural background. Born in 1906 in the Belgian Ardennes, he grew up, as he said, in an organic society:

> *At home we ate black bread, often without coffee. Everyone was friendly. My father was a bourgeois and the lawyer and doctor were bourgeois too. But they greeted the blacksmith and the tanner as they passed their doors because the blacksmith and tanner earned their living as they did, and, like them, had many children: they were all honest, respectable working men.*[1]

[1] R. Brasillach, *Léon Degrelle* (Plon, Paris, 1936), p. 15.

From here he moved on to a Jesuit education and then to the
University of Louvain, where, as a flamboyantly religious student,
he was attracted by strong spiritual ideals which he was convinced could be put into practice. His hero was Charles
Maurras and like large numbers of Catholic students he read the
editions of the *Action française* with the devotion of a disciple.
Even when Maurras was condemned by the papacy in 1926 the
ideas of the French movement continued to influence Degrelle,
but with his hero disgraced he turned increasingly to his own
potential. Curious and sensitive, he began to make long trips
round the country to experience the ordinary life and suffering of
the people. He wrote a little poetry and then suddenly went to
Mexico under false papers, to 'suffer with the Catholics there
who were dying for their faith'. He joined a secret Catholic
grouping called 'Soldiers of Christ the King', and listened
emotionally to stories of Catholic martyrdom, which he later
sold to American newspapers on his way home.

When he returned to Belgium he was not yet twenty-five. He
came back to a country which, like Britain, was locked in an
economic crisis but was still politically stable. Belgium was a
monarchy where the king was widely respected. In a parliamentary system three parties predominated, the Catholic Party, the
Socialists and the Liberals. Since 1918 they had ruled in differing
coalitions, no one party ever obtaining a sufficient majority in
the elections to rule alone. At a time when party politics were
being criticized and questioned all over Europe it was not surprising that the changing Belgian coalitions aroused opposition
in the twenties. Spokesmen of the middle classes complained of
the cynical professionalism of the politicians; declining tradesmen
and industrialists accused parliament of subservence to high
finance, and idealistic students denounced corruption, inefficiency
and inaction. On grounds such as these, voices began to be raised
for a reform of politics which would bring greater power to the
executive and more security to society. The ideas of the *Action
française* were tailored exactly to these demands.

The economic slump increased this discontent, but at no point
was the Belgian parliamentary system in danger of collapse. What
was new was the multiplicity of small groups who stood opposed
to the system altogether, and although they were always divided

they had a weakening effect on the democratic confidence of the people. This economic insecurity and political suspicion became the raw material of Degrelle's movement, as of fascisms all over Europe. In Mexico Degrelle had served 'Christ the King' and back in Belgium he had joined a Catholic publishing business with the same name, *Christus Rex*. In 1932 he and several friends issued their own Catholic paper with identical inspiration but called simply *Rex*. With the symbols of crown and cross it launched indignant attacks against political corruption and social materialism. It was a moral campaign, urging a return to purity and spiritual values, and with its slogan *Rex vaincra* ('*Rex* will conquer') it became a crusade. By 1935, building on a year of meetings and public speeches, Degrelle had become the leader of a movement, loosely organized at first and with imprecise aims, but with a membership which grew rapidly as the circulation of the paper, in several editions, increased.

It was in this year, 1935, that the great personal talents of Degrelle became established as a political force. Devoted followers flocked to hear his diatribes against party politics. They paid to sit at his feet, for no meeting of *Rex* was free—the movement needed all the money it could raise. In June its membership became open to all Belgians and thereby lost its particular Catholic character. Degrelle actively encouraged this development. As Brasillach, the French Fascist writer, punned, Degrelle was a man of 'irresistible *Rex* appeal who wanted everyone to follow him'. As a result even the patronage of Catholicism became a curb on his individual dynamism, and in November 1935 he made a flamboyant, insulting speech at a congress of Catholic associations and circles, branding many of the Catholic leaders as corrupt politicians.

It was now *Rex* against the whole established order, and from this point the Fascist side to Degrelle's moral campaign became increasingly apparent. He denounced politicians and financiers indiscriminately, herding them into his basest category, that of *les pourris*, the corrupt and rotten. He described the Belgian system of government as '*la dictature des pourris*' and demanded a great national purge. There was just enough substance to his attacks, and there were just enough minor scandals within

Belgium or larger ones like the Stavisky scandal in France, to give credibility to his denunciations, but those who followed him were not all public protesters and moralists. Like Fascist movements everywhere, Degrelle's movement fed on a wide variety of discontent and insecurity, from intellectual restlessness to economic bitterness. One thing remained dominant, and that was the element of student idealism and revolt. Degrelle, like the Italian Futurists and José Antonio in Spain, knew how to build on the conflict of generations.

The climax came in 1936. With yet another acknowledgment towards *Action française*, Degrelle brought out a newspaper called *Le Pays Réel*—the real, organic nation which Maurras had proclaimed since the Dreyfus Affair. It was founded to fight the parliamentary elections which would, the Rexists hoped, lead to a conquest of the government. Degrelle himself decided not to stand, a decision he came to regret when the polls brought astonishing success to his chosen colleagues. Twenty-one Rexists were elected to a parliament which numbered 200 seats: one in every nine Belgians had voted for the party of Fascist purity. From student gesturing to political significance, *Rex* had moved at almost impossible speed in a matter of months. The leaders of fascism elsewhere began to take greater interest. Financial grants from Mussolini became substantial, Hitler welcomed Rexist success, and Brasillach in France published a flattering history and portrait of Degrelle and his movement.

There were other Belgian movements which had Fascist aims and methods. *Verdinaso*, led by the brilliant Joris van Severen, was an example with its violent Flemish nationalism, its authoritarianism, its militia and its Fascist salute, but neither this nor other smaller groups stimulated the Belgian imagination as Degrelle's movement did. After the electoral successes of *Rex*, numbers well beyond its voting strength watched for signs of a creative policy which would fulfil its colourful promise. The question 'What does *Rex* want?' became a persistent one.

It soon appeared that Degrelle had few answers. He had no economic or political programme beyond the vague outlines of a Corporate State and a 'healthy' nation. His social ideas were closer to those of *Action française* and Salazar in Portugal than to those of Hitler, but he showed a certain admiration for the

Léon Degrelle, leader of the Belgian *Rex*, in 1938

Nazi Führer which alienated many Belgian nationalists. He was hostile to communism and had used the slogan '*Rex* or Moscow?' in the election campaigns, but he went on to support a number of workers' strikes and thereby kept the main body of industrialists at a suspicious distance. Nor could he depend on Catholic support since his speech of November 1935. Wherever one looked there seemed to be Rexist sympathizers, but the party and policy of *Rex* was something of a mirage. Degrelle's own personal magnetism was the only constant in the movement.

Like Britain, therefore, Belgium needed more than an emotional leader and a wave of discontent to unsettle its equilibrium. The government kept control and the three main parties as well as the trade unions did not lose their morale. When Degrelle stood against the Prime Minister, Paul van Zeeland, in a by-election in Brussels in April 1937, he was decisively defeated by the established parties, who all coalesced behind the principle of parliamentary rule. *Rex* had failed to present a workable alternative. It had destroyed with power but its constructions were weak and ambiguous.

For the rest of the thirties *Rex* was a shadow of its former self. Degrelle finally entered parliament in 1939 and his speeches round the country continued to electrify the credulous, but he was essentially powerless. His support ebbed and the number of Rexist M.P.s dropped from twenty-one to four. Like Doriot in France he could rise only on the external defeat of his country. When this came in 1940 with the German occupation, Degrelle offered himself to Hitler as the natural ruler in a Fascist Belgium, but there was still opposition, this time from conservative collaborators, and Degrelle left Belgium to fight on the Eastern Front against Russia. Here, finally, he made his case for leadership: decorated by Hitler for military valour, he was, by 1944, the Führer's choice for power in Belgium. This power he was unable to enjoy. The Allies liberated Belgium before *Rex* could conquer and fulfil its oldest slogan. Degrelle fled by air to Spain, the Spain of General Franco.

3 JOSÉ ANTONIO AND THE SPANISH *FALANGE*

Fascism in Spain seems a curio of history, like communism in Russia. Both ideologies would appear to need an advanced economic environment in which to appear and yet both Russia and Spain were predominantly rural and, in many areas, feudal societies. If fascism is held to be a desperate last stand by frightened capitalists against encroaching socialism then Spanish fascism would need a great deal of explaining, but such a definition is quite inadequate. What Spanish fascism exemplifies is the strong vein of irrational, romantic nationalism which is as much a feature of fascisms everywhere as is capitalist insecurity. Spanish nationalism therefore is the best area in which to search for signs of growing fascism. Few parallels with the rest of Europe are helpful, though a comparison of early 20th-century Spain with late 18th-century France might help to set certain perspectives. In both countries the dominant problems were social ones: the coexistence of vast landed wealth and working-class or peasant misery; the autocratic control of the Catholic Church, which maintained a strict social hierarchy, and the gradual development of towns with attendant separation of bourgeois and proletariat. Again, in both countries these problems were easily pushed aside by the constant fluctuations in the political scene, breeding frustration and revolutionary ideals on the one side and authoritarian reaction on the other. France between 1780 and 1830 was in a constant state of change, uncertainty and civil enmity: ideas proliferated, and political solutions were kaleidoscopic. Revolutions and revolts occurred, dictators were produced, constitutions written and broken and old monarchs restored. Spain between 1875 and 1939 presents a not dissimilar picture. It had little in common with the Europe of Kaiser Wilhelm II and Lloyd George or of Hitler and Neville Chamberlain, but this Europe was drawn into Spanish politics by the passionate infection of the Spanish Civil War. What the volunteers who fought in the Civil War discovered was the very particular nature of Spanish life and problems, and historians are now at pains to emphasize this fact. Spain must be examined in Spanish terms.

This is especially true of Spanish nationalism. It was barely in evidence in the 19th century: provincial differences were strong and staunchly defended and Spain was not involved, like Britain and France, in building an empire or fighting other European powers. Between 1909 and 1926 it was engaged in a losing battle in Morocco which left the military anxious and dissatisfied, but nationalism was not born from issues of foreign policy. All the major conflicts were internal ones. Economic development was slow and uneven and its benefits confined to small numbers; wages were as low as any in Europe and industrial methods often little more than primitive. The so-called

constitutional monarchy which had ruled since 1875 was inert
where action was most needed, and its few advances towards
democratic liberty and equality were resisted by entrenched
conservatives and scorned by growing circles of anarchists.

Under the stress of so many unsolved problems, ideas and
politics began to polarize. Extremes became more common and
more organized. Respect for the faltering efforts of the constitutional régime and its middle-class politicians was at a
minimum. Nationalism, therefore, like Spanish anarchism and
communism, developed as an extreme answer to Spanish internal
problems. It stressed the need for a strong executive, a revival of
traditional institutions like the Church and an élitist culture
which would be purely Spanish.

It thus seemed a straight expression of nationalism when a
jovial, sensual Andalusian general, Miguel Primo de Rivera,
staged a successful *coup* in 1923 and ruled as dictator until
January 1930. Frequent comparisons were made between the
General and Mussolini, and indeed meetings between the two
gave the appearance that they had much in common. But Primo
de Rivera's *coup* and dictatorship were in a firmly established
19th-century tradition, that of the *pronunciamento* ('pronounce-
ment' leading to *coup*). When the country was deemed by the
military to be threatened by incompetent politicians then they
'reasserted the national will' by a timely *coup d'état*. Primo
de Rivera's hold on Spain was closer to this accepted image
than to any contemporary fascism. He had no real party
and little ideology. He was acceptable to the conservatives and
owners of capital and land because he brought order and
simplicity to government business. Beyond that there was
nothing endurable, and when he lost the confidence of his
supporters due to his economic failures there was no structure
to maintain him. He had preached national unity and had relied
on the backing of the Church. To a large extent he had aroused
patriotic fervour, but he failed to achieve any national solidarity
and he fell from power in 1930, when there was no one prepared
to fight for his continued rule. The King, Alfonso XIII, fell from
power a year later and a republic was proclaimed with festivities
and optimism, which merely veiled the deep divisions and social
bitterness which were still unresolved.

It is against this background of a growing nationalism and the failure of its first political leader that Spanish fascism developed. The dictator was seen as too moderate, too unimaginative and too reliant on the old conservative forces who had finally betrayed him. He had failed to appeal to the working classes and had no driving ideological belief. The new leader would be more conscious of old and new, of capitalist interests and trade-union demands, of traditional Spanish beliefs and new dynamic ideas. In short, a synthesis was needed which would be neither conservative nor anarchist, neither ultra-Catholic nor anti-clerical, neither capitalist nor Socialist, but which would contain skilfully blended elements of them all.

It is one of the astonishing facts about José Antonio Primo de Rivera, the dictator's son, that he worked carefully and consciously towards just such a synthesis. In the years following his father's fall he reflected intensively both on his father's mistakes and on the betrayal of the dictator by the conservatives. He was not alone in this reflection: among those who were reaching in the same direction was Ramiro Ledesma Ramos, a young, unsociable student of philosophy who was by 1931 a clerk in the postal service. In 1931, admiring and emulating Hitler, Ledesma founded an explicitly Fascist party of ten members all with university backgrounds. He called himself a national-syndicalist and his paper *La Conquista del Estado* ('The Conquest of the State') proclaimed the aim of the movement. José Antonio had many points of contact with Ledesma but was of an entirely different character. In some respects he was an idol like Degrelle in Belgium: talented, charming, poetic and with the confidence of his wealthy social background, he was able to sway and inspire his university friends, and he remained the firm favourite of idealistic students.

Like Ledesma, José Antonio was interested not in a conservative but in a revolutionary nationalism. His antipathy for the old reactionary Spain became as strong as his love for the Spanish spirit of independence and vitality which he was determined to harness into a vigorous movement. He was greatly influenced by the élitist ideas of the great Spanish sociologist Ortega y Gasset, whose brilliant book *The Revolt of the Masses* affected most subsequent nationalism in Spain. Ortega had not supported the dictatorship of Miguel Primo de Rivera, since he believed that the living values of Spanish culture could best be preserved by a combination of all parties, from which the national leaders would emerge. José Antonio was less impressed by this ideal political formation than by Ortega's cultural élitism which lay behind it. He felt it was necessary to have a party of his own. In this way a 'creative minority' could forge the weapons of the new Spain.

In 1933, with the help of a well-known aviator, Julio Ruiz de Alda, José Antonio founded the *Falange Española* (Spanish Phalanx). Financed partly by nationalist businessmen, the new party began to attract the student population in Madrid. The way it emerged and the nature of its first support showed how consciously idealistic and ideological it was. There was little economic fear or social insecurity behind the early *Falange*: it thought and spoke with the poetic romanticism of young literary men who had worked out a solution for divided Spain. The Republic had failed either to create social harmony or to appease nationalist sentiments: the students round José Antonio called for a new cause and a new leader.

On 29 October 1933, the young aristocrat presented his ideals to a political meeting at the Comedy Theatre in Madrid.

> The Patria *is a total unity, in which all individuals and classes are integrated:* the Patria *cannot be in the hands of the strongest class or of the best-organized party.* The Patria *is a transcendent synthesis, an invisible synthesis with its own goals to fulfil: and we want this movement of today, and the state which it creates, to be an efficient, authoritarian instrument at the service of an indisputable unity, of that permanent unity, of that irrevocable unity that is the* Patria.[1]

He went on to state that 'there must be no shrinking from violence' if violence was necessary, but José Antonio was to show later how reluctant he was to unleash forces of destruction and assassination. In this speech, however, the *Falange* was launched as an aggressive nationalist movement which flouted the old nationalism of the twenties by using left-wing revolutionary

[1] Quoted in S. G. Payne, *Falange* (Stanford U.P., 1962), p. 39.

terms and syndicalist slogans. For this reason it was regarded with suspicion by most of the Spanish conservatives and for three years it struggled for a real foothold in Spanish politics. Where it quickly established itself was in the streets of the capital. Increasing civil bitterness was producing street clashes between anarchists and conservatives, between Communists and clericals, and the *Falange* swiftly became the object of left-wing attacks. It was seen from its beginning as a Fascist movement even though José Antonio refused the label of fascism since it came from outside Spain. But such distinctions were lost in the unsubtle warfare of terrorism and assassination. Before long young Falangists fell to the knife and bullet of the Spanish Left, and as the numbers rose José Antonio authorized actions of revenge. When he did so he could no longer claim to represent all aspects of Spanish life and politics. Increasingly his movement was pushed towards the Right, though he fought this tendency until his death.

Pressure on José Antonio came also from within his own party. Like Mussolini before the Matteotti murder, he was urged by extremists in his militia to extend the conflict and increase the revolutionary aims of the movement. The Falangist militia was less interested in ideology than in the basic struggle for power, and the leader's poetry and ideals had only superficial effects on their activism. He could not, however, afford to curb their activities: the situation in Spain moved steadily towards civil war and armed followers were a necessity for aspiring national leaders.

After a year of existence the *Falange* was still a very minor political grouping. Numbering only five thousand regular members, it had not succeeded in wresting revolutionary initiative from the Left nor in attracting powerful figures from the Right. The party's finances were in a poor condition and but for José Antonio there would have been little romance in the movement. By early 1935 he was undisputed *Jefe* (leader) after a challenge from Ledesma had failed and the latter had returned to provincial obscurity.

Hugh Thomas, historian of the Spanish Civil War, has called José Antonio 'the Hero in an Empty Room', and in 1935 the independent stature of the leader did become a form of lonely heroism. He rejected possible ties with other European fascisms, even though a photograph of Mussolini remained prominent in his office, and he reasserted the *Falange*'s ideas of synthesis which excluded it from both Right and Left in Spanish politics. As a speaker José Antonio continued to present his ideal country: 'We do not love this wreck, this decadent physical Spain of today. We love the eternal and immovable metaphysic of Spain.'[1] It was a language which explains why the *Falange*'s members were mostly under twenty-one and attached to universities or intellectual circles. This élitist composition was to José Antonio's liking: despite his ideology, which called on all classes to join the *Falange*, he was not a popular orator like Hitler or Doriot. There exist few reliable statistics on the sociology of the movement, but those that do exist show that the working class preferred their Communist or anarchist movements to the intellectual claims of the young aristocrat.

The year 1936 brought change and disaster. In the elections the *Falange* was loosely associated with the Right and therefore shared its considerable defeat. A Popular Front of left-wing parties appeared to have gained Spanish approval for the Republic. The various groupings of nationalists, army leaders and conservatives who had fought the régime since 1931 were faced with the alternative of submission or revolt. In the atmosphere of street violence and recurrent political murders revolt became the only 'honourable' course. The *Falange* was forced to share this decision. Since the elections several more members had been shot down in the streets, and as Falangists accelerated their own programme of murder and brutality the government arrested the leaders, including José Antonio. From his prison the *Jefe* negotiated with the plotting army generals and other right-wing conspirators, but his bargaining power was limited. When the generals' revolt was finally staged on 17 July 1936, the *Falange* was swept along with events: it did not determine them.

The revolt brought civil war, and civil war led to the intervention of Italy, Germany and volunteers from the democratic countries. The events and importance of this brutal war will be presented later.[2] As will be seen, the triumph of General Franco

[1] Quoted in S. G. Payne, *Falange* (Stanford U.P., 1962), p. 80.
[2] See pp. 127–33.

and the nationalist cause did not benefit the *Falange*. At first there was a rush of new members and conscripts into the militia: the *Falange* became an effective police and terrorist arm of the generals' campaign. But the price was a high one. Its independence was lost and its ideology absorbed into a more traditional nationalism. Its hero and leader could not change or check this development. Early in the war his death before a Republican firing squad left a gap which no other personality could fill. It was symptomatic of the *Falange*'s romanticism that many refused to believe that José Antonio could be dead. He had inspired an ideal of a living, permanent Spain, and they waited for his return.

CHAPTER SEVEN

The Thirties: Consolidation of Fascism

'The lamps are going out all over Europe; we shall not see them lit again in our lifetime.' Edward Grey's celebrated remark at the beginning of World War I was echoed more desperately and tragically throughout the thirties. There can be few decades which have lived so permanently under the actuality and threat of destruction. In Britain and France they are called the *pre*-war years, but already in 1931 Japan was at war with Manchuria, in 1935 Mussolini waged war against Abyssinia, in 1936 the bloody civil war in Spain erupted and in 1938 Hitler seized Austria and intensified the war economy under which Germany had been living since his arrival at power. The decade began with the largest economic depression in the history of modern Europe: it ended with the most devastating war. Between the two, the hold of fascism over the lives and minds of millions of Europeans tightened and expanded. There were few areas of life which were not in some way menaced or attracted by its forceful appeal. People sensed, even more than they had done in 1914, that Europe was facing the end of an era.

The poetry of Louis MacNeice captures with subtlety this sense of catastrophe in Britain:

> *Hitler yells on the wireless*
> *The night is damp and still*
> *And I hear dull blows of wood outside my window;*
> *They are cutting down the trees on Primrose Hill.*

The wood is white like the roast flesh of chicken,
Each tree falling like a closing fan:
They want the crest of this hill for anti-aircraft,
The guns will take the view
And searchlights probe the heavens for bacilli
With narrow wands of blue.
And the rain came on as I watched the territorials
Sawing and chopping and pulling on ropes like a team
In a village tug-of-war; and I found my dog had vanished
And thought 'This is the end of the old régime'
But found the police had got her at St. John's Wood station
And fetched her in the rain and went for a cup
Of coffee to an allnight shelter and heard a taxi-driver
Say 'It turns me up
When I see these soldiers in lorries'—rumble of tumbrils
Drums in the trees
Breaking the eardrums of the ravished dryads—
It turns me up; a coffee please.[1]

Brought together by MacNeice are the trivia of daily events and
the shadow of violent death, the coffee and the roast flesh, the
lorries and the tumbrils. But in Britain they could still be
separated. In 1938, when this poem was written, war had not
arrived and the energies of politicians were fully exerted to
perpetuate peace. In Italy, Spain and Germany the thirties were
different: violent death was counted among the trivia of daily
events: what was shadow in Britain was substance in these
countries.

1 ITALY

In Italy a Fascist encyclopaedia of 1931 proclaimed that
'Nothing is ever won in history without bloodshed'. Mussolini's
régime incorporated this language of war and struggle into the
ordinary speech of day-to-day politics. There was a 'battle' to
increase wheat production, a 'battle' to raise the birth rate, a
'battle' to reclaim unproductive land and a constant 'warfare'
against internal enemies. This last feature of Fascist rule had been

[1] L. MacNeice, from 'Autumn Journal' in *Collected Poems of Louis MacNeice*
(Faber).

aggressively proclaimed in Mussolini's speech which closed the Matteotti affair. It became the hallmark of his system. Opposition parties were first prohibited then crushed. Critics were mostly silenced by imprisonment or forced into exile. Some were even pursued into their countries of adoption. One notable opponent, Carlo Rosselli, was savagely murdered in Paris by Mussolini's hirelings eight years after leaving Italy. The victims inside the country were those belonging to minority groups, such as the Slavs and the Tyrolean Germans, or those who resisted the uniformity of Fascist thought and politics as imposed by the party officials and the local *squadre*. The violence which had been so successful between 1920 and 1922 became an instrument of rule, and local leaders continued to have considerable independence, enabling them to solve problems in their area in true Fascist 'style', against which no argument was possible. Under this régime of force the parliament and the king became no more than cyphers and even the Grand Fascist Council, introduced by Mussolini as the highest organ of government, was bound by the whims of the *Duce*. Mussolini stood at the head of everything. In 1926 he numbered among his offices those of Prime Minister, President of the Grand Council, Foreign Minister, Minister of the Interior and Commander-in-Chief of the armed forces. To give colour and prestige to his rule he showered honours on his favourites, entertained lavishly, postured as a Caesar-like figure on a white Arab horse and encouraged a belief that he worked all hours of the night, played the violin with artistry and was a model husband and father. In short, Mussolini cloaked every act of dictatorship with disarming respectability. A British biographer of Mussolini, the Reverend Alexander Robertson, spoke for a wide European opinion when he wrote in 1929:

> *In one of the great speeches which Mussolini made shortly after being called to power, he uttered these words which I have used as the motto to this chapter: 'I have undertaken the task assigned to me by King Victor Emmanuel III to give material and moral greatness to the Italian people.' And from my personal knowledge I can testify that during the seven years he has been in power he has done that with*

*marvellous success, and he has done more than that, for he
has not only improved the condition of the Italian people
materially and morally, but also spiritually.*[1]

It was an image which Mussolini carefully cultivated with the
skilled editor's eye for the public. Robertson was particularly
impressed by Mussolini's eye-catching statement 'The New
Testament is the best book I know of in the world' and in 1929
the *Duce* furthered his religious standing by an agreement with
the Pope. This agreement—the Lateran Treaty—was a historic
achievement, and Mussolini was fêted throughout the Catholic
world as a new defender of the faith. The Papacy had withdrawn
from Italian affairs in protest at the seizure of Rome by the
newly unified Italy in 1870. For fifty-nine years Church and
nation were in theory, and largely in practice, unreconciled.
Succeeding Popes had made a number of concessions allowing
Catholics to participate in national politics, but mutual recrimination was the norm. Mussolini's agreement ended this 'cold war'
and brought Church and State together. In return for papal
support Mussolini conceded full freedom to church organizations.
Dictatorship, it appeared, stopped short of religious control.
Christian opinion throughout Europe was impressed by this
admission.

In the years that followed the Lateran Treaty it became clear
that the State had gained more than the Church. Mussolini had
eased the consciences of Italian Catholics and in return he gained
their political allegiance. He even felt secure enough to retract
some of his concessions and persecute Catholic Action, the large
youth organization run by the Church. Its independence
threatened the Fascist dominance over young Italians and its
position was gradually eroded. Protests from Pope Pius XI
brought some improvement in Catholic interests, but Mussolini
retained control. Like all his window-dressing, Mussolini's
display of religious fervour carried just sufficient conviction to
hide the harsher realities that lay behind.

This was particularly true of his social policies. His achievements in land reclamation, road and house building, educational
reform and leisure-time provisions were by no means sensational.

[1] A. Robertson, *Mussolini and the New Italy* (Allenson, 1929), p. 176.

There were peaks of success such as the draining of the Pontine Marshes, but in most undertakings the notorious corruption and inefficiency of the party officials acted as a form of sabotage. Yet public opinion was bombarded by the wonders of social progress in the new Italy, and the real facts of the situation were kept from the national consciousness. When one considers the central-ized power Mussolini had at his disposal, it remains incredible that he achieved so little. Display was unaffected by failure, how-ever, and Mussolini played on the gullibility of the public. In 1928 he declared triumphantly: 'In an Italy which has been completely reclaimed, cultivated, irrigated, disciplined, that is to say, a Fascist Italy, there is room and bread for ten million more people.' In his autobiography he added: 'A new sense of justice, of seriousness, of harmony and concord guides now the destinies of all the peoples and classes of Italy . . . Many have finally opened their eyes to this serene and severe truth: the Italians feel themselves of one fraternity in a great work of justice.'[1] It was an idle but theatrical boast.

Social programmes in Fascist as in democratic countries depend on economic strength, and the weakness of many of Mussolini's undertakings was the weakness of the economy. The economics of fascism are the subject of a later chapter,[2] but to understand Italian fascism of the thirties one must note the failure of Mussolini's régime to bring industrial greatness to Italy. His much-vaunted ideal of a Corporate State interlocking employers and workers in a great national enterprise of pro-duction was a hollow shell. The promises, the evocations of prosperity and the revolutionary ideas were there, but the policies foundered on the central weakness of Fascist Italy: egoism backed by corruption. 'Mussolini is always right' proclaimed the hoard-ings: it was not a sound economic principle. The *Duce*, brilliant at self-advertisement, was caught in a hall of mirrors: the reflection of his military chest covered in medals or his proud, peasant profile as he sat at the wheel of a tractor blinded him to objective reality. Under the pomp and the Fascist 'style', behind the extended arms saluting his progress through the villages and

[1] B. Mussolini, *My Autobiography*, trans. R. W. Child (Hurst and Blackett, 1936), p. 224.
[2] See p. 196.

behind the ecstatic cries of '*Duce! Duce! Duce!*' the party
administrators and political hacks bargained and bribed, and
authority was inseparable from personal gain. 'A party', said
Mussolini, 'which entirely governs a nation is a fact entirely new
to history; there are no possible references or parallels.' Like the
Futurists, Mussolini was infatuated by novelty: the newness of a
situation was its own justification. He did little to ensure that
novelty worked.

Such a judgment appears to contradict the view of Mussolini
as a pragmatist, but a man who moves a step at a time according
to events is not necessarily a practical and efficient organizer.
Mussolini's pragmatism, like his social and economic programmes,
suffered increasingly from his egoism. He turned more and more
to ideology and in 1932 this high priest of fascism, impressed by
the number of similar or derivative movements throughout
Europe, decided to define the orthodoxy of the new faith. His
treatise was called *The Political and Social Doctrine of Fascism* and
it became the handbook of the Italian party. It opposes the
materialism of Marxist ideals and announces the regeneration of
Europe through the Fascist State:

> *The State as conceived and realized by fascism is a spiritual*
> *and ethical entity for securing the political, juridical and*
> *economic organization of the nation, an organization which*
> *in its origin and growth is a manifestation of the Spirit. . . .*
> *Far from crushing the individual, the Fascist State multiplies*
> *his energies, just as in a regiment a soldier is not diminished*
> *but multiplied by the number of his fellow soldiers.*[1]

The simile was significant. The 'new man', the 'Fascist man'
would necessarily be a warrior, for 'War alone brings up to its
highest tension all human energy and puts the stamp of nobility
upon the peoples who have the courage to meet it'. This is the
pivotal point of Mussolini's doctrine. A movement born out of
war, social unrest and violence could not adapt itself to the
subtler arts of economic progress, social reforms and peace. Its
blustering convinced many that it had endurable peacetime ideas,
but it was a façade covering a deep-seated scorn for peaceful
values. Mussolini admitted this:

[1] B. Mussolini, *Fascism. Political and Social Doctrine* (Ardita, Rome, 1935),
pp. 27–9.

*As regards the future development of mankind . . . Fascism
does not believe in the possibility or utility of perpetual peace.
It therefore discards pacifism as a cloak for cowardly supine
renunciation. . . .*[1]

Here was the struggle for survival elevated to the sphere of
international conflict, for only by taking the whole nation to
war could Mussolini show the individual, the party and the State
to be one. Violence within Italy was not enough: persecution of
minorities within the country must lead to elimination of weaker
elements on the world stage. From conquest of national power
Mussolini was pulled by his ideology into international war. To
this extent his earlier pragmatism was swamped by doctrine and
he was drawn to policies which no careful pragmatist would have
considered. Hitler was similarly betrayed by his own doctrinal
fanaticism. Fascism may have been the dominant reality in
Europe for over a decade, but it was feeding on illusions which
in the end caused its destruction.

In Italy the inevitable call to arms was sounded in 1935.
Mussolini's legions sought to recreate the ancient Roman Empire
by imperial conquest of Abyssinia. The adventure was justified
by Mussolini with a passion which recalled the days of
d'Annunzio's Fiume. Abyssinia had inflicted a humiliating defeat
on colonial Italian forces in 1896: this defeat at Adowa rankled
in nationalist circles as a slur on modern Italy. To re-establish
Italian prestige, Mussolini threw a huge army into the field
and within a year the Abyssinians were crushed. The Italian
enterprise became a European crisis. Abyssinia was a member
of the League of Nations: this entitled her to support from
other members, since Italy was clearly the aggressor. Anti-
Italian emotion ran high in Britain and France and there was
a call for economic and, if necessary, military sanctions against
Mussolini. When a secret plan hatched by the Foreign Ministers
of Britain and France, Samuel Hoare and Pierre Laval, was
revealed as giving considerable ground to Mussolini, the emotion
doubled. The ministers were dismissed and it looked as if fascism
was to be met with determination, but the fears of a generation
which had so recently fought a prolonged and disastrous world

[1] B. Mussolini, *op. cit.*, p. 19.

war were on Mussolini's side. The two democratic governments had social and economic problems at home and the public was in the final resort more interested in peace than in Abyssinia. Sanctions in a few economic categories were half-heartedly applied, just enough to antagonize Mussolini and to reassure him that democracy was decadent and worthless. His conquest was unaffected. Fascism had gained prestige and the aura of success. Even those Italians who had begun to chafe under the dictatorship were impressed by Mussolini's achievement. A new imperial Rome was more widely envisaged. In France the various Fascists were delighted: in Germany Hitler skilfully gauged the extent of Anglo–French weakness and accelerated his programme of military revival. Fascist movements were beginning to achieve a European momentum.

The Abyssinian war gave the Italians a temporary diversion from economic failures at home, but in the same year that Europe accepted the Italian conquest, Mussolini was forced to admit that his plans for economic expansion had yielded less than he had prophesied. In a speech to the nation he painted a picture of reduced prosperity common to all Europe: 'We are probably moving towards a period when humanity will exist on a lower standard of living.' The cost of the Abyssinian campaign was not mentioned, but it was clear that Italian fascism was surrendering all hopes of peaceful prosperity for the speculative gains of war.

Economic progress was not the only victim of Mussolini's colonial adventure. By expending arms and money so lavishly on this African campaign he forfeited much of his power in Europe. One aspect of Italian foreign policy, for which she had entered World War I, had been to contain Germany and Austria within their frontiers and prevent their expansion into the Mediterranean. In pursuance of this, Mussolini declared in 1925 and again in 1930 that Germany and Austria should not be allowed to unite. Their combined strength would present a threat to Italy which Mussolini pledged himself to avoid. When Hitler came to power in 1933, one of his repeated aims was to unite the Germans of Austria with the *Volk* of the German fatherland. However much Mussolini might sympathize with Hitler's Nazism, on this national issue he appeared firm. In July

1934 he mobilized Italian troops along his Austrian frontier when a Nazi *coup* in Vienna led to the murder of the Austrian Premier, Dollfuss. The *coup* failed and Hitler was forced to dissociate himself. Mussolini had shown a forceful awareness of Italy's national interests. He seemed a powerful barrier against Nazi expansion.

His preoccupation in Abyssinia destroyed this balance of power. Returning from Africa with reduced manpower and armaments, Mussolini was faced with a Nazi Germany several times stronger than his own Fascist Italy. His choice lay between co-operation with France and Britain, who had opposed his Abyssinian conquest, and a new working relationship with Hitler, who had openly encouraged him in his ambition but who threatened Italian interests in Austria. All the force of Fascist doctrine pushed him into the latter alliance and between 1935 and 1939 Mussolini, the father of fascism, became the junior and submissive partner in a Rome–Berlin axis.

2 GERMANY

This partnership with Hitler underlined the vast changes produced in Europe by the Nazi seizure of power. Hitler had been appointed legal Chancellor of a weak but still constitutional republic in 1933. By the end of 1935 he had fashioned all the constituents of a totalitarian régime more powerful and destructive than any other in modern history. By comparison Mussolini's rule was fumbling and moderate. Where Mussolini declaimed and postured, Hitler organized and acted. A. J. P. Taylor has called Hitler a 'great literalist': he put into practice ideas which others played with, but they were not merely the ideas of others, they were also the fanatical convictions of his own fantasy world. This one man's vision of supreme power dominated European history for twelve years. For the first seven he had nothing but success.

The party which both terrorized and protected German society in the crisis years 1930–3 was easily converted into a tight machinery of government. The smoothness with which it assumed political, economic and legal power has an appearance of inevitability. On 27 February 1933, less than a month after

Hitler's accession to the Chancellorship, the Reichstag (parliament) building was burnt down. The fire was started by a young Dutch Communist, Marinus van der Lubbe. It is certain that German Communists had no hand in this operation. If van der Lubbe was a tool of anyone it was of the Nazis themselves, who wanted an excuse to eliminate communism from national politics. Hitler at once used the fire to his advantage, issuing a decree of emergency regulations 'for the protection of People and State', but he needed the legal approval of the Reichstag before such decrees could become the normal method of government. In the March elections the Nazis used every method of physical and psychological pressure to increase their vote. Despite this unprecedented propaganda campaign, Hitler failed to gain an overall control of parliament, but by a combination of force, eloquent persuasion and attractive promises he achieved the necessary two-thirds majority when a bill enabling him to rule by decree was presented to the Reichstag. The political suicide of those parties, particularly the Catholic Centre, who voted for this bill is one of the lowest points in Germany's political history. Occurring when a general election had shown over half of Germany to be hostile to Nazism, the weakness of the deputies is difficult to understand, but the strength of Hitler's persuasion should not be underestimated. He promised concessions to Catholic interests and displayed an eminent respectability at the opening session of the Reichstag in Potsdam Church on 21 March. The ceremony took place in the presence of the ageing President Hindenburg, who was surrounded by dignitaries of high social and military prestige. The occasion was a testing one for the little corporal in unaccustomed tailcoat and starched shirt, but Hitler rose rhetorically to the occasion:

> . . . By a unique upheaval, in the last few weeks our national honour has been restored and, thanks to your understanding, Herr General-Feldmarschall, the union between the symbols of the old greatness and the new strength has been celebrated. We pay you homage. A protective Providence places you over the new forces of our Nation.[1]

[1] Quoted in A. Bullock, *Hitler: A Study in Tyranny* (The Hamlyn Group of Publishers, 1952), p. 243.

Outside the church the two symbols, the army and the S.A., presented a guard of honour. Hitler and Hindenburg emerged to saluting guns, a tumult of drums and the genuine acclamation of the crowd. The Nazi pretence to constitutional rule was firmly grounded. It was sufficient to undermine the Centre's opposition to the Enabling Act and on 23 March 1933 Hitler became the sole determinant of legality in Germany. The decrees of persecution began.

Within six months of the Act Nazism had a stranglehold on all aspects of German life except the army. The trade unions lost all power of collective bargaining and were then abolished; the political parties were disbanded one by one and the Nazi Party remained the only political organization in the country. The various states of federal Germany were forced to surrender their independence and for the first time in history Germany became a centralized nation, an achievement which became the basis of Hitler's claim to have surpassed the historic German role of Bismarck.

As insidious as any of these dictatorial measures was the first sign of official racialism. Between 1 and 4 April, under the direction of Julius Streicher, a boycott of Jewish shops and businesses was organized. The effect was to begin that legal alienation of Jews from the rest of society which ended in their isolation, dehumanization and destruction. In the town examined by W. S. Allen the effect on the Jews was cataclysmic. One Jew, Gregor Rosenthal, and his wife 'could not at first believe that it would take place. But when they saw the two S.A. men posted before their door the full significance of it broke upon them. They did not dare to leave their home at all that day and Gregor Rosenthal sat crumpled up in his chair for hours repeating, "Was it for this that I spent four years defending my Fatherland?" ' [1]

Persecution of this sort was always excused in the first years of Hitler's Reich as a defensive measure. The Communists were said to be plotting treason, the trade unions to be undermining productivity, the Jews to be planning an international conspiracy: Nazism promised protection against all such threats. To convince the public of the reality of these dangers an immense expansion of propaganda was necessary, and Nazism invaded

[1] W. S. Allen, *The Nazi Seizure of Power* (Eyre and Spottiswoode, 1966), p. 211.

The first Nazi boycott of Jewish shops, April 1933. The placard says 'Germans! Defend yourselves! Don't buy from Jews!'

every sphere of communication in order to control not only actions but thought. In this lies the totalitarianism of Nazi Germany. In Italy by comparison there was an element of freedom: the great liberal philosopher Benedetto Croce continued to publish his journal *La Critica*, and some political opposition was possible until 1929. In Germany criticism was dead within less than two years. Through the propaganda network of Joseph Goebbels and the publishing monopoly of Max Amann, a systematic control of ideas, scholarship and opinion allowed Nazism to dictate reality. Truth and falsity were determined by the will of the Führer: the power to reason and choose was removed from the individual.

The growth of this totalitarianism was piecemeal: move by move, decree by decree and arrest by arrest. There was no single revolution which might have shocked Germany into reaction. Each act of persecution was worse than the one before but the change did not seem very great at the time. It was only when the whole edifice was built that its monolithic nature became apparent, but by then it was impregnable. Hitler may have been vulnerable before 1935, but after that date opposition was powerless. Germans still ask themselves why this gradual Nazi stranglehold was not broken in the two early years and the answer usually given is that Hitler combined social reconstruction with his measures of persecution. Unemployment figures fell rapidly as he initiated government-sponsored public works, road building and arms production. His policy of economic self-sufficiency gave a stimulus to industries to produce a range of goods hitherto provided by imports, and his regimentation of labour after the suppression of the trade unions kept the employers happy. All these measures had been planned in Italy also, but the difference in execution was crucial. Mussolini's régime could never match the iron efficiency with which Hitler's Reich carried every detail of theory into practice. The result in Germany was an economic progress which staggered the rest of Europe and which diverted the German people from the growth of tyrannical power. Hitler had promised to solve the economic crisis and he was successful.

At the start of his rule it was easy to ignore the calculations behind this recovery, but from his very first decrees to reduce unemployment in the spring of 1933 to his final mobilization of young teenagers to fight in Berlin in 1945, Hitler based his social policy on a war economy. All productivity was designed to strengthen Germany for one major purpose—the conquest of power in Europe. With this declared aim he had attracted millions to German nationalism before 1933. After 1933 it was a vision held out to the party, the people, the industrialists and in particular the army. A reading of Hitler's speeches in the thirties leaves little doubt that the aggressive designs of *Mein Kampf* remained Hitler's consistent policy: destruction of the Jews, repudiation of Versailles, unification of all Germans under one Reich and the conquest of living space (*Lebensraum*) in

Eastern Europe. A book which he wrote in 1928, but which was not published at the time, continued with better arguments these themes of *Mein Kampf*, in particular the inevitability of war against Russia. Hitler probably left the book unpublished because it contained severe criticisms of the conservative nationalists with whom he formed an alliance shortly after, but it provides yet more evidence of Hitler's fanatical adherence to ideas which germinated during and immediately after World War I.[1]

Consistency of idea was backed by opportunism of action, but Hitler was never carried along by events. The methods were just as much his own as the ideas, and he rarely responded favourably to advice. In 1934, when a strong challenge to his methods was mounted by the S.A., he showed how ruthless he could be in maintaining control. Hitler had promised the stormtroopers that a revolution would follow the conquest of power. Mostly socially underprivileged, the members of the S.A. looked to this revolution as something belonging particularly to themselves. The leader of the S.A., Ernst Röhm, encouraged this belief and nurtured his own ambition that the S.A. would become the standing popular army of the new Reich, thus usurping the position of the official army, the Reichswehr. Röhm was known as 'the Führer's best friend' and had been on intimate terms with Hitler since before the Munich *Putsch*. He had built the S.A. into a movement far larger than the army and had provided the force and much of the organization behind the Nazi success. He had once been a member of the Reichswehr but had resigned when the more violent attraction of an independent army was presented. The S.A. was his life, and supreme military power his ambition.

In the first few months after January 1933 the S.A. was heavily involved in the extension of Nazi control over all Germany, but control was seen to be insufficient while so many of the old régime continued unmolested—in particular the army officers, the industrialists, the financiers and the upper strata of society. The revolution was nothing if it left these heads untouched. Like the extreme Fascist *squadre* at the time of Matteotti's murder, the S.A. called for more positive action. This demand had been anticipated by a branch of the Nazi Party which had been led by Gregor Strasser. From the mid-twenties

[1] *Hitler's Secret Book*, trans. S. Attanasio (Grove Press, N.Y., 1961).

Strasser, in the north of Germany, had placed more emphasis on the Socialist side of National Socialism, while Hitler, in the south, had avoided any doctrinal commitments. In the critical months before 1933 Strasser broke with Hitler but still remained a potential rival exerting influence in favour of a 'second revolution' to destroy the old capitalist society.

Hitler had come to power on a subtle balance of violence and respectability. He had no intention of altering a combination which brought so much success. He needed mass terror and extreme methods but he also needed the sympathy of the army, which was aristocratic and highly respected, and provided a valuable link with Germany's imperial past. He already had the support of General von Blomberg whom he had made Minister of Defence, and the army had not interfered with his dictatorial measures of 1933. The ideas of Röhm and Strasser were therefore in danger of disturbing the smooth workings of a profitable collaboration. Even more, Röhm's S.A. was growing less essential as a popular army due to the huge increase in Himmler's S.S. which numbered over 100,000 by 1934. Himmler was a more skilful man than Röhm and saw the advantage of implicit obedience towards Hitler: he was in a position to gain significantly from the elimination of Röhm.

The climax was reached in June 1934. There is no evidence that Röhm's criticisms of Hitler ever crystallized into a plan for an armed rising, but Hitler, encouraged by Göring, Goebbels and Himmler, decided to anticipate any further challenge. The S.A. were due to disperse for a month's holiday on 1 July. On 30 June the S.S., with some co-operation from the Reichswehr, moved against a pre-arranged list of victims. With no concern for the niceties of arrest and trial, over eighty 'traitors to the Reich' were slaughtered in cold blood. Some were shot in their beds, others taken to one of the centres in Berlin or Munich and shot by an S.S. firing squad. Most of the murdered were S.A. leaders. Röhm was among them, caught, Hitler claimed, in the middle of his homosexual practices, and executed for plotting the overthrow of the government. With each murder went immediate justification in terms of national security, but it was difficult to disguise the settling of old scores and the elimination of monarchists, leaders of Catholic Action and personal rivals of Hitler such as Gregor Strasser and General von Kahr, who had opposed Hitler's Munich *Putsch* in 1923. Kahr's body was found hacked to pieces; another general, von Schleicher, who had challenged Hitler for power in January 1933, was shot with his wife when he answered the doorbell. The murders continued on 1 July and by then the public was learning the events with stunned horror. They were forced also to read tales of Röhm's orgies and of the intricate plans for insurrection which had been discovered. The propaganda machine of Goebbels worked as hard as the S.S. murderers. Germany had to be convinced that the purge was both necessary and legal. After a newspaper and wireless barrage of self-justification the government issued a blanket decree: 'The measures taken on 30 June and 1 and 2 July, to repel the treasonable and mutinous attacks, are legal and in accordance with the State's right to self-defence.' It is difficult to assess how many people believed in the justice of the events, but the army was one section of public opinion which felt pleased with Hitler's action: the threatened industrialists and upper classes were others. The dying Hindenburg expressed his gratitude to Hitler for his quick remedies to a national crisis: terror and respectability had again proved a potent concoction.

After 30 June the S.A. were eclipsed by the S.S. and Hitler himself became even more the godhead of the Nazi universe. By comparison, the Reichswehr, though saved from a collision with the S.A., lost a great deal of influence. In condoning a brutal slaughter of this kind it forfeited much of its independence. It was the first major step in the humiliation of a proud officer caste which for two centuries had epitomized German honour.

The Röhm Purge is a microcosm of the whole Nazi rule. It had all the ingredients of brutality, persuasiveness, authority, licence, calculation and spontaneity which marks the foreign and internal policy of Hitler. In particular, it is instructive because it was followed by no effective protest either within or outside Germany. This too was to be a familiar feature. The values of fascism had not conquered the whole of Europe but they had paralysed its will to oppose.

With supreme confidence Hitler built on his success. When Hindenburg died in August 1934, Hitler amalgamated the titles of President and Chancellor and became sole ruler of Germany

in name as well as fact. The armed forces swore an oath of
loyalty to their new official leader: 'I swear by God this sacred
oath that I will render unconditional obedience to Adolf Hitler,
the Führer of the German Reich and nation, the Supreme
Commander of the Armed Forces, and that I shall be ready, as
a brave soldier, to lay down my life at any time for this oath.'
It was an oath to Hitler in person rather than to an institution,
and caused agonies of conscience later during the war when
many officers felt that Hitler should be overthrown in the
interests of the country. But in 1934 the alliance of Führer and
Reichswehr was firm and it provided a basis for Hitler's growing
assertiveness in foreign affairs.

In October 1933 Hitler had withdrawn Germany from the
League of Nations since he could not, he stated publicly, accept
the level of disarmament forced on his country by international
pressure. The withdrawal was deplored by other members, but
only in words lacking the power to intimidate. Hitler proceeded
with his rearmament. When France increased its military service
in March 1935 Hitler took the opportunity to announce com-
pulsory military service in Germany as a counter-measure. The
limits imposed by the Versailles Treaty on the German army
were broken, and again the reaction was slight. A year later he
remilitarized the Rhineland, which had been guaranteed by
Versailles as a demilitarized zone in order to create a wide area
between French and German armies. The move was overwhelmingly popular in Germany. The occupying troops were
crowned with flowers, but Hitler was not without anxiety. He
said later, 'If the French had then marched into the Rhineland
we would have had to withdraw with our tails between our
legs, for the military resources at our disposal would have been
wholly inadequate for even moderate resistance.' His gamble
succeeded, however. The French were in the middle of a
ministerial crisis and the British were not too alarmed at Hitler's
illegality. So many of the clauses of the Versailles Treaty seemed
irrelevant to the new situation of the thirties and Hitler's action
was a small affair compared with Mussolini's recent Abyssinian
conquest. If the latter could be achieved without European
intervention, then Hitler could be reasonably optimistic about
his own plans for Germany's military revival.

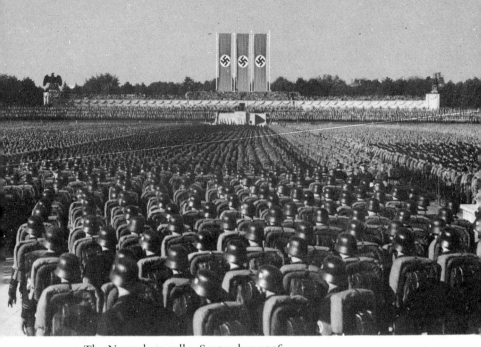

The Nuremberg rally, September 1936

These three years (1933–6) of Nazi consolidation were portrayed to the outside world as the achievement of a united nation. In plebiscites held in November 1933 to confirm withdrawal from the League and in August 1934 to endorse Hitler's succession to Hindenburg, the pro-Nazi vote had been about 95 per cent of the whole. On 29 March 1936 after the re-militarization of the Rhineland the figure rose to 99 per cent. Opposition had dropped from over half of the voters in Germany in March 1933 to little more than 500,000 in 1936. These results cannot be taken at their face value due to the intensification of dictatorial methods, but for Hitler they provided a statistical buttress to his illusions of omnipotence. What particularly impressed the rest of Europe was the display of this 'unified' Germany. The mass meetings; the thousands of parading Nazis with arms stiffly raised in salute and the thunderous shouts of 'Heil Hitler!'; the huge swastika flags; the martial singing which concluded Hitler's emotional speeches; the disciplined squads of Hitler Youth, the League of German Girls and the Labour Front, who marched and dressed with the precision of soldiers, and behind it all the wheels of industry turning with ferocious power and efficiency: these symbols of strength attracted as much as they repelled. Nevile Henderson, the British Ambassador to Germany from 1937 to 1939, wrote:

> To my own countrymen I would for instance particularly recommend the labour camps. Between the age of seventeen and nineteen every German boy, rich or poor, the son of a labourer or of a former reigning prince, is obliged to spend six months in a labour camp, building roads, draining marshland, felling trees or doing whatever other manual labour may be required in his area. In my humble opinion these camps serve none but useful purposes. In them not only are there no class distinctions but there is on the contrary an opportunity for better understanding between the classes. Therein one learns the pleasures of hard work and the dignity of labour, as well as the benefits of discipline; moreover they vastly improve the physique of the nation. The average weight a German boy puts on during those six months is thirteen German pounds, or a little over a stone of bone and muscle.[1]

This opinion does not mean that Henderson admired the whole of Nazi ideology, which he calls 'odious', but it illustrates the considerable attraction which Nazi authority and power were able to exert. In September 1936 Lloyd George remarked about Hitler: 'He is a remarkable man. His head has not been turned by adulation. Contrast him with Mussolini. He seems essentially modest.' Such impressions could be multiplied to show the quality of Hitler's appeal. The Third Reich in 1936 recommended itself as a triumph of vigorous policy.

But the Nazi flags of unity waved over mass arrests and mass fear: the new authoritarian Germany covered destruction with its façade of creative productivity. In September 1935, before a vast Nazi Party rally at Nuremberg, the first inhuman laws against the Jews were promulgated. Marriages and extramarital relations between Jews and 'citizens of German or kindred blood' were forbidden. Jews were also forbidden 'to employ as servants in their households female subjects of German or kindred

[1] Sir N. Henderson, *Failure of a Mission* (Hodder and Stoughton, 1940), p. 24.

Nazi congress at Nuremberg in 1934, with Julius Streicher on Hitler's left

blood who are under the age of 45 years'. Hitler and Julius Streicher, who edited an anti-Semitic newspaper, *Der Stürmer*, had both been obsessed in their youth by the vision of pure Aryan girls raped by Jewish monsters, and in these laws their crude fantasies were verbalized. Jews became second-class citizens, prevented from claiming German rights and 'polluting the Aryan blood'. The boycott of 1933 had turned into a permanent racial war. Overnight the Jews were stripped of all status and a terrified expectancy of ruin and imprisonment became their common social attitude. Many of them chose suicide: one who did this was a well-known actor, Joachim Gottschalk, who killed his Jewish wife and children as well. The Nazis were delighted at what they called a confession of guilt and inferiority. The rest of Europe had known about German concentration camps since early 1935: now they knew who were to be the majority of prisoners. In Germany it was better *not* to know these things: life was more secure in ignorance. There is nothing which underlines the totalitarian success of Nazism more strongly than this wilful avoidance of fact. In varying degrees it affected all Europe

3   SPAIN

In 1936, the year of Mussolini's Abyssinian conquest and
Hitler's move into the Rhineland, a bitterly divided Spain
erupted into civil war. The savage conflict which racked the
peninsula for three years at once became the focus for the ideals
and illusions of the thirties. In particular it was seen as a direct
battle between communism and fascism, and these two ideologies
appeared to be contesting the future not only of Spain but of
Europe. The Spanish Civil War became a vibrant symbol of
this conflict of ideologies.

The war began in July with the revolt of several army garrisons
in Spanish Morocco against the Republican government in
Madrid. It spread at once to the mainland and in the next month
the whole country became passionately involved. As neighbouring
areas declared for different sides it became clear that Spain was
not contesting the rights and wrongs of the army rebellion, but
rather the very nature of Spain itself. The army, led by Generals
Sanjurjo, Franco and Queipo de Llano, was buttressed by the
highly conservative Catholic Church, the political parties of the
Right including the *Falange*, and the economic interests of the
great landowners. They stood for a traditional Spain, clerical,
hierarchical, spiritual and authoritarian, and they fought in the
name of God and the Nation. Their immediate enemies were the
Republicans of the government but behind these lay the more
extreme forces of anarchism, syndicalism and communism,
equipped with ideologies to destroy old Church and old State
and to replace them with the revolutionary values of the working
class. Though at first neither the rebels nor the government were
controlled by extremists, the brutal and uncompromising nature
of the fighting brought with it a more desperate and extreme
political conflict which threw the Spaniards, often against their
will, into fanatical positions. By 1938 the Communists dominated
the Republican cause, and on the Nationalist side General Franco
had become a dictator with methods similar to those of his
Fascist supporters, Mussolini and Hitler. Atrocities were committed on both sides. Hugh Thomas in his book *The Spanish
Civil War* gives examples of the common barbarity. In Navarre
the Nationalists told one prisoner 'to extend his arms in the form

of a cross and cry "*Viva* Christ the King" while each of his limbs was amputated. His wife, forced to watch, went mad as he was finally bayoneted to death.' In Ciudad Real, Republican extremists were equally inhuman: 'At Alcazar de San Juan, a young man distinguished for his piety . . . had his eyes dug out . . . A crucifix was forced down the mouth of a mother of two Jesuits. Eight hundred persons were thrown down a mineshaft.' Every account of the war, whether by participant or historian, mentions atrocities such as these, not for sensational reasons but in order to illustrate the central character of the struggle. Life was cheap: the cause, Republican or Nationalist, Communist or Fascist, was everything.

With ideals at such a high or extreme level, the war gained a romantic, heroic image reminiscent of the Greek War of Independence in the 1820s. Just as Byron idealized the bitter fighting in Greece, so poets of the thirties rose to the colour, the heat and the atmosphere of Spain and gave the war a poetic status which neither of the world wars obtained. The death of the great Spanish poet Lorca at the hands of the *Falange* in August 1936 led to an interwoven theme of poetry and martyrdom which later claimed the English poet John Cornford, killed on his twenty-first birthday. These lines of Cornford's are typical of the idealism invested in the Spanish tragedy:

> *Freedom is an easily spoken word*
> *But facts are stubborn things. Here too, in Spain*
> *Our fight's not won till the workers of all the world*
> *Stand by our guard on Huesca's plain,*
> *Swear that our dead fought not in vain,*
> *Raise the red flag triumphantly*
> *For Communism and for liberty.*[1]

Cornford was one of the many volunteers who joined the International Brigades to fight for the Republic. Organized by Communists from all over Europe, these Brigades were composed largely of two groups: workers drawn straight from factories and mines and intellectuals who were passionately anti-Fascist. They were the only help gained by the hard-pressed

[1] John Cornford, a poem entitled 'Full Moon at Tierz: Before the Storming of Huesca', taken from *John Cornford: A Memoir*, ed. Pat Sloan (Cape, 1938).

Republic from the democratic countries. Almost as soon as war broke out the governments of Britain and France suggested and carried through a Non-Intervention Pact according to which no military aid should go to either side. Italy, Germany and Russia all signed this agreement and all three broke it, but Britain and France remained adamant and even recruiting for the International Brigades was made illegal.

The result was a total imbalance of foreign aid to the two Spanish sides. The Republic had only the support of Stalinist Russia which reached a peak in men and arms in 1937–8 but dwindled and was finally stopped before the war ended. On the other hand Franco and the Nationalists received the dedicated help of Mussolini in every aspect of the fighting, and the support of Hitler who sent considerable numbers of his young army and air force to be blooded in the Spanish battles. Fascist parties elsewhere, particularly in France, also adopted the Nationalist cause as their own, and by 1937 the Spanish Civil War appeared to have crystallized a European Fascist alignment which had already been partly visible during Mussolini's Abyssinian campaign. It was this and the Russian involvement which gave the war its simplified character of a Communist–Fascist confrontation.

By this argument all Spanish Republicans and their supporters were Communist and all Nationalists were Fascist. The truth was more complex. On the Republican side there were constant group and party conflicts for power and office from the moment war broke out. The opportunism of the Communists, who were controlled, equipped and financed from Russia, did indeed give them superiority over their rivals. By the end of 1938 they occupied almost all positions of power in the Republican army and government, but in reaching these positions they alienated large numbers of Republicans and bitterly shattered the illusions of those who had believed communism to be a spontaneous, heroic ideal of the masses. Many young intellectuals who had left Britain and France with enthusiasm for Communist values returned with cynicism. Communism was unmasked in Spain as a ruthless extension of Stalin's foreign policy. As such it was unacceptable to the majority of Republicans, especially those Spaniards who favoured the native, anarchist movement, which gave far more scope to the individual's sense of revolution. On the Nationalist side it is interesting to note the virtual elimination of original Spanish fascism, despite all appearances to the contrary. Under the more traditional nationalism of Franco, the *Falange* lost first its power and finally its separate identity. Its leader, José Antonio Primo de Rivera, was the victim of Republican war justice on 20 November 1936. He was arrested and executed for crimes against the Republic and his death removed one of the most talented exponents of fascism in Europe. He was immediately regarded as a martyr by the rest of the *Falange*, due in part to the story of his last hours told throughout Spain by his sister Carmen who had visited him on the night before he was shot:

> *He had grown thinner. The Reds who witnessed the interview did not miss a single word and their faces mirrored admiration for a man who, on the threshold of death, possessed such stout courage.*
>
> *I had brought a crucifix and gave it to him.*
>
> *'Simply by looking at it, full pardon is given to you at the hour of death,' I said. 'I bring it to you just in case . . .'*
>
> *With great pleasure he took the crucifix and showed it to those standing around. . . . José Antonio embraced us for the last time and then went back to his cell.*
>
> *On the next day, November 20th, at twenty minutes to seven in the morning we ourselves heard the volley which ended his life. The execution took place in the courtyard of the provincial prison. His last words, spoken in farewell to the warden shortly before they came for him, were:*
>
> *'Warden, if I have done anything to disturb or annoy you, forgive me.'*[1]

The *Falange* did not at first show signs of this loss. It continued to gain in numbers and its terrorist activity increased. It was also used by the military leaders as a special police force, equivalent to the S.S. in Germany. Squads of Falangists patrolled the streets of Nationalist territory checking papers and seizing suspicious persons. The German aircraft manufacturer, Willy

[1] Quoted in *The Civil War in Spain*, ed. R. Payne (Secker and Warburg, 1962), p. 134.

Messerschmitt, said of these Falangist patrols that they were 'merely young people for whom it is good sport to play with firearms and round up Communists and Socialists'. This was a comment on their lack of driving ideas, one which was increasingly justified as the *Falange* drifted through the first year of the war with less and less ideology and more and more spontaneous activity. It was by no means at the head of all Nationalist atrocities, though its share of barbarous incidents was not a small one. Its methods had in fact been adopted by the whole Nationalist side, and its Nationalist rivals, the Carlists, had their own military formations (called *Requetés*) who exceeded the Falangists in brutality. Falangists and Carlists were the only permitted parties within Nationalist Spain. They were as distinct in theory as Hitler's Nazis and Hugenberg's Nationalists, but in April 1937 Franco ordered their amalgamation. The *Falange* submitted. Over twenty of its oldest members were arrested at Franco's orders to forestall opposition, but the movement was too aimless to find strength to fight for its independence. In the new monolithic party its name and many of its ideas, as well as its salute, were continued and Franco paid lip-service to Falangist theories of economic organization, but in all questions of power and authority the original party had been eclipsed. The military dictatorship of Franco, based on emotions far more traditional and conservative than José Antonio would have acknowledged, was the mark of Nationalist Spain, and it cannot be exactly equated with Falangism. The Spanish *Falange*, like the fascism of Italy, Germany and France, had combined nationalism with a new ideology which came near to socialism. In contrast, Franco was an army general with a love of conventional Spain: he was an élitist who had no interest in mass politics and only an abhorrence of socialism. He took over the *Falange* not in order to make its fascism more effective but to destroy any vestige of rival ambition which it contained. Had José Antonio lived, the differences between Franco and fascism might have been clearer. In the event Franco seemed to be a completely Fascist leader; a Spanish Mussolini or Hitler. In reality the Spanish Civil War was as much the grave of idealistic fascism as idealistic communism, but the success of Franco's armies aided by Italy and Germany obscured this fact. It appeared that the *Falange* was triumphant.

The end of the war came in March 1939, by which time
Europe was facing the threat of a vaster conflict. The support
of Hitler and Mussolini had lasted to the final victory of Franco
—the collapse of Madrid on 28 March. The two dictators, however, had not shown identical policies towards the war. For
Mussolini, Spain was almost a continuation of Abyssinia. His
victorious troops had returned from Africa with nothing to do
and their reintroduction into civilian jobs was totally alien to
Mussolini's philosophy. Spain gave them another cause, the
fight against communism in Europe, and this was the reason
Mussolini and his Foreign Minister, Ciano, gave for intervention:
Spain must not be overrun by the Reds; its long national heritage
must be preserved. To achieve this, Mussolini sent 763 aircraft
to Spain, 1,672 tons of bombs and thousands of guns, and at the
highest point in mid-1937 there were probably about 50,000
Italian forces involved in the fighting. In Italy the Spanish war
was seen as something of a crusade, particularly by the Catholic
Church, which was horrified by the anti-clerical atrocities of the
Republicans. Priests blessed the departing Italian soldiers and
Mussolini thrived on his reputation as the bulwark of
Mediterranean culture. The number of Italians killed was about
6,000 and the main political result was to bring Mussolini
even more into dependence on Hitler. The Rome–Berlin axis
was created during the war and by 1939 it had become a tight
alliance.

Hitler also spoke of the 'Red peril' in Spain and encouraged a
missionary zeal in support of Franco, but his intervention was
far more calculating than Mussolini's. He used the fighting in
Spain as a diversion from his own military build-up in Germany
and as a practice ground for new military and aerial tactics. The
new German air force, the *Luftwaffe*, under the command of
Göring, was particularly quick to profit from Spanish experience.
A special air force unit for service in Spain, the Condor Legion,
learnt the power of terror bombing and diving attacks on convoys
of lorries and pedestrians. It was responsible for the most noted
single atrocity event of the war, the destruction of Guernica.
This small Basque town near Bilbao in northern Spain was
strongly Republican, and on 27 April 1937 the front of the
fighting was about twenty-five miles away. Just before five

o'clock on that day, when local farmers were bargaining in the busy Monday market, German planes appeared and began bombing and machine-gunning the streets. Wave upon wave of aircraft followed for three hours, dropping high explosives and incendiaries and firing at anybody running through the streets. The centre of the town was destroyed and 1,654 people killed. Nine years later, in 1946, Göring admitted that Guernica had been a valuable testing ground. This was the reality and spirit of German intervention. The actual numbers of Germans sent to fight and the quantity and quality of armaments is not exactly known, but at a Condor Legion parade in Berlin in May 1939 after withdrawal from Spain 14,000 veterans took part. They were nearly all young Nazis who had to some extent volunteered for service in Spain as part of their military and ideological duties. Idealism was not limited to the Republican supporters in the International Brigades. The Nazis went with dedication. 'We shall be marching onwards, if all else crashes about us. Our foes are the Reds, the Bolshevizers of the world.'

The Spanish Civil War was thus a military playground for European fascism. The spectre of communism, which Fascists saw in Spain, convinced them that their interests lay together whatever their national differences. Mussolini and Hitler drew closer in their aims: the P.P.F. in France became the open advocate of reconciliation with Germany; Mosley's Black Shirts in Britain were vociferous supporters of Franco, and Léon Degrelle in Belgium placed his Rexist movement firmly behind Mussolini's Spanish policy. Degrelle himself later escaped to Spain at the end of his wartime collaboration with Hitler. Ironically, only Spanish fascism was in the end missing from this European alignment. The old *Falange* was lost in the broader nationalism of Franco, and the victorious Spanish general would have no part in anything European. After March 1939 he kept Spain in political isolation, and even Hitler was unable to coerce him into the world conflict of 1939–45. For Franco the Spanish Civil War had been about traditional Spain, not about fascism, but without Fascist intervention he might never have created the Spain which he desired.

During the Spanish war Europe became accustomed to a new degree of human savagery. Horrific stories of torture and political murder filtered through to the democratic countries and were read over the breakfast table. In the Fascist countries selected reports were used for propaganda purposes and Nazism in particular learnt much from the public reaction to brutality. If Guernica could not provoke Britain and France, then Hitler could perhaps go further. By these successive steps the world of politics and diplomacy came to know bestiality as an everyday occurrence. The Civil War is a central factor in the degeneration of Europe during the thirties to a point where acts of unparalleled inhumanity could be planned and carried out in almost a vacuum of public opinion.

It was an indication of fascism's power in this decade that the rest of Europe was drawn to a level of political compromise which has since been cause for guilt and recrimination. Non-Fascist Europe seemed unable to meet fascism with either confidence or conviction. It was not until Hitler's insatiable ambition demanded a full-scale war that the indecision was finally shaken off. By then the two terms 'appeasement' and 'collaboration' had entered the vocabulary of politics, indicating just how far European history had come to revolve round fascism, though by 1939 it would be more correct to say, round Nazi Germany.

CHAPTER EIGHT

Appeasement

1 THE ARGUMENT OVER APPEASEMENT: BRITAIN AND FRANCE

A month after Hitler's accession to power these words were spoken in the House of Commons:

> *What is this new spirit of German nationalism? The worst of the all-Prussian Imperialism, with an added savagery, a racial pride, an exclusiveness which cannot allow to any fellow-subject not of pure Nordic birth equality of rights and citizenship within the nation to which he belongs. Are you going to discuss revision with a government like that? . . . Germany is afflicted by this narrow, exclusive, aggressive spirit, by which it is a crime to be in favour of peace and a crime to be a Jew. This is not a Germany to which we can afford to make concessions.*[1]

The speaker was Austen Chamberlain, a politician who had worked to bring Germany back into the concert of powers after the harsh peace of Versailles had isolated her. He saw what many did not—that the change of régime in Germany would need a reappraisal of British foreign policy: concessions to the Weimar Republic might have been justified, but would it be wise to give any encouragement to Hitler?

By 1937 this problem was even more acute. Hitler had always demanded the total destruction of the Treaty of Versailles and once in power he proceeded to demolish its restrictions. Without negotiations he cut away the remaining shackles of the treaty and

[1] *Hansard*, 13 April 1933. Quoted in M. Gilbert, *Britain and Germany between the Wars* (Longmans, 1964), p. 75.

launched his programme of national rearmament. During the
Spanish Civil War it became obvious that Germany was geared
to heavy military development, and constant reports from the
British ambassadors in Berlin, Sir Horace Rumbold and Sir Eric
Phipps, emphasized Nazi aggression, violence and ruthlessness.
In retrospect the war mentality of Hitlerism appears blatant.

At the time the issue was not so clear. There were some in
both Britain and France who pointed to the dangerous nationalism of the Hitler régime, arguing that he should be checked,
even at the risk of war, before he grew too powerful. There
were others, however, who believed that the policy of the
twenties should be continued: Germany should be treated with
concern and favour and her reasonable requests met with sympathy. Even Hitler, they continued, had reasonable demands
and nothing should be done to antagonize him. Rather he should
be encouraged to negotiate and to express his demands so
that the rest of Europe could arrive at a settlement. Any other
course, they believed, would precipitate war.

These two attitudes to Hitler furnished the great debate of the
thirties: whether or not the Nazi Führer should be met with
force. Those who advocated a strong line became known by their
opponents as 'warmongers'. Those who advised concessions were
labelled 'appeasers'. Until 1939 the appeasers seemed to have the
most convincing arguments and it was their policy which determined British and French attitudes to Hitler in the last years of
the thirties. It was not a new policy. Mussolini had not been
firmly opposed in 1935 when he conquered Abyssinia, and the
Spanish Civil War had failed to stir the democracies into action.
Appeasing Hitler was therefore an easy way to adopt: it did not
require a reversal of existing ideas. Moreover, it had most of the
public of both countries behind it: pacifist ideas were widespread
and few people would have chosen war unless their own
countries were threatened. It was firmly believed by the
appeasers that peace could be kept if they avoided all the
mistakes made before 1914. They therefore repudiated secret
diplomacy, refused to indulge in an arms race and tried to avoid
economic or colonial conflicts. They felt they had learned the
lessons of history: the tragedy would not be allowed to recur.

Heartened by these attitudes, Hitler increased his requests, in

particular the obsessional demand that all Germans should be
reunited in one Reich. With careful propaganda he played on the
foreign governments, stressing that this was his only demand:
once united, he promised, the greater Germany would be a
powerful force for peace. The argument was not without its
appeal and the resistance of Britain and France was gradually
weakened. In March 1938 Hitler believed he could move
without reprisals. Faking a situation of unrest and hostility to
the government within Austria, he marched in and annexed his
country of birth. Austria had 'come home' to the fatherland.

Despite a poignant broadcast by the Austrian Premier re-
pudiating the German reasons for invasion, the statesmen of
Britain and France preferred to accept Hitler's excuses. They
were undoubtedly correct in believing that no one would fight
to keep Austria and Germany apart: the issue was, for most
people in France and Britain, a trivial one. Hitler increased this
complacency by assuring the world that the *Anschluss* was a
peaceful move entirely in accordance with Austrian wishes, but
the logic of his policy pointed to other Central European
countries as his next victims, for they too had Germans living
within their borders. He was therefore demanding nothing new
when in the summer of 1938 he announced his intention to
annex the part of Czechoslovakia known as the Sudetenland,
which was populated largely by Germans.

It was over the Czech issue that the problem of appeasement
raised the controversy which still impassions writers and
historians. In Britain the government of Neville Chamberlain
(brother to Austen) was quite clear that war must be avoided.
In France the Premier, Daladier, was hesitant, but the influence
of Britain and of his own Foreign Minister, Georges Bonnet,
pulled him into appeasement. Chamberlain, working at a level
of high drama, made a series of air journeys to meet Hitler, and
persuaded him to postpone his invasion. At the same time he
and Daladier, aided by Mussolini, exerted pressure on the Czechs
to concede the Sudeten area to Germany. At Munich on 29–30
September Chamberlain informed Hitler that the Czechs had
agreed: a settlement was signed and the French and British
Premiers returned to the cheers of London and Paris. War had
been averted and Hitler had promised to be content with the

Sudetenland. Only the Czechs had to face the brutal realities of the Munich appeasement.

In March 1939 Hitler broke his agreement. The German armies advanced on Prague and conquered the rest of Czechoslovakia. In Britain and France the cold shock of events led the governments to take rearmament more seriously. They also began discussions with Poland and agreed to defend the Poles if Hitler turned his aggression in that direction. This Polish guarantee was an exception to the policy of appeasement, and no sooner was it signed than Chamberlain began to look for ways to forestall a Polish crisis. Helped by Nevile Henderson, the Ambassador in Berlin who had replaced the anti-appeaser Phipps, the British government put pressure on both Hitler and the Poles to come to an agreement, suggesting even that the Poles, like the Czechs, should make territorial concessions. The moves failed. Hitler was impatient and on 1 September his armies crossed into Poland.

Under the guarantee Britain and France were bound to aid Poland. Reluctantly both countries declared war. Appeasement had failed and Chamberlain above all was shattered by this failure. To the House of Commons he said:

> *This is a sad day for all of us, to none is it sadder than to me. Everything that I have worked for, everything that I have hoped for, everything that I have believed in during my public life has crashed into ruins.*[1]

Europe was at war, although for almost nine months it was little more than a phoney war. Instead of striking against Germany while Hitler was engaged in Poland, the armies of Britain and France waited in the west, their governments still hoping that the Nazi leader might return to peace. Hitler, however, had no such intention and in May 1940 he turned the overwhelming power of the German war machine against his reluctant enemies. As the West fell or retreated before this onslaught the record of appeasement grew blacker in retrospect. Would Europe have been submitted to Hitler's régime had he been checked in the mid-thirties? If the words of Austen Chamberlain had been followed and not the policy of his brother, would Europe still have been at peace?

[1] *Hansard*, 3 September 1939.

Fascist supporters saluting Sir Oswald Mosley at a meeting in
October 1938

These tantalizing questions will provide an argument without
end, but there is a second controversy about appeasement which
is of particular interest here. As Chamberlain and his colleagues
pursued their policies the accusation grew that they were
sympathetic to fascism. It was said that they were impressed by
Hitler's strength and authority, were awed by his Nazi demonstrations of power and were grateful for his uncompromising
stand against communism. In summary, the accusation reads, the
appeasers made willing concessions not only to an aggressive
country but to an evil ideology. How true are these allegations?
Did the appeasers fall within the orbit of European fascism? The
case for both sides must be presented.

In defence of the appeasers three main points argue that
although their policy was ill-fated their motives and attitudes
cannot be suspected of fascism.

Firstly, their record in home politics distinguishes them at
once from Fascists of all degrees. They remained basically convinced of the rightness of parliamentary democracy and the
freedom of the individual. In Britain most of the appeasers
expressed either publicly or privately their dislike of Mosley, and

where they seemed tolerant of him this was frequently due to a concern for the freedom of expression. Thomas Jones, a friend of the leading appeasers, wrote in October 1937 after a lunch with Samuel Hoare (Home Secretary) and Lord Halifax (Foreign Secretary):

> *Hoare bothered with the Mosley processions but does not wish to squash them in a hurry because the Civil Liberties group in the House is numerous and vocal.*[1]

Most appeasers shared the view of Stanley Baldwin when he was Prime Minister in 1934: 'Mosley won't come to any good and we need not bother about him.' There was no attempt by the government to imitate Fascist methods and throughout the period of appeasement its critics like Duff Cooper and Churchill, even if ignored, were not forcibly silenced. In France, Daladier, himself a Radical, was no nearer the French Fascist groups than Chamberlain was to Mosley. He had been the object of attack by right-wing leagues on the night of 6 February 1934, and he remained critical of political violence and unconstitutional procedures. Bonnet was more unscrupulous and seized on appeasement as a simple, clear policy, pursuing it with almost fanatical intensity, but even he had no relationship with the French Fascists and no open sympathy for their ideas, although he became a collaborator during the war.

Secondly, the appeasers formulated their policy with the explicit aim of preserving peace, not of encouraging Nazi expansion. Like the majority of the British and French people, they feared the mass destruction which the advent of aerial warfare in 1917–18 had promised for a future world conflict. Chamberlain himself had an almost obsessive dread of war and viewed it as the ultimate evil. A. L. Rowse, a critic of appeasement and a participant in heated discussions with appeasers at All Souls, Oxford, picks out this characteristic for derision:

> *They were 'men of peace', i.e. no use for confronting force, or guile, or wickedness. That they did not know what they were dealing with is the most charitable explanation of their failure; but they might at least have taken the trouble to*

[1] T. Jones, *A Diary with Letters* (O.U.P., 1954), p. 368.

> *inform themselves. There were plenty of people to tell them,
> but they would not listen . . . One way or another they had
> none of the old 18th-century aristocrat's guts—they were
> middle-class men with pacifist backgrounds and no knowledge
> of Europe, its history or its languages, or of diplomacy, let
> alone of strategy or war . . . The plain truth is that their
> deepest instinct was defeatist, their highest wisdom surrender.*[1]

It is a hard, insensitive portrait which fails to understand the
merits of pacifism, but in its very exaggeration it underlines the
point at issue. Appeasers in Britain were motivated by inner
convictions about peace; convictions held, however naïvely, by
a large section of the British public. Chamberlain, once a
businessman and accustomed to rational negotiations round a
table, was determined to secure a peace guarantee by talking
openly to Hitler. At Munich, after the dismemberment of
Czechoslovakia had been decided, he obtained the signature of
Hitler to a declaration of peaceful intentions. This 'piece of
paper' seemed to justify the whole of his policy. Speaking to
the welcoming crowds in Downing Street he said:

> *My good friends, this is the second time in our history that
> there has come back from Germany to Downing Street peace
> with honour. I believe it is peace in our time.*

Despite the fact that over 800,000 Czechs had been transferred
to Hitler's brutal régime and that Hitler had achieved this
through threats and fanatical outbursts, Chamberlain really
meant both parts of his statement. Returning to France,
Daladier, less proud of the Munich settlement and expecting
the insults of a scornful crowd, turned up his coat collar, but his
reception was no less jubilant than Chamberlain's in London.
Most of France, like Britain, was overwhelmingly relieved to
know that war had been averted. Chamberlain could also
remember the cheers of the Germans when they, too, warmly
welcomed the envoy of peace, much to Hitler's disapproval.
The whole episode of Munich, in the eyes of the appeasers,
was about peace and the concessions made were, according
to them, to be seen entirely in this light. All talk about

[1] A. L. Rowse, *All Souls and Appeasement* (Macmillan, 1961), p. 19.

'throwing Czechoslovakia to the wolves' was irrelevant to
them.

Thirdly, only a small minority of opinion coupled appeasement
with fascism. The more general attitude over Munich was that
Chamberlain had been successful in *restraining* Hitler, not that
he had encouraged his ambition. Chamberlain himself voiced
this opinion when he said, 'I have no doubt, looking back, that
my visit alone prevented an invasion for which everything was
prepared.' At the time the full facts of Hitler's persecution and
tyranny were little known and his final extermination of the
Jews had not begun. It was not surprising that the average citizen
of Britain or France felt that war would be a greater evil than
Hitler's expansion into the Sudetenland. This can be seen by the
attitude of the public to Czechoslovakia while the issue was still
in doubt. In Britain there was an increase in church-going to
pray for peace and to pray that Czechoslovakia would be co-
operative, and the press to a large extent placed the decision of
war or peace in Czech hands. After Munich the gratitude to
Chamberlain came from all sections of the public: letters poured
in and columnists vied with each other in articles of praise,
though few went as far as the broadcaster and writer Godfrey
Winn, who had exclaimed even before Munich: 'Praise be to
God and to Mr. Chamberlain. I find no sacrilege, no bathos, in
coupling these two names.'

Even among the critics of appeasement it was not the accepted
practice to accuse the appeasers of having Fascist sentiments.
Churchill thundered his opposition and maintained that submission to Hitler over the Sudetenland would open Europe to
Nazism, but he did not arraign Chamberlain as a crypto-Fascist:
he saw him rather as a traitor to the proud British tradition of
international justice. Munich, he declared, was a 'total and
unmitigated defeat' and he concluded his parliamentary attack
with these words:

> *This is only the beginning of the reckoning. This is only the
> first sip, the first foretaste of a bitter cup which will be
> proffered to us year by year, unless by a supreme recovery
> of moral health and martial vigour we arise again and take
> our stand for freedom as in olden time.*[1]

[1] *Hansard*, 5 October 1938.

In Churchill's eyes Chamberlain was both foolish and cowardly;
but the possibility that the appeasers might have Fascist intentions
was not mentioned.

Who did, then, accuse the appeasers of having Fascist
sympathies and how does their case compare with the three
arguments above?

The most outspoken accusers were the British and French
Communists, who, between 1935 and 1939, maintained a constant barrage of criticism against the Western 'friends of Hitler'.
They were joined by young anti-Fascist intellectuals, many of
whom declared their disgust for appeasement by fighting for the
Republic in Spain and by continuing to run anti-Fascist leagues
once the Civil War was over. Together the Communists and anti-
Fascists pointed to the non-involvement in the Spanish war, to
the acceptance of the *Anschluss* and finally to Munich, as evidence
of close collaboration by Britain and France with the Fascists in
Europe. The Communist newspapers, *L'Humanité* in France and
The Daily Worker in Britain, saw fascism as the last degenerate
stage in the history of capitalism, a stage in which the capitalist
governments of Britain and France were inevitably involved.

In Britain the government's policy was also attacked as pro-
Fascist by certain left-wing members of the Labour Party, notably
Sir Stafford Cripps and Aneurin Bevan, who tried without
success to organize a Popular Front of all anti-Fascists. The
various accusations seemed to be given substance by the information contained in *Tory M.P.*, a book analysing all the Conservatives in Parliament and pointing out the Fascist sympathies
of many of them.[1]

When the substance of these attacks is considered, its strength
rests on the following two points. In the first place, the methods
of the appeasers in obtaining their ends were suspect. Chamberlain was high-handed and autocratic: he ignored the normal
channels of diplomacy, bypassing his own Foreign Office and
relying on a few chosen men who had his full confidence. In
Cabinet meetings he rarely listened to contrary arguments and
never entrusted his colleagues with all the facts of the situation.
This led to severe reproaches from those like Lord Vansittart and
Duff Cooper who felt that Chamberlain was pursuing his policy

[1] S. Haxey, *Tory M.P.* (Gollancz, 1939).

blindly and obstinately. When he began his personal meetings with Hitler, Chamberlain became even more impervious to criticism: like Nevile Henderson, the British Ambassador in Berlin, he shut out the more unpleasant aspects of the Nazi régime and concentrated on the personality of Hitler, which he felt to be impulsive but not beyond reason. This refusal to face facts in their entirety was shared by most of the other appeasers. Geoffrey Dawson, editor of *The Times*, slanted the news which came from Germany in order to show Hitler in the most favourable light, and Horace Wilson, Chamberlain's right-hand man in Downing Street, carefully selected the information he knew the Prime Minister would like to see. Not only did the appeasers respond generously to Hitler's claims, they also suggested to Hitler ways in which he could gain colonial territory and strengthen his economy. These proposals meant little to Hitler, but they were signs of an extreme willingness on the part of other countries to ingratiate the powerful dictator.

The corollary of this generosity to Hitler was a ruthlessness towards Czechoslovakia. Once Chamberlain had decided that the Sudetenland should be conceded to the Nazi Reich the interests of the Czechs were brushed aside. France was equally domineering, despite her longstanding agreement to protect Eastern Europe against German expansion.

Such single-minded dedication to appeasement and wilful avoidance of fact does suggest that the appeasers were not viewing Nazism with an objective eye. They saw what they wanted to see and this was not the brutal, savage side of the Hitler régime. Throughout the thirties they showed a willingness to treat foreign fascism with understanding. As Henderson said in his memoirs: 'Peace was my big objective and my influence with the Germans would be nil if I prejudiced the Nazis from the start . . . I did not go to Berlin to curse, but where possible to bless.'[1]

Secondly the social conservatism of the appeasers and their fundamental hostility to communism led them to approve certain aspects of German and Italian fascism, which they compared favourably with the Stalinism of Russia. The ideology of communism with its emphasis on social revolution and the

[1] Sir N. Henderson, *Failure of a Mission* (Hodder and Stoughton, 1940), p. 36.

overthrow of capitalism was seen as a greater threat to the industrialist, the businessman and the owner of property than the social policy of fascism. The diplomacy of appeasement reflected this. Stalin was omitted from all consultations over Czechoslovakia, and when a mission was sent from Britain to Moscow to discuss the possibility of an agreement it had none of the prestige, power or urgency of similar missions to both Italy and Germany. Where Hitler was trusted, Stalin was suspected, and where fascism was given the benefit of the doubt, communism was seen in none but the worst terms. This was particularly true of Chamberlain's own attitude, which, as appeasement advanced, became more and more the single determinant of British foreign policy. After Munich he confidently told the House of Commons that Hitler's word could be trusted:

> It is my hope and my belief that, under the new system of guarantees, the new Czechoslovakia will find a greater security than she has ever enjoyed in the past.[1]

But of Russia he wrote in March 1939:

> I must confess to the most profound distrust of Russia. I have no belief whatever in her ability to maintain an effective offensive, even if she wanted to. And I distrust her motives, which seem to me to have little connection with our ideas of liberty and to be concerned only with setting everybody else by the ears. Moreover she is both hated and suspected by many of the smaller states, notably by Poland, Roumania and Finland.[2]

It could be said that Chamberlain's suspicions were justified, since in August 1939 Stalin set his seal to a Nazi–Soviet non-aggression pact, and thus became an appeaser himself, to the unwarranted indignation of Britain and France. The question remains, however: would Stalin have signed such a pact had he not been conscious of the West's hostility to communism and believed that Anglo–French appeasement was encouraging Hitler to turn against Russia?

[1] *Hansard*, 3 October 1938.
[2] Quoted in K. Feiling, *Life of Neville Chamberlain* (Macmillan, 1946), p. 403.

The appeal to order and tradition at the headquarters of the British
Union of Fascists

These two points of accusation, citing appeasement's question-
able methods and its anti-communism, stand up well to historical
analysis. This is equally true of the three earlier points defending
the appeasers' motives. A summary must therefore present
something of a contradiction. It would seem that the appeasers
were in no sense Fascists, for they made no attempt to embrace
a Fascist ideology or practise Fascist methods of government, but
they were clearly conditioned by their passionate desire for peace,
their suspicion of communism and their preference for the social
policies of Mussolini and Hitler, to see something of value in the
Fascist countries and to entertain naïve hopes for the future of
Nazi Germany. They trusted and to some extent admired those
aspects of the Fascist synthesis which had already attracted the
social conservatives in Italy and Germany: the order, the
authority and the respect for hierarchy—values which were
common to the society to which most of the appeasers belonged.
Appeasement, therefore, is worth studying in a history of fascism
because it forms a powerful illustration of the Fascist appeal. At
one end of the scale Hitler and Mussolini could inspire the brutal,
revolutionary hopes of brown- and black-shirted thugs: at the
other end they were capable of duping the well-intentioned
leaders of democratic governments.

2 THE ATTITUDE OF THE PAPACY

Chamberlain and Daladier were not the only exponents of appeasement. The Pope and the Roman Catholic hierarchy also kept their criticisms of fascism to a minimum and in many areas supported its aims, particularly against communism. The Vatican's policy in this period, like that of the unwitting followers and appeasers of fascism throughout Europe, is proof of the wide degeneration of principles and ideals in the face of the Fascist challenge. Some critics of the Vatican, particularly the German playwright Rolf Hochhuth in his play *Der Stellvertreter* ('The Representative'), echo the accusations levelled against the appeasers. The intention is to show Pius XI (1922–1939) and Pius XII (1939–58) to have been pro-Fascist and to have ignored the vast questions of human justice raised by the Nazi persecution of the Jews. It has not been difficult to make out a good case in support of this harsh indictment. For a body which had claimed the monopoly of religious and moral truth and set itself the highest aims of justice and philanthropy, the record of Roman Catholicism under Hitler and Mussolini was compromising. Compared with Pius IX's outspoken denunciation of liberalism in the 1860s and the continued hostility of his successors to radicalism, socialism and communism, the attitude of the Papacy to fascism of all varieties was one of cautious appeasement. In the long list of statesmen excommunicated for their sins against God and the Church, the name of Hitler could not be found. He remained till his death a member of the Catholic community. It was also beyond question, though not beyond apology, that the Vatican did not openly and firmly condemn the horrific persecution of the Jews during the war. Guenther Lewy in his study *The Catholic Church and Nazi Germany* ends his chapter on the Jewish Question with these words:

> When Hitler set out on his murderous campaign against the Jews of Europe, truth and justice found few defenders. The deputy of Christ and the German episcopate were not among them. Their role gives a special relevance to the question the young girl in Max Frisch's Andorra asks her priest: 'Where were you, Father Benedict, when they took

away our brother like a beast to the slaughter, like a beast to the slaughter, where were you?' The question still waits for an answer.[1]

Answers have of course been given, and many of them have the same well-reasoned value as the defence of Anglo–French appeasement. It is necessary to recognize that the Catholic Church, though generally understanding towards fascism, was by no means uncritical. Pius XI roundly condemned Mussolini for his interference with Catholic freedom in his encyclical *Non abbiamo bisogno* in 1931. What was clear in Italian fascism, he said, 'was the intention of monopolizing the young from their earliest childhood till maturity, for the sole and exclusive benefit of a party or a régime, on the basis of an ideology which expressly resolves itself into a veritable pagan glorification of the State . . .' and this, he proclaimed, was totally unacceptable to the Catholic doctrine. Later, in 1938, when Mussolini introduced anti-Semitic legislation into Italy, Pius XI uttered a series of censures on 'this grave and gross error of racialism' and accused the Italians of slavishly imitating Germany.

Towards Nazism the Vatican was also critical when certain circumstances demanded. In particular, Pius XI reacted strongly when Hitler persecuted the Church. In 1933 Hitler had signed a concordat with the Pope guaranteeing the free exercise of the Catholic religion in Germany, but, like Bismarck in the 1870s, Hitler could not tolerate an outside source of authority governing the minds and actions of native Germans. By 1937 he had attacked Catholicism in so many ways, imprisoning clergy and closing their schools, that Pius issued a strong warning against the false doctrines of National Socialism. The encyclical known as *Mit Brennender Sorge* was smuggled into Germany and despite Nazi confiscations and arrests was read from many pulpits. Nazism, said the Pope,'takes the race or people or the State or form of government . . . and deifies them with an idolatrous worship'. Protests were also launched from Rome against the removal of crucifixes from schools and against the Nazi introduction of euthanasia and sterilization. During the war and the pontificate of Pius XII there was less public protestation from

[1] G. Lewy, *The Catholic Church and Nazi Germany* (Weidenfeld and Nicolson, 1964), p. 308.

Rome, but it has been argued that Pius XII saved hundreds of Jews by giving instructions to convents and monasteries to shelter the hunted. After the war a deputation of Italian Jews, freed from concentration camps, called to thank the Pope, who welcomed them in the Hebrew language.

Finally, the answer given to Hochhuth, Lewy and other accusers pleads the difficulties of the situation. The Pope, it is claimed, had to protect the widespread community of Catholics: in each country the situation was complex and nowhere was the hierarchy in a position to defy the political powers. Had he denounced Hitler and called on all Catholics to oppose him, he might have divided Catholicism and unleashed a new wave of mass murder in which thousands of innocent Catholics would have suffered for the words of their spiritual, but not political, head. Would any other leader, asks the Vatican, with such vast responsibilities, have taken this risk?

So far, the argument as presented shows the accusers as concentrating on Rome's failure to pronounce openly and consistently against Nazi evils. In reply the apologists can point to several examples where the Church did take a firm stand. But the accusation goes deeper by giving many examples and instances of outright Catholic support for the forces of fascism. Again, there is a reputable historical case. In 1929 Pius XI spoke of Mussolini as a man of providence, summing up seven years of Catholic co-operation with the Fascist government which the Church had warmly accepted after the march on Rome. The Vatican had taken the side of Mussolini against the liberal Catholic leader of the Popular Party, Don Luigi Sturzo, and had officially dissociated itself from Sturzo's criticisms of the Fascist State. In the mid-thirties, despite the encyclical of 1931, the Church stood solidly behind Mussolini's foreign policy. Towards Spain the hierarchy pursued an uncompromising line in favour of Franco and thereby in support of Mussolini's aid to the Nationalists. When the story of the Guernica bombing was relayed to the Vatican by two indignant Basque priests who had witnessed the massacre, Pius XI would not discuss the incident, and his Secretary of State, Cardinal Pacelli (later Pius XII), showed them the door with the cold remark, 'The Church is persecuted in Barcelona.'

During the war the evidence of Papal sympathy towards fascism diminished. More is made of what Pius XII did not say than of what he did. Nevertheless it can be shown that the Vatican, despite appeals for peace and offers of mediation, was slow to dissociate itself from Fascist aggression, though diplomatic notes went to Berlin protesting against the persecution of Catholic priests in occupied countries. At best, the accusation reads, Pius was neutral, and even this neutrality covers a continuous sympathy for Mussolini's régime until 1943. In October 1942 Himmler visited the *Duce* and reported to Hitler that opposition to Mussolini from the Catholic hierarchy was unlikely: 'The Pope was not going to make things too difficult for him and he was after all an Italian at heart.'[1] At this point the case against Pius is taken up by the indictment already stated: that not once during the war did he openly mention the Jews, either to plead for their lives or to condemn the extermination policies of Hitler.

Just as Chamberlain's policy was rejected by some Conservatives like Churchill and Duff Cooper, so the Pope's appeasement had its Catholic critics throughout Europe. No history of Catholic–Fascist relations can ignore the courageous resistance of thousands of unknown Catholics and hundreds of well-known clergy against every aspect of Fascist barbarity. Their actions would figure prominently alongside those of Communists, Liberals and other men of anti-Fascist convictions if this were a history of European Resistance. Nevertheless, the conclusion is that despite this widespread Catholic resistance, despite the moments of Papal firmness against Mussolini and Hitler, the leaders of Catholicism, like the leaders of France and Britain, were unwilling to make their partial criticisms of fascism into a full denunciation.

In the perspective of Catholic politics this position of the Papacy is not surprising. Since the 18th century the Catholic fight had been directed against the revolutionary challenge from the Left. From this direction had come all the attacks on Catholic doctrine, clerical privileges and the whole status of Catholicism in social and political circles. The Catholic Church throughout the

---

[1] Quoted in F. W. Deakin, *The Brutal Friendship* (Weidenfeld and Nicolson, 1966), p. 55.

19th century was militantly conservative. Furthermore the Papacy
was located in Rome, a city owned and ruled for hundreds of
years by the Church. In 1870 it was taken over by the Italian
Republic and the Pope retired behind his Vatican walls and
outlawed the usurpers. The tradition therefore of Church against
left-wing politics was carried on into the 20th century, and the
advent of irreligious communism in 1917 seemed to underline
this conflict more forcibly. Almost everything therefore conditioned the Papacy to respond gratefully to the anti-communism
of Italian fascism and later of German Nazism. The concordats
were made and socially the Church benefited from the authoritarian, hierarchical nature of Fascist society. It might well have
been suicidal for the Church to resist the limited friendship
offered by the two régimes, though the effect on public opinion
had it done so is incalculable. What is clear is that its initial
commitment to the Fascist régimes drew it into a series of
compromise statements and actions which some label squalid
and others defend as diplomatic and necessary.

Whatever the final judgment on this issue, and it will have to
wait until the Vatican's archives are available, it would seem
that the emotions provoked by the controversy are due in part
to the previous history of the Papacy. If over the centuries it
had claimed less for its wisdom and understanding and had
issued fewer statements on political and social questions,
then less might have been expected of it in the difficult situation
created by fascism, for the critics of Catholic policy have judged
it by the very highest standards—standards which the Church
has always claimed for itself. By lower standards the record is
no better or worse than that of appeasers throughout Europe.
Fascism revealed the insecurity and fallibility of many well-
established, historic institutions.

CHAPTER NINE

Hitler's War

Thomas Mann, the great German novelist, wrote from exile in 1940:

> *Is there any sense in shutting the eyes to the truth that can indeed burn through closed eyelids?—namely that the deeds and scenes and everything without exception that happened in Germany since this gang came into power carried the inevitable implication of war.*[1]

This was a view which Mann had proclaimed throughout the thirties: that Nazism was a romance of war and that Hitler's policy could lead only to international disaster. It was a view which was contested at the time of appeasement by those who saw in Hitler a man of peace. Events proved Mann to be right and the appeasers wrong. Even if one still believes that Hitler was an opportunist with no detailed plan for world war, one is forced to admit that he both provoked and welcomed a state of European conflict. Out of this conflict, which he hoped to control, he intended to emerge with a united Reich dominating a reconstructed Europe. He had made this his aim in *Mein Kampf*; he repeated it in his second, unpublished, book in 1929; he reiterated it throughout the thirties and he made it the basis of his war aims after 1939.

This single-minded ambition of Hitler leads the historian Trevor-Roper to write:

> *The Second World War was Hitler's personal war in many senses. He intended it, he prepared for it, he chose the moment for launching it; and for three years, in the main,*

[1] T. Mann, *This War*, trans. E. Sutton (Secker and Warburg, 1940), p. 12.

*he planned its course. On several occasions between 1939
and 1942 he claimed to have won it. It was—or would have
been—a personal victory, for although the aims which he
sought to realize were old nationalist aspirations the policy
and the strategy for their realization had been imposed by
him.*[1]

As a total explanation of why war broke out this would be
inadequate. The evil genius of Hitler stalking firmly through the
history of the thirties towards war in 1939 is an alluring but
simplified vision. But the central emphasis on Hitler at this point
is perfectly acceptable for the general history of fascism.

At the time of the Spanish Civil War, fascism, although to
some extent united in general aims, was still a mosaic of different
national parties, each with its own atmosphere, policy, emphasis
and leader. But between 1936 and 1940 the power of Nazism
and the European successes of Hitler began to dominate the
other national movements. Fascisms in Italy, France and Belgium
lost much of their individuality and became shadows of Nazi
Germany. Most of the Fascist leaders fell into line behind Hitler,
echoing his attitudes and imitating his extremism. When war
broke out due to Hitler's aggression they followed him and
endorsed his plans for a new Fascist Europe. The future of a
widely diffused ideology thus became narrowly linked with the
fortunes of Hitler's national armies.

This submission to Hitler lasted long enough to give to World
War II an ideological character. Because Mussolini in Italy,
Doriot in France, Degrelle in Belgium and leaders of smaller
Fascist groups elsewhere were the staunchest supporters of
Hitler, it appeared as if fascism had united and declared war
against democracy. For many people this was and remains the
character of the war, but to accept this interpretation is to forget
that 1939–45 was essentially Hitler's war fought in the interests
of Nazi Germany. It was not automatically in the interests of all
Fascist movements in Europe and by 1942 many Fascists had
fully recognized this fact. As they did so, they turned back to
their own ideals and accused Hitler of betraying an ideology for
nationalist German ends. The war thus brought only a temporary

[1] H. R. Trevor-Roper, *Hitler's War Directives* (Pan, 1966), p. 13.

alliance of fascisms throughout Europe. In 1942 this alliance began to crack and by the end of the war it was in pieces. There were some non-German Fascists who remained loyal to Hitler until the end, but there were others who came to see Hitler not as their ideal leader but as an enemy of their cause. Thus in 1945 Fascists in Western Europe were still disunited, but their subservience to Hitler, if only for a brief period, had left them identified with his system and his war aims. When Hitler fell, the victorious Allies were in no mood for subtle distinctions between different Fascists. The ideology and all its practitioners were judged by the excesses of the Nazi régime. Fascism as a creed and a political system stood totally condemned, and in the wave of official trials and popular justice which accompanied the end of the war Fascists of every degree were swept to their death or to prison.

At a distance it is possible to re-establish some of the distinctions which were blurred in 1945. Hitler's influence obliterated many of the differences among Fascists, but some remained and some were even accentuated. This complexity becomes evident when the situations in Italy and France are examined (see the following two sections), after which there is an examination of the particular nature of Hitler's war and his own defeat and death.

1 THE DISINTEGRATION OF ITALIAN FASCISM

The rule of Mussolini was never as totalitarian as Hitler's control of Germany. He himself had none of the ruthless consistency of the German Führer and the Italians were less interested than the Germans in efficient organization and uniformity of ideas. Though the *Duce* ruled as a dictator with unpredictable whims executed by a subservient party and militia, he depended on the support of the Italian people. This support he frequently abused, and despite his propaganda and public image he had little respect for the masses. Nevertheless, Italian fascism was built on the relationship between Mussolini and the people, and when this relationship weakened and the people lost confidence in their leader Mussolini was undermined and easily overthrown.

There had been moments in the thirties when the relationship had been strained. Mussolini had failed to bring the promised economic millennium and had been forced to tell the people that fascism could not perform miracles: he had also alienated Catholic Action and sent Italians to fight and be killed in Abyssinia and Spain. In 1937 he adopted Hitler's anti-Semitism and introduced it into an Italy which cared little for the fanatical racism of Hitler and saw no need to persecute Italian Jews. Finally, despite the objections of many of his own Fascist colleagues, he followed Hitler into war after committing Italy to a German alliance which bound the two countries 'like a pact of steel'.

None of these actions was completely popular, but victory in both Abyssinia and Spain had silenced the dissenting voices and there were many Italians who approved of Mussolini's independence of the priests. Even the racial decrees were not sufficient to stir the country into action against Mussolini, and the 'pact of steel' would have been acceptable had it shown quick and beneficial results. From the start, however, Mussolini's part in Hitler's war was a fiasco, and between 1940 and 1943 his hold on the Italians diminished. As it did so, a strong opposition group within the Fascist Party developed and Mussolini was finally rejected by his own subordinates.

In 1939, however, when the 'pact of steel' was announced, Mussolini's pro-German policy did not seem dangerous or perverse. His allegiance to Hitler was a logical outcome of the Abyssinian crisis and the Spanish Civil War. Both had shown that Mussolini's severest critics were in the democracies whereas Nazi Germany both admired and flattered him. In particular, Mussolini was deeply impressed by the tributes paid to him by Hitler and overawed by the immense military power which he saw on his visits to Germany. Though long-standing national interests still divided Italy and Germany, the new common ground between Hitler and Mussolini seemed more significant. Fascism was determined to recast the politics of Europe into a new mould.

On this understanding Mussolini was able to carry his party

and Italy with him. The future looked secure and Hitler's diplomatic successes in 1938 and 1939 seemed to justify Mussolini's claim that democracy was decadent and fascism the only strong régime of the twentieth century. There were even Fascists surrounding Mussolini who were more pro-German than himself. Farinacci greatly admired the Nazis, and the leader of the Fascist militia, Galbiati, was strongly in favour of Hitler's war. Others, especially Count Dino Grandi and the ideologist Bottai, were opposed to such a tight co-operation with Hitler but in 1939–40 their criticisms were slight.

In 1940 began the sequence of events which raised these criticisms of Mussolini into a full denunciation and turned Italy from Fascist rule to civil war. Firstly, the Italians were told by Mussolini that they were at war with France; then France was overrun by Hitler and an armistice declared, thus robbing Italy of the chance of sharing the spoils of French defeat. Secondly, they were told they were at war with Greece and Yugoslavia; but the Italian campaign was so ill-prepared and unsuccessful that the Germans had to take over and make the invasions effective. Thirdly, in 1941, when Hitler turned his war against Russia, the Italians were informed that troops would go to the Russian front to fight for the Fascist cause against communism; but in 1942 the Russians held Stalingrad and the Italian divisions, weaker than the German, were largely destroyed in the months of heavy, close fighting. Fourthly, in 1942, the French North African colonies (which Mussolini coveted) fell to the Anglo–American forces. Lastly, in July 1943, the Allies invaded Sicily and began their advance through the Italian peninsula. Mussolini's gamble had failed: his own forces had been unable even to defeat Greece, and the apparently invincible armies of Hitler had met decisive resistance. The war had turned out to be a war of German expansionism, in which Italy provided no more than a fumbling sideshow which impressed no one, least of all the Italians themselves.

As the defeats and humiliations followed each other and it became clear that Italian interests were radically different from those of Nazi Germany, the groups and institutions which had buttressed Mussolini's power began to look for a change of government. The King, Victor Emmanuel III, who had kept his throne only by the most complete submission to Italian fascism, began to assert himself and intrigue with the army chief-of-staff, Marshal Badoglio. The Pope and the Vatican bureaucracy found increasingly more issues on which to reprove Mussolini and by 1943 had begun to shelter the enemies of fascism and the victims of Hitler's war. Within fascism itself the growth of opposition was even more remarkable. Mussolini was by this time both ill and disillusioned with his own foreign policy, and showed none of his old flair and determination in meeting this opposition. While his colleagues and subordinates planned his removal he appeared inert and disinterested, a factor which increased the confidence of his critics.

During the winter of 1942 Mussolini's position was eroded. The average Italian, especially in the towns, was tired of making useless efforts for a régime which showed no results, and reacted with increasing scorn to the exhortations and promises of the government. This mounting disaffection had its effect on the embryonic opposition groups. They came more into the open and acted with conviction and urgency. The Fascist opposition struck first. Under the leadership of Bottai and Grandi they staged a dramatic meeting of the Fascist Grand Council on 24 July 1943, a fortnight after the Allies had landed in Sicily. There was a sense of doom among many of the conspirators, some of whom expected violence or death to be the outcome of the meeting. Grandi, one of the earliest Fascist leaders who had controlled the *squadre* and party in Bologna, had been to confession and carried two hand grenades with him. It was he who denounced Mussolini to his face in a speech which was bitter and outspoken. He accused Mussolini of betraying Italian fascism by his personal rule:

> *The real enemy of Fascism is the dictatorship. From the day when the old motto 'Liberty and Fatherland' inscribed on the action squads was replaced by the other 'Believe, obey, fight' Fascism was finished. The narrow, absurd formula of the Fascist war has brought the nation to ruin. The responsibility for this disaster lies not with Fascism, but with the dictatorship. It is the latter which has lost the war.*[1]

[1] Quoted in F. W. Deakin, *The Brutal Friendship* (Weidenfeld and Nicolson, 1962), pp. 443–4.

Bottai, in more measured tones, endorsed this verdict, pointing to an 'inefficient machinery of command' which had led to the disasters of the last three years.

Farinacci, one of the most violent of the Italian Fascists and closer to Nazism than any of the others at the meeting, also rejected Mussolini's personal rule, but for a different purpose. His aim was to strengthen the Fascist government under the King, to purge the army of all inefficiency and to throw a rejuvenated Italy against the invading Allies. 'In my motion,' he declared, 'I call for an even closer union with our ally Germany in the conduct of the war.' Turning to Grandi, he accused him of dividing fascism and weakening its moral force just when the country was threatened: 'You cannot continue this underground and cannibal war against us.'

There was a chance here for Mussolini to make concessions to Farinacci and then join him in a counter-attack against the moderates who wanted an end to the war. But the *Duce* was apathetic and the meeting ended in the early hours of 25 July with a decision that Mussolini should cease to be leader. The voting was nineteen to seven, and the incredible had happened. A Fascist leader had been removed from power by a democratic vote. Moderates had triumphed over extremists and a Fascist war policy had been reversed, not by anti-Fascists but by Fascists themselves.

This decisive meeting of the Grand Council might well have become an historic event in the history of Italy had not its importance been overshadowed at once by the action of the King and Marshal Badoglio. When Mussolini left the King's palace on 25 July after visiting Victor Emmanuel to discuss the situation, he was forced into a car and driven off to arrest and imprisonment. The Fascists had rejected Mussolini but it was the King and the army who overthrew him. In the face of this action the Fascist régime disintegrated. The inheritors of Imperial Rome and the ideologists of force and action did nothing. The King's *coup* succeeded and twenty years of fascism disappeared overnight. Its façade of strength, order and permanence had cracked and there was nothing substantial behind. Hitler's war had brought disaster to the first Fascist movement of Europe. Nazi Germany continued to fight in Italy purely for its own ends,

The first meeting of Hitler and Mussolini after the latter's rescue in September 1943

and the visions of a Fascist Europe became nothing more than obstinate illusions.

Undoubtedly the events of July 1943 brought the end of Fascist Italy, but the political career of the *Duce* was not at an end. Within two months he had been traced by Hitler's spies and rescued from his place of imprisonment. He was flown northwards behind the German lines and taken to Hitler, who recreated him leader of Italy. It was almost an empty title since the Allies were beginning to occupy most of the peninsula and the King had changed sides and joined them, but where the German forces were still entrenched in Northern Italy there Mussolini's rule was re-established. He was little more than a puppet of Nazi Germany and the Italians under his rule were conscious of his crumbling fortunes: there was none of the old grandeur and confidence of the Fascist régime.

The new reality was civil war—Mussolini's republic in the north, under the watchful eye of Hitler, attempting to rally Italians to continue the war against the Allies, and in the south and centre of Italy a confused combination of Allied soldiers, the new régime of the King, and partisan underground fighters who wanted to free Italy for a Communist or at least Republican future. The passions aroused by this chaos of conflicting politics and ideologies were bitter and Italy took on the agonized character of Spain in the thirties.

Two features of this complex situation are important in the history of fascism. Firstly, many of Mussolini's old colleagues and subordinates disappeared completely from political life. The majority of those who had voted against Mussolini in the early hours of 25 July became lost in the general turmoil. Some went back to their Italian businesses, others went abroad. The two major opponents of the *Duce*, Grandi and Bottai, separated; Grandi became a wealthy salesman with considerable success in South America, and Bottai, idealist to the end, left Italy to join the French Foreign Legion. Fascist Italy thus showed no solidarity in defeat. Once the régime had been broken the individuals who had buttressed and exploited it revealed no consistent desire to continue the fight underground.

Secondly, Mussolini's Republic in the north centred at Salò produced a revival of early Fascist ideology. Freed from respectable connections with monarchy, Church and aristocracy, Mussolini's youthful Republican and Socialist spirit was rekindled, and his pronouncements in 1944 echo his activist ideas of the years before the march on Rome. Surrounded by the strength of German arms he could afford a last gesture of individualist power. With no concern for old services and loyalties he arrested many of his opponents of 25 July who were still within his territory, and had six of them shot, including his son-in-law Ciano. Other orders to discourage desertion and disloyalty went regularly from his headquarters on Lake Garda and with them the reassertion of 'pure' Fascist principles. The word 'revolution' was used again by Mussolini to signify an uncompromising attitude to the enemies of fascism, and the action squads regained much of their old independence. With the anti-Fascist partisans growing in strength, the conflicts resembled those of 1920–1. Fascist Italy had returned to its origins.

A new ingredient in all this was the attempt by Mussolini to apply Socialist principles to the industry that remained under his rule. Ideas were formulated to bring workers and employers together in the running of industrial production under the overall direction of the Republic. One of the objects was to tie industry more closely to a war effort which was rapidly losing all support; another was to outbid the growing appeal of communism among the workers. Several biographers of Mussolini have made much of this socialism, suggesting that the 'real' Mussolini had at last emerged. It is difficult to say. The Socialist decrees met with little enthusiasm from employers or workers and the complete collapse of Mussolini's power in the spring of 1945 ended the experiment prematurely. It had certainly failed to bite during the short life of the Republic but the conditions were hardly encouraging for a radical reorganization of society. Whether it was anything more than another facet of Mussolini's opportunism is open to debate.

The end came in April 1945 when the military situation in Northern Italy was desperate. The occupying German forces had surrendered at Milan and Mussolini was left with a small band of friends and subordinates at Como; he had no army, no administration and a meaningless title. Refuge was refused to him by the Archbishop of Milan: flight or suicide were the only alternatives. He chose to try and lose himself but was arrested by partisans at a road-block. On 28 April Mussolini and Clara Petacci, his devoted mistress, were put up against a wall and shot. The partisans had preferred to exact their own vengeance despite orders to deliver Mussolini alive for trial. As a final humiliation the *Duce* was mutilated and strung up by his feet from the roof of a petrol station in Milan. The body was largely ignored: Italy had lost interest in its leader.

2 COLLABORATION IN FRANCE

When Hitler turned against the West in May 1940 and launched his *Blitzkrieg* he accompanied it with powerful propaganda. The German forces proclaimed the New Order, an ideal of a Europe ruled by new men with new ideas; the Fascist civilization. French Fascists responded to this ideal with enthusiasm. Although their country was at war with Hitler they could not treat the invading Nazis as enemies. Their real enemies were their opponents in France and they accepted the defeat and German occupation as an opportunity to turn on these internal enemies with the borrowed power of Nazi authority. In this way a civil-war situation was created in which those Frenchmen who collaborated with the Germans found themselves fighting fellow countrymen who resisted.

To some extent this civil war had been latent throughout the thirties. The Third Republic, which had survived so many crises, was by 1939 a sick régime. It was undermined on all sides, and when Daladier's government ended its appeasement in September 1939 and declared war on Hitler it was a weak and divided country which responded. At first this was not apparent. The French had great confidence in their defence system, based on a vast line of concrete fortifications stretching along the frontier with Germany and known as the Maginot Line. For eight months over seventy French divisions manned this line with little fighting to do, since Hitler was still occupied in defeating Poland, but in May the gigantic force of the German army was turned against France and Belgium, and the phoney war of the previous months became a real war of proportions totally unexpected by the French military command. Concentrating on the main roads leading into France, the German army struck with such speed and intensity that the French were soon routed and in retreat. Their British allies were of little help. The British army on the Continent was weak and was quickly forced to retreat to Dunkirk and from there back to England on a flotilla of small ships. The French faced the invaders in some areas with desperate courage but in others with panic and defeatism. As the Germans swept towards Paris, *Luftwaffe* aircraft strafed the roads with shells, scattering and terrifying the hordes of refugees who were escaping from the threatened towns and villages. Belgians and Frenchmen from the north and east crowded into the areas where the French forces were trying to re-establish their defence.

The effect of this stream of refugees was catastrophic. French soldiers had no incentive to stay and fight when they saw thousands in headlong flight. Defeat appeared certain and what man wants to be killed when the war is so nearly over? This was the observation of Marc Bloch, who described the dramatic collapse of France in his book *L'Étrange Défaite* ('Strange Defeat'). It was not just a military collapse. As he saw at the time, the German invasion revealed the real weakness of France, its deep political and ideological divisions. Retreat and defeatism were due not only to German power and the *Luftwaffe*, but also to the many groups of Frenchmen who had opposed war, who had urged Daladier to continue his

appeasement or who had advocated a settlement with Hitler.
As the French army began to collapse, these forces came to the
surface and the war effort was sabotaged. On the Fascist side,
followers of Doriot urged the French to welcome the bringers
of strength and National Socialism, and at the high level of
government, voices began to insist on surrender and an armistice
before the whole of France was overrun. This opinion seemed
more and more reasonable as the Germans moved first into
Paris and then beyond. By mid-June it had enough supporters to
become official policy. The war government fell and Marshal
Pétain, the old and venerable hero of World War I, was called
on to head a new government and make peace with the
Germans. Another much younger and almost unknown military
figure, General de Gaulle, crossed to England in protest and
from London called on all true Frenchmen to continue the fight.

But it was Pétain and not de Gaulle who carried French
opinion with him in June 1940. An armistice was signed. France
was divided into two parts: the north occupied by the Germans,
and the south ruled by Pétain's government from the fashionable
resort of Vichy. The Third Republic was dead. Its leaders were
discredited: they were accused of mismanaging France in the
thirties and leading her to a disastrous defeat. In Vichy new men
came to power, not young men, but men of nationalist and
conservative attitudes: the men who read *Action française* and
called for a moral purge of the nation; men who were anti-
Communist and anti-Republican. They had been the outsiders
of the thirties. They were now in power and they had old scores
to settle. Vichy was a parade of counter-revolutionary France in
which Nazi Germany took the salute.

It was in the logic of the armistice that the government of
Pétain would co-operate, if not collaborate, with the Germans.
The victors held the whip hand and could apply pressure at
any moment by extending the occupation. This was done in
November 1942 when the whole of France was occupied by
Nazi authorities, but the Vichy government was allowed to
remain, and in the person of Pierre Laval, Pétain's Prime
Minister, it was even capable of independent action. Laval, a
shrewd business man and a political individualist, shared few of
the conservative ideals of Pétain and his colleagues, but he had

been no less of an outsider between the wars. Although twice
a minister, his policies had been rejected each time and he had
been dismissed from office. He had no party and no ideology.
He was a complete opportunist.

Accepted reluctantly by Pétain, who mistrusted him, Laval saw
collaboration as a way of preserving France from the worst evils
of occupation. To this end he went to extreme lengths of
appeasement, even at one point publicly announcing that he
hoped for a German victory against the Allies. But, he maintained, by saying this he prevented the tightening of the Nazi
hold on France and thus spared thousands of Frenchmen from
deportation and death. This too was his excuse when he agreed
to persecute the Jews: he claimed that although he sent several
thousand alien Jews to Germany he managed to protect
thousands of French Jews from a similar fate by bargaining with
the Germans. His whole case rests on the assumption that evil is
worthwhile if it prevents greater evil. The Germans, he fervently
believed, would have crushed the whole of France as the
Resistance movements began to have effect: they would have
treated the French as they treated the Czechs and Poles, as
animals. A statesman was therefore necessary to give them a
little of what they wanted, so that they would not demand
everything. This was Laval's role as he saw it, and it was in his
eyes a role of providence just as important for France as Pétain's
or de Gaulle's. Laval was tried and shot in 1945 before his case
could be objectively argued. Only now is it beginning to be
treated with some respect. At the time of France's liberation,
however, he was the symbol of the hated *collabos*, men who were
seen as betraying France unscrupulously to the enemy.

Charles Maurras too was brought to trial and found guilty of
helping the enemy. His career under Vichy shows an embittered,
vitriolic old man casting about for an attitude which would be
true to his ideology of *Action française*, but producing nothing
but articles of hatred. His nationalism now looked hopeless and
pretentious, his rantings against Jews and Resisters became
pathological and his monarchism disappeared under the cult
of Pétainism. He claimed in 1945 that he had continued to
preach patriotism and for this reason he opposed the Resisters as
he had once opposed the Dreyfusards, accusing them of dividing

France. In almost every detail, however, his newspaper writings
had taken on a Fascist intensity. Maurras became under the
occupation the extreme propagandist of the Vichy conservatives,
and just as they were drawn to collaborate by the very fact of
the occupation, so Maurras, in vilifying the Jews and Resisters,
appeared to be pro-Nazi. This he denied strenuously at his trial,
in a spirited, eloquent defence which reads like an apology for
pre-revolutionary France, but the evidence would seem to
suggest that the Vichy period saw the *Action française* at its most
degenerate. It had begun as a vigorous nationalist movement pro-
tecting France against internal and external enemies. It ended as
a sordid branch of fascism, conscious of its impotence but unwilling to alter its attitude. For Maurras, the great nationalist
and fervent anti-German, to be condemned for anti-nationalism
and pro-Germanism, was an ironic twist of history. Maurras
went off to prison musing on this fact: 'It is the revenge of
Dreyfus!' he exclaimed.

In occupied Paris the Nazis ruled from the start. They at once
made illegal all the old parties of pre-war France, leaving a
vacuum of French expression. The streets had been deserted and
the shutters bitterly closed when the Germans entered Paris and
marched in triumph down the Champs-Élysées. But the silence
and withdrawal were not complete. Out of the social and
political underworld emerged the supporters of fascism, the
admirers of Hitler and the idealists who believed in the promised
New Order. Defeat had brought them an unexpected importance:
they were the only groups who would be tolerated by the
Nazis: this was their moment of history in which the Fascist
revolution could be established.

The leaders of this new Parisian élite were Jacques Doriot and
an ex-Socialist Marcel Déat. They were very different in
character. Doriot was a man of action and force. He might
have become a leading Communist but he preferred his own
ideas and methods to those of the party. His worker's background gave him an appeal in the factories and on the streets.
His forceful nature led him to encourage violence and ruthless
repression. He became more and more of a Nazi, adopting first
the anti-Semitism, then the brutal mentality and finally the
uniform. Déat was more of an intellectual, moving by argument

and persuasion. He had left the Socialists and devoted the last years of the Third Republic to demanding peace at almost any price. His brand of pacifism became defeatism in 1940 and open collaboration with the Germans by 1941. To expand his views on the new Europe which he hoped would emerge under Hitler he founded his own party, the *Rassemblement National Populaire* (R.N.P.) and embraced most of the Fascist ideals. With his round face, small moustache and flattened hair he seemed to be modelled on Hitler, but in fact was more philosophic, more rational and less demonic.

Together, part colleagues part rivals, Déat and Doriot symbolized the men of the New Order. In many ways they were little more than puppets of the Nazi occupation, echoing the attitudes and executing the policies of the German command. It is impossible to gauge accurately how many Frenchmen supported them, but they were not the only spokesmen of native French fascism. Other leaders of small Fascist groups who had cut sinister or almost comic figures in the inter-war scene came into their own and strutted on the Paris stage, entertaining German officers and publishing vindictive newspapers against the Jews, the Allies, the Communists and the old Third Republic. Marcel Bucard, once the leader of the *Francistes*, and Eugène Deloncle, organizer of the cloak-and-dagger *Cagoulards* (The Hooded Men), were Fascist-collaborators of this type.

Even more active and dedicated to the Nazi cause was Joseph Darnand, the French Himmler. Darnand was an adventurous and courageous soldier whose actions in World War I and in the few months of World War II had gained him the highest merit, but between the two wars he had become influenced by the Fascist and nationalist ideas of the right-wing French groups. He was also a fervent admirer of Pétain. In the early years of the occupation he formed his own group of veterans which rapidly became the equivalent of the Nazi S.S. Known as the *Milice*, it acted brutally against all Resisters and achieved a reputation for cold, cynical barbarity wherever it moved. Under Darnand's command the *Milice* mutilated and murdered innocent village Jews who were unlucky enough to be in its path as it searched the country for evidence of Resistance activities. At his trial

Darnand pleaded that he was a sincere revolutionary, willing to follow out his ideals of a social transformation in France: 'I do not claim to have played a double game. I went in *one* direction. I'm proud of what I did. I was mistaken but I acted in good faith. I believe I have served.'[1] This defiance against the court, which was a formal prelude to the inevitable death sentence, was the mark of the active Fascist in occupied France. Doriot, Darnand and their followers worshipped action for its own sake, idolized strength and saw virtue in ruthlessness. This was the Fascist morality.

Quite different was the romantic Fascist idealism of Robert Brasillach and Drieu La Rochelle. The novelist Brasillach wrote in his wartime diary that 'there are certain universal laws, the most rigorous of which is the necessity of maintaining the eternal spirit of creative youth'.[2] The Fascist ideology and the Nazi spirit of power and vitality seemed to Brasillach to obey this law and to proclaim life. For him the German occupation was the start of a genuine new order, not of new politicians 'but of revolutionary ideas, emotions and creativity'. 'Only French fascism can collaborate with this new world', he wrote, and in the newspaper *Je Suis Partout* ('I Am Everywhere') he struck out vigorously at all remnants of sterile France, which is how he saw the politics of the Third Republic. Under the eye of the Nazis much of this romanticism gave way to crude anti-Semitism and attacks on the Allies. As Brasillach himself said, this became more and more unsatisfactory to him, but it was too late to change sides and when the Liberation came he gave himself up, conscious of his pro-Nazi record. He pleaded his literary talents but they were disregarded, and like Laval and Darnand he was shot for relations with the enemy.

Drieu La Rochelle, a novelist of even greater talent, and friend of a wide cross-section of French intellectuals, believed passionately in a united Fascist Europe as the hope of the 20th century. Here was a Fascist who was a genuine internationalist, but at the same time had a nostalgia for the old France, its virility and its sense of life. He called the modern French an ugly and sex-obsessed generation which had no concept of the 'whole

[1] *Les Procès de Collaboration* (Michel, 1948), p. 257.
[2] R. Brasillach, *Journal d'un homme occupé* (Les Sept Couleurs, 1955), p. 180.

man' in whom sex would be merely one aspect of a vibrating totality. Similarly he wanted 'whole politics' (neither left-wing nor right-wing, but a full unity), and this led on to his concept of a Europe which would transcend the petty nationalisms of the various countries. This idealism he invested in collaboration, pinning his hopes on the German promises, but in 1943 he became racked with disillusion in the face of Nazi realities. He saw nothing but brutal nationalism and the slavery of France. His collaboration diminished and he acknowledged personal as well as ideological disaster. In 1944 he began a series of suicide attempts which finally succeeded in March 1945.

From these few examples of prominent collaborators it can be seen how wide was the appeal of fascism and how varied was the response. Collaboration in France was partly a shifty, guilt-stricken compromise, partly an attempt at political bargaining, and partly an open welcome to an ideology which promised a new era of civilization. Illusions were built up and shattered. At their most persuasive they brought excitement and a new sense of freedom. Jean-Paul Sartre in his trilogy of novels *Les Chemins de la Liberté* ('Paths to Freedom') makes Daniel the homosexual into a collaborator. Daniel has been a social outsider in pre-war France but he watches the Germans arrive in Paris with feelings of delight and expectation. In a deserted square he feels free—he could even take off his trousers and no one would object. The old world had collapsed and the inheritors were the former outcasts. This was the psychology and the politics of collaboration. The appeal of Nazi Germany was, to many, irresistible. Brasillach summed it up when he wrote in January 1944:

> *I was not a lover of Germany before the war, nor even at the beginning of the period of collaboration. I was following my reason. Now things have changed. It would seem that I have had an affair with the spirit of Germany. I shall never forget it. Whether one likes it or not, we cohabited together. Frenchmen of several different attitudes have during these years slept with Germany. They have had quarrels, but the memory of the experience remains sweet.[1]*

[1] R. Brasillach, *Journal d'un homme occupé* (Les Sept Couleurs, 1955), p 354.

3   A WAR OF EXTERMINATION

Hitler's war, in which Mussolini was an inferior partner and other Fascists little more than collaborators, was in many ways a nationalist war like any other in modern history. It was fought by politicians and armies for territorial gain and international power. Some historians have shown that Hitler's aims were scarcely more extreme than the war aims of imperial Germany in 1914, and there is considerable evidence to support this argument. Churchill summarized it at an early stage when he called the two world wars 'one work in two volumes', and the continuity is certainly apparent. But to this pattern of German expansionism Hitler added his own ingredient: the venom of his racial theories.

Already by 1939 the Jews in Germany, Austria and Czechoslovakia were persecuted as enemies of the Germanic, Aryan race. They were subjected to personal humiliations, imprisonment and loss of property rights, and the S.S. under Himmler and Heydrich were already supervising their transportation to camps of forced labour within Germany.

In 1941 the anti-Semitic campaign was intensified. Hitler by now had conquered all of Western Europe except Britain and in the east had begun his war against Russia, after occupying Poland, Yugoslavia and Greece. Most of Continental Europe lay at his feet and Jews of all nationalities were within the range of his persecution. Ever since his days as a young, unsuccessful artist in Vienna Hitler had talked of exterminating the Jews. At times it had seemed little more than the outrageous metaphor of a petty demagogue but since his arrival at power it had assumed increasing reality. In November 1941 the first stage of what was to become literal extermination was announced:

> *Jews who do not hold jobs essential for the economy will be deported to a city in the east in the course of the next few months.*

Ghettoes in which Jews were herded and later killed like animals had already been established by the S.S. in Warsaw and other Polish cities, and to these were added the death camps which began to function in 1942. A Final Solution to the Jewish

The German Occupation of Poland. Polish Jews being deported to a concentration camp

problem was agreed to be necessary by Hitler, Himmler, Heydrich and Göring, after suggestions for resettling Jews in other parts of the world had been dismissed as impractical. This solution was openly barbaric. Beginning with the assumption that Jews were racial parasites eating their way into the pure races and destroying them by intermarriage, it became a question of preventing the reproduction of Jewish life. This could not be done by enforced sterilization or separation of the races since the Jews were held to be too clever and too determined to be restricted in these ways. The alternative was therefore a simple one. All Jews must be killed. Their race must be eliminated. Only then could the Aryans remain uncontaminated.

The fact that the Final Solution was ever adopted testifies to the unprecedented power of Hitler and the Nazi régime. His hold over the lives and minds of millions of people allowed him to order one part of the nation to destroy the other. In obedience to his insane belief that he was saving the world from racial vermin, thousands of men, women and even children took part in the mass murder of six million fellow human beings.

The methods were determined by a terrifying mixture of sexual sadism and inhuman efficiency. In some places the S.S. marched into the ghettoes and mowed down the Jewish inmates as they huddled in corners or sat helplessly on the pavements. In Warsaw the thousands of Jews were shot, starved or burnt alive when the ghetto was first isolated and then destroyed by fire. Elsewhere Jews were taken in special trains to country districts, were marched to wide, open fields and told to dig their own mass graves. They were then ordered to remove their clothes and stand naked in closed ranks. The nakedness increased their humiliation and gave pornographic stimulation to the guards, who frequently mutilated the exposed bodies before the order for mass shooting was given.

In the death camps the gas chambers, referred to as 'hot baths', were favoured as the quickest and most effective method. The gas was turned on once the last of the line had been pushed in at the point of a bayonet, and was turned off once the screaming had stopped. The bodies were then removed by other Jews and taken by them to be burned. In this way the individual Jew was made an accomplice in the murder of his own people, filling him with self-disgust and guilt. Some of the few who survived are still reliving this trauma in mental hospitals throughout Europe.

The extermination was not a hole-in-the-corner activity. It was well organized, fully documented and frequently recorded by film or photographs. The figures were relayed to Hitler, who expressed pleasure or impatience according to the rate of destruction. As he began to lose the war so his determination to settle the racial question increased. Throughout the whole of the Final Solution he and his underlings maintained a pseudo-scientific detachment. Hitler was convinced that history and evolution were on his side. With the same confidence he ordered medical research on those who were fit objects for vivisection, sterilization, castration and experiments with drugs. The victims here were frequently the nomadic gypsies, who were rounded up and treated with the same inhumanity as the Jews. Women had agonizing operations performed on their wombs and men on their testicles. Many doctors refused to perform these experiments, but the Nazi power of persuasion was always sufficient to find others willing to obey orders from the top. The concentration camps in which most of the murders, sadism and medical operations were carried out were a microcosm of Nazism. The camp commander was a little Führer who ruled over a community divided into superior and inferior beings. The superior ones—the staff, guards, doctors and mechanics— were rigidly organized into hierarchies so that many of them when put on trial after the war claimed that they were mere cogs in a machine, knowing nothing of what happened either above or below them. They either obeyed or lost their own lives, although there are some examples of doctors who contravened orders given to them but were too valuable to be killed. Among the inferior beings there was also a structure. At the bottom were the racially impure: Jews, gypsies and sometimes Slavs, who were liable to be shot or gassed at any moment. Above them were the old or weak prisoners who would be worked until they collapsed and died, and at the top were those who were considered part of the German work force, the slave labour on which Nazism more and more depended as the war progressed. Himmler saw this slave labour as an opportunity to increase the armaments of his S.S. and build it into a vast army, and for this reason he tried to keep the death toll of the camps within his control. But in this he failed. The camps were disease-ridden, exposed to fierce cold in the winter and subject to fits of sadistic killing by the officials and ordinary guards. Like Nazi Germany itself, the camps were controlled by force, which in the end became inefficient. As more of the slave labour died, so the desperation and savagery of the camp authorities increased. Similarly, as Hitler lost his armies and saw defeat closing in on Germany, he became more destructive and struck out blindly in all directions.

Thus the extermination spread beyond control as the Nazi panic increased. For a country fighting a war on several fronts and needing vast resources of manpower, the useless destruction of people other than the 'racially impure' was a monument to the incompetence and personal rivalries of the Nazi officials. Gerald Reitlinger in his history of the S.S. writes:

Deaths of Aryan internees in concentration camps, properly

*so called, may well have exceeded a quarter of a million
between 1933 and 1945. This massacre by ill-treatment was
only fractional as compared with the deliberate extermination
of Jews . . . Nevertheless it stands comparison with the entire
German civilian losses from Allied bombing. It was not a
deliberate ideological policy like the extermination of the
Jews, nor was it an inevitable part of total war like the air
raids on civilians. It was not in the budget and it was
admitted to be a mistake.*[1]

A régime which could destroy so many of its potential workers
'by mistake' was caught in a whirl of self-destruction. The concentration camps vividly illustrate both how Nazism ruled and
why it collapsed. The tragedy for Europe was that its self-
destruction came so late. When the camps finally broke up or
fell into Russian hands and Germany was defeated, Hitler's war
of extermination had lasted over five years and had involved
millions of victims from all over Europe. But figures in millions
tend to blur the picture of savagery. Clarity and horror come
from the particular incident, and for every unit added to the
number of dead there was a body, mutilated, shot or burned
alive in a hell which only the creative writer can fully evoke:
the language of the historian is inadequate.

4   THE DEATH OF NAZI GERMANY

The military successes of Germany between 1939 and
1942 established Hitler as one of the most effective war leaders
in history. Not only were the policies of expansion the product
of his own particular vision but the actual control of the army
lay also in his own hands. The power of Hitler's appeal to the
conservative nationalists in Germany has already been stressed
and nothing illustrates it more clearly than the subservience of
the army to Hitler's war ambitions. The German army was
barely touched when Hitler came to power. Under the Weimar
Republic it had been a small, efficient and brilliantly organized
unit with a high ratio of officers to men. The senior officers

[1] G. Reitlinger, *The S.S.: Alibi of a Nation* (Heinemann, 1956), p. 269.

continued to be something of a special caste, conscious of their social status, their historical traditions and their non-political role in the State. Disdainful of the petty party intrigues and the business of parliament, they stood above Republican politics. Many of them were aristocrats from old Imperial families and their attitudes were conservative, nationalistic and authoritarian.

At first they were superior and distrustful towards the Nazi corporal whose political demagogy had brought him to supreme power, but Hitler needed their support if his reconstruction of Germany was to succeed. The Röhm Purge of 30 June 1934 showed how willing he was to appease their suspicions. The mass murder of S.A. leaders was a sacrificial offering to the old military forces in society and they responded with indulgence. From 1934 until 1944 the army gave Hitler its calculated blessing, though at times it showed flashes of independence and dissension. In particular Generals Fritsch and Beck were critical of Hitler, and when in 1938 Himmler and Göring produced a police dossier showing that Fritsch was guilty of homosexual practices, Beck urged him to a *coup d'état* to save his and the army's honour. Fritsch declined, but Beck continued his opposition throughout the Czech crisis in 1938 and in August of that year resigned his post of Chief of Staff in protest against Hitler's ambitions. His action was an individual one and was not followed by other officers. A more general picture is given by General von Blomberg in 1945: 'Before 1938–9 the German generals were not opposed to Hitler. There was no ground for opposition since he brought them the successes they desired.'

It was just this continuous success of Hitler which disarmed all opposition. While the country was growing stronger, while diplomatic gains were constant, while industry was booming and society was free from revolution, the army could ignore the more unpleasant sides of Hitler's rule. They were bound to the Führer by an oath of personal allegiance and this could not easily be broken in a period of stability and consolidation.

This situation continued into the first years of the war. The army was the spearhead of the conquest of Europe, and established German authority in the occupied countries. It was flanked by the S.S. and the Gestapo, with whom it worked in sometimes tight, sometimes strained, collaboration. At the head of all operations stood Hitler with a new machinery of war control, the *Oberkommando der Wehrmacht* (O.K.W.), the High Command of the Armed Forces. Through this carefully staffed machine Hitler's orders for war and occupation were disseminated to the commanding generals in the field. The strategy for conquest was invariably his, and the chiefs of the O.K.W., Generals Keitel and Jodl, were entirely ruled by his decisions. They were pliant and unquestioning subordinates who remained under Hitler's orders through the years of success and disaster, appearing together after the war to be judged and hanged by the Allied Nuremberg tribunal for their unswerving enactment of Hitler's war crimes.

In 1943–4, despite this rigorous organization and the history of army co-operation, the war effort began to disintegrate. The successes had stopped and the Allies were gaining control of the war. Inexorably the Germans were heading for defeat. In the east the Russians were moving onto the offensive; in Italy the Allies took Rome on 4 June 1944; and in France they landed on the coasts of Normandy on D-Day, the night of 5–6 June. The vast Nazi empire was caught in a pincer movement and the Allies would accept nothing less than total surrender.

Hitler, however, would not hear of defeat. He rejected all talk of surrender and continued his fantasies about invincibility. He was confident that German scientists were about to produce the greatest weapon of all time and on this he pinned his belief in ultimate victory, but as the Allies advanced and the satellite countries were gradually liberated, this belief became a desperate and personal one. Others were unable to share it and groups within the army and within Nazism itself began to contemplate alternatives to Hitler.

Thus in the face of defeat after ten years of dictatorship Germany stirred against its Führer. There had been courageous movements of resistance against Hitler throughout this decade, but they had been broken by the police state and the indifference of the mass of Germans. Their history is one of isolated heroism but of political futility. Hitler was never seriously troubled by resistance: he had good reason to believe that Germany was behind him. In 1944, however, the discontent and determination of his opponents was more articulate and better organized than ever before. In the army a group of senior officers became convinced that Hitler must be killed if Germany were to survive. The officers were led by General Beck and Count von Stauffenberg and were in association with various civilian groups who had a wide variety of motives and political opinions, but who were all in opposition to Hitler. Most famous among these were the conservatives Carl Goerdeler (once Mayor of Leipzig), Ulrich von Hassell (the former German Ambassador in Rome) and the circle formed round Helmuth von Moltke in Kreisau which condemned Hitler on moral and religious grounds. They were divided on method, only some being prepared for assassination.

In July 1944 the loose strands of a *coup d'état* were woven together and the outlines of an alternative government were sketched. Individual plotters were in contact with sympathizers behind the Allied lines and several churchmen were involved, in particular the radical theologian Dietrich Bonhoeffer. It could not be said that they were all in one co-ordinated plot: communication was made difficult if not impossible by the changing state of the war, by the ruthless hounding of the Gestapo, and by the suspicion of the Allied leaders who had little interest in distinguishing one German from another.

On 20 July 1944 Count von Stauffenberg brought the major plot to its climax when he attended a military conference at Hitler's headquarters at Rastenburg in East Prussia. In his briefcase he carried a time-bomb which he deposited under the table a few feet from the Führer's seat. Shortly after his arrival, he left the conference and had the satisfaction of seeing the room explode as he hurried to catch a plane to Berlin. Convinced that Hitler was dead, he put into operation the plans for a new government. The plotters in Berlin surfaced and success appeared within reach, but communication with Hitler's headquarters had not been efficiently cut and Goebbels in Berlin heard by telephone that Hitler was still alive. The plot was undermined by this devastating news: despair and sheer disbelief turned the plotters into tragic figures as their plans collapsed and they stood exposed to the furious revenge of Hitler. To many he seemed after all to be a man of providence who eluded even the most certain death. Four of those at the conference had been killed and the room had been wrecked, but Hitler had escaped with minor cuts. It seems that one of the officers had accidentally pushed the briefcase behind a table leg, and this had diverted the blast away from Hitler.

The failure was complete and Germany plunged on to self-destruction in another nine months of suicidal war. The trials of the plotters were a mockery of justice and their savage death, hanging by meat hooks through their necks, was the ultimate in Nazi barbarity. Arrests, forced suicides (including that of Field-Marshal Rommel) and executions involved hundreds of Germans as Hitler purged every suspicion of treachery. It was a violent reassertion of his power and a convincing answer to those who contemplated an alternative leader.

The Nazis themselves remained loyal to Hitler throughout the course of the July Plot—there was no Nazi equivalent of the Fascist Grand Council meeting which had rejected Mussolini. But the solidarity behind Hitler began to dissolve in the winter of 1944–5. Individual Nazis explored the possibility of dividing the Allies by suggesting a new alliance with Britain and America against Russia. In Italy the surrender of the German troops was agreed to by the S.S. General, Karl Wolff, after secret negotiations with the Americans—an act of treachery which reduced Hitler to impotent rage. It was impossible for him to control all the crumbling outposts of his short-lived empire, and despite a continuous stream of orders forbidding any surrender, the Nazi authorities in the conquered territories attempted to make their own terms.

Among the senior Nazis, Göring became the most independent. His drug addiction had progressively immobilized his powers of swift thought and action, and his control of the *Luftwaffe* degenerated into incompetence. At the same time his vanity increased until he saw himself as Hitler's successor. In the last month of the war he made a half-hearted bid at succession which was as futile as any of the last despairing actions of Nazism. Himmler, with his powerful hold over the S.S., was more of a threat to Hitler, but he concentrated more on saving his own future than in destroying that of his leader. In the last few months of the war he put a brake on the Final

Solution, received money for the lives of prominent Jews and turned a blind eye to those of his subordinates who sought their own peace terms with the Allies. Although Hitler ordered complete destruction of everything as the German forces retreated, Himmler did not fulfil these orders to the letter. Some concentration camps fell to the Russians with their hellish buildings intact and small groups of emaciated survivors left to tell the details of mass persecution.

Goebbels, the third of the big four, was rewarded at the very end by the post of Chancellor when Hitler dictated his final testament in April 1945. By then Germany was in ruins and Berlin was surrounded. In his underground headquarters, the famous Berlin bunker, Hitler continued to be defiant. In his testament he declared:

> It is untrue that I, or anyone else in Germany, wanted the war in 1939. It was desired and instigated solely by those international statesmen who were either of Jewish descent or worked for Jewish interests.

He then turned to his own martyrdom:

> After six years of war, which in spite of all set-backs will go down one day in history as the most glorious and valiant demonstration of a nation's life-purpose, I cannot forsake the city which is the capital of the Reich . . . I have decided therefore to remain in Berlin and there of my own free will to choose death at the moment when I believe the position of Führer and Chancellor can no longer be held.[1]

That moment came on 30 April 1945. The day before, Hitler learnt of the death of Mussolini and during the night he made elaborate plans for his own destruction which would prevent a fate similar to that of his Italian partner. He had married the devoted Eva Braun during the preceding night and he planned their combined deaths down to the last detail. After lunch on 30 April Hitler and his wife retired to their rooms. After a short interval Hitler shot himself through the mouth and Eva Braun took poison. Together, according to Hitler's instructions, they

[1] Quoted in A. Bullock, *Hitler: A Study in Tyranny* (The Hamlyn Group of Publishers, 1952), p. 725.

The end of Nazi Germany. A Russian soldier in the Berlin bunker where Hitler committed suicide

were solemnly burnt in the garden of the bunker. Goebbels was among those who watched. He later shot himself, his wife and his children. With the Russians in the suburbs of Berlin, the centre of Nazism destroyed itself with a sense of occasion. An S.S. officer who watched the scene in the garden turned away in grief. 'The Führer is dead,' he said, 'he is burning outside.'

Others too had burned, in ghettoes, death camps, villages and towns. Six million Jews were dead, over twenty million Russians had been killed, the Western Allies had lost nearly two million soldiers and civilians, and Germany herself had a total of four million killed by war, suicide, execution or illness. The devastation of countries left millions without homes, families and friends. Insanity was a widespread result of terrifying war traumas, and bitterness was universal. The war had been a forcing-house of destruction: the American atomic bomb had emerged, the British had killed 135,000 in the bombing of Dresden, and men everywhere were geared to death and conflict.

This was Hitler's war. It had involved in its course the diverse forces of fascism, but it had remained basically his war. Those who supported him in other countries rapidly became his puppets: Quisling in Norway, the archetypal collaborator, Mussert in Holland, Degrelle in Belgium and Doriot in France. Mussolini also can be listed. Fascism cannot, however, be left as completely synonymous with servile collaboration. Even in a Europe dominated by the power of the Nazi Führer, there were Fascists who held out for independence and dissociated themselves from the Nazi line. They were found mostly in Italy and France, where there were strong ideologies of fascism which conflicted with the fanatical nationalism of Hitler. Had it not been for the war, Fascists in these countries might have grown old in politics as the dictator Franco has done in Spain, or Salazar in Portugal. Had they done so, the ideology of fascism might have changed. As it is, caught up in the destruction of war, fascism retains the image of a young, violent movement which brought opposites together in a dynamic assertion of primitive and modern man. This was the character of both its life and its death, and for this reason the war appears consistent with Fascist ideology. If destruction breeds destruction and violence turns in on itself, then fascism ended logically in Hitler's war—but it was a logic which fascism had not fully anticipated. The future which the Fascists proclaimed envisaged war but not defeat, for defeat, they believed, was confined to the inferior, those who were less than men and whom history would not tolerate. By their own standards they may be judged.

PART THREE

Approaches to Fascism

CHAPTER TEN

Psychological Approaches

How does a knowledge of Hitler's infancy help one to understand the rise of Nazism? Doesn't psychology tend to excuse and explain away the evils of Fascist rule? How can psychologists analyse people who are dead? These are some of the familiar questions which stem from a suspicion of psychology as soon as it is applied to recent history. In fact they indicate more than suspicion. There is also a fear that psychology will upset the black-and-white view of fascism which has been prevalent since 1945; that it will demand a more generous understanding than we are prepared to give or that it will find fascism to be less abnormal than we have assumed. In short, it may make us reconsider well-established judgments.

Of course the opposite could also be argued: that psychology will underline and endorse the evaluations made by politicians and historians and that it will confirm and not destroy our judgments. But do we need to argue in either way? It is surely preferable to start with important questions about fascism and then see if we can possibly ignore psychology in answering them: clearly we cannot. If we want to know why Hitler was so fanatically anti-Semitic or why violence is so recurrent in all fascisms or why so many people welcomed authoritarianism, then the approach of the psychologist will be as important as that of the political historian or the economist.

As yet, psychological studies of fascism are few in number and limited in scope. Hitler and Nazism have been and continue to be the obvious subject for psychologists interested in violence, aggression and extreme behaviour, and there are many projects of research into this area, but when one turns to Spanish, Belgian or British fascism, or to Doriot's P.P.F. or even to the leaders of the Italian *squadre*, there are vast areas untouched by psychological research. Generalizations are therefore unwise and there is no such thing as a single psychological interpretation of fascism: there is not even one accepted psychological interpretation of Hitler. Some conclusions, however, can be drawn from the work so far done, though it must be stressed that further knowledge and research may soon make even these rather obsolete.

High on the list of books banned to all Germans under the Nazi Reich stood the works of Freud. It is therefore not surprising that the Nazi leaders have been submitted to critical Freudian examination. Hitler in particular has aroused much interest among those who believe that events in early childhood determine later psychological developments. Adolf Hitler was born on 20 April 1889 at Braunau-am-Inn in German Austria, into a lower middle-class family. His father was, before his early and frustrating retirement, a low-grade civil servant who demanded strict obedience from his children: he was also said to be something of a drunkard. Hitler's mother on the other hand was a quieter, more indulgent person who is said to have suffered periodically from drunken beatings by her husband. It is further claimed that Hitler, as a young child, was forced to accompany his father back from the drinking houses to his crowded home where the scenes of anger and assaults must have deeply affected him. Oedipal love for his mother might have been intensified by the sight of his father's brutality towards her. When Hitler was thirteen years old his father died, and it could be expected that the

Adolf Hitler in 1923

young Hitler would feel both guilt and relief. Left with a mother who tended to spoil him, the boy probably entered adolescence with unresolved childhood strivings towards her which he could not admit or overcome. In later life Hitler's obsession with the rape of Aryan womanhood by inferior men might well be a product of his childhood, when he had identified strongly with his mother against the personality and drunkenness of his father.

Such an analysis has been taken further by those who believe, on incomplete evidence, that Hitler was sexually impotent. This would indicate the inhibiting guilt which Hitler felt, due to his strong oedipal affections. It would also account for much of Hitler's aggression: he would desperately need to prove his masculinity and would be easily drawn to violence of word and action. It is not easy to substantiate this, but Hitler did show some signs of sexual inhibition or perversion: in particular his strange relationship with his niece Geli Raubal, which ended in her suicide (or was it death at Hitler's hands?) in 1931, gave some credibility to rumours of impotence which had started when he was poor and unemployed in pre-1914 Vienna.

One other interpretation also connects Hitler's early childhood with his personality as dictator. This is the view of Hitler as a person whose psychological growth was arrested at the child's stage: just as a small child sees the world revolving round himself, so Hitler as an adult had an egocentric view of reality. He had child-like fantasies of being all-powerful: he raged when he was thwarted and his outbursts of anger vanished once he obtained what he wanted. This infantilism is perhaps the most clearly marked of Hitler's characteristics. It was also successful: for twelve years he stood at the centre of the stage, demanding and obtaining the most childish and fantastic things, forcing his subordinates to indulge his wishes like a mother spoiling her child. Why should Hitler's development have been arrested at this early stage? Possibly it was because his life after infancy became increasingly insecure and difficult: he was therefore con-stantly forced back to the earliest stage when at least he had received gratification without a painful struggle.

For many experts on Hitler these conclusions about his psychosexual difficulties as a young child are too speculative

They prefer to concentrate on a later period, the period of Hitler's adolescence in pre-war Vienna. The evidence here is different but the conclusions are not dissimilar. Hitler's schooling at Linz was not a success and he was seen as a difficult pupil. His mother died when he was seventeen, and Hitler left for Vienna where he failed to secure a place as an artist or architect in the Academy of Fine Arts. This frustration is the best-known feature of his early career and is documented by the memoirs of an artist friend of these years, Josef Greiner. By itself it might not have been too traumatic for Hitler, but it was one in a series of failures. He also failed to create a successful relationship with a fair-haired model whom he clumsily assaulted and whom he later saw in the street with a Jew, a scene which provoked him to an outburst of anti-Semitic rage. Finally, he was unable to find either a stable job or secure housing in Vienna, and drifted in and out of cheap doss-houses where he regarded his fellow sleepers and vagrants with unconcealed dislike. In a city where anti-Semitism was an organized political feature, Hitler's eyes were opened to what he came to see as the source of his misery and failure—the Jew. It was not merely the wealthy Jew he came to hate, but also the poor, refugee Jew who had fled from the Russian persecutions, who still dressed in his East European Jewish costume, and who competed with the unemployed Germans and Czechs for jobs in the Austrian capital.

Here is the psychology of frustration, insecurity and failure. It led to the paranoia and racial fanaticism which marked the rest of Hitler's career. But it is only one side, although the most significant, of Hitler's personality. During and after the war he discovered his talents as a political speaker and leader and this brought confidence and a sense of power to the aggressive young man. When fused together, the insecurity and power made a formidable combination which proved capable of exploiting the social and political divisions of Germany.

Some other Nazi leaders were more accessible to the psychologists than Hitler. In 1945 the victorious Allies staged their legal revenge on the Nazi war criminals in a series of trials held at Nuremberg. Among those who had contact with the prisoners before their execution or long imprisonment was the American psychologist G. M. Gilbert, who carried out a number of tests

Hermann Göring in 1923, and in 1945 in his cell at Nuremberg

and interviews. In his book, *The Psychology of Dictatorship*,[1] he presents several case studies, including one on Hermann Göring, Hitler's second-in-command for most of the Nazi period.

Göring was a man of high intelligence with a sharp, cynical attitude to men and events. He was not an intellectual like some of the more cultured German leaders, but he had projected himself as a man of taste and discernment by his collections of art and antiques. Gradually under interview he exposed his own background and childhood. His family was wealthy and almost aristocratic, his father owning a castle and serving in the Prussian army as a cavalry officer. It was in the romantic atmosphere of the castle under the authoritarian control of his wealthy father that Göring grew up. He appears to have been naturally exuberant and aggressive and to have baited the Jews of the village as a childish sport. Whenever his aggression became too open he was punished severely by his father, which prompted more aggression, more punishment and so on, a cycle which was played out against the child's developing interest in war and historical periods of German greatness. At sixteen he entered the

[1] G. M. Gilbert, *The Psychology of Dictatorship* (Ronald Press, New York, 1950).

tough Academy for Officers at Lichterfelde near Berlin, and during World War I he became a brilliant, courageous pilot. Both situations, the Academy and the war, were ideally suited to Göring's aggressive needs.

Defeat and peace brought nothing to Göring except inactivity and boredom, and when he joined the Nazi Party it was in the hope of action. 'I joined the party,' he said to Gilbert, 'because it was revolutionary, not because of the ideological stuff.' By that time Göring was not only a man of unusual aggression, he was also highly narcissistic, believing himself to be a superior, talented person who was undervalued by society. Such an exalted view of himself must have been difficult to sustain during the twenties when both Göring himself and the Nazis had little success. It might therefore be seen as an extension of his narcissism when he began to take drugs in addictive quantities: they would help him to preserve his self-esteem.

It was this sadistic, self-opinionated drug addict who brought to Hitler an active dedication which lasted until the last months of the war when he was tempted to assert himself against his Führer. Perhaps his most revealing statement to Gilbert was the confession: 'I have no conscience: my conscience is Adolf Hitler.' As a child he had known little but the pleasure and pain of aggression; as an adult he had no values other than action and self-gratification.

This picture of Göring has much in common with the personality of Benito Mussolini. The Italian *Duce* was by no means the son of a high-class family, but like Göring he projected a public image of an artistic man, in his case through his grossly exaggerated ability as a violin player. In his autobiography he wrote:

Benito Mussolini as musician

*In the eighteenth century there was a Mussolini in London.
Italians never hesitate to venture abroad with their genius or
their labours. The London Mussolini was a composer of
music of some note, and perhaps it is from him that I inherit
the love of the violin which even today in my hands gives
comfort to moments of relaxation and creates for me
moments of release from the realities of everyday.*[1]

This may be genuine, but the much-publicized stories of
Mussolini practising until the early hours of the morning after
a day of State administration are probably attempts to conceal
his nights with Clara Petacci, his mistress. Whatever the
immediate purpose of such distortions, they betray Mussolini's
permanent egoism and his need for adulation. He was born in
1883, the son of a Socialist blacksmith. The family was poor but
the father's Socialist activities, at times leading to his arrest,
brought an atmosphere of energy and excitement; he constantly
urged his son to protect himself, if necessary, by violence, and
it is known that Mussolini once broke open a boy's head with a
jagged stone and later was expelled from his school for stabbing
a fellow pupil. This was an action as much against the school, a
Catholic boarding establishment, as against the pupil in question.
He had hated being sent away from home, regarding it as a
punishment. In the school records he is noted as being 'of a
passionate and riotous nature . . . solitary . . . revengeful'. At his
next school he showed the same characteristics and was again
expelled, this time for 'having beaten up three schoolfellows at
play'. As a result his inconsistent father thrashed him with the
same energy that he threw into his political activities.

Mussolini's aggression, stimulated, like Göring's, by paternal
punishment, spread during adolescence from actions into words.
He began to make inflammatory speeches at his teachers' college,
and these, together with his anarchist style of dress, alienated
him from the authorities. He did, however, qualify as a teacher,
but found it difficult to obtain teaching posts and impossible to
keep them. He drifted from one to another, playing all the time
with revolutionary politics; this led in 1908 to a prison sentence

[1] B. Mussolini, *My Autobiography*, trans. R. W. Child (Hurst and Blackett,
1936), pp. 18–19.

of three months. His trial gave him a stage and an opportunity to inflate his achievement, and made him decide that politics was his vocation. From this point he moved more deeply into revolutionary socialism and from there to his own Fascist activism.

Mussolini could perhaps be called a neurotic, but his level of aggression and egoism was not unusual in fringe politics. Compared with the image of the pipe-smoking, pig-rearing British Premier, Stanley Baldwin, he looks pathological, but there are other comparisons with 20th-century leaders which put his aggression and narcissism more into perspective. He never approached the monomania of either Hitler or Stalin.

For those who believe that all Fascist, and certainly all Nazi, leaders had abnormal childhoods, there is one major figure who presents a considerable problem. This is Heinrich Himmler, the head of the S.S. and organizer of the Final Solution against the Jews. One would expect such an apparent monster to have had at least an unusual background. He may have done, but as yet the evidence is lacking. His father was a Bavarian schoolmaster who appears to have been a pedantic but humanistic man. There is nothing to suggest that Himmler was repressed by him nor that the two ever quarrelled. His mother is barely known but seems to have been rather matriarchal and perhaps sparing in her love towards her son. The family could not be called unstable or exceptional.

Only one thing stands out and that is Himmler's puritanism. The excerpts which survive from his diary show his emphasis on self-control, particularly during his period of Catholic schooling. His mind appears to have been

Heinrich Himmler, head of the S.S.

fastidious and narrow. He took an attitude of strict self-denial in sex until he was in his mid-twenties, and was harsh in his criticism of more expansive colleagues. Already he showed signs of being addicted to colds and minor physical ailments, and might well have been jealous of his elder brother, who was more talented than he was and had the satisfaction of joining the army during World War I, something Himmler coveted but was too young to achieve.

At school and agricultural college Himmler was noted for very little: he was not gifted intellectually nor artistically, and was not a great success at the job for which he was trained—farming. His failures do not seem to have been traumatic, however, although his failed marriage with a nurse six years older than himself may be symptomatic of disorders in his personality. He was never at ease with women, and if lack of maternal love *were* a factor, then he may have had homosexual drives which he could not openly face or control.

Once he became a Nazi, signs of abnormality increased: he became obsessed with the career of Henry the Fowler, a Duke of Bavaria in the early Middle Ages who had fought the Slavs and Hungarians, and he may have seen himself as the Fowler's reincarnation, destined to lead another Germanic revival. He also became a complete hypochondriac, nursing himself through imaginary illnesses helped by a carefully selected range of pills and a bevy of doctors, and by the time he was leader of the S.S. he was already a crank about things as diverse as genealogies and natural food. These obsessions, together with his calculating subservience to Hitler and his sadism towards political and racial prisoners, make him as complex as any character in the history of fascism. He committed suicide in 1945 before he could be examined and analysed, and the clues to his cold, emotionless character may never be fully known.

These few examples of a psychological approach to individual Fascist leaders can only be supplemented by wide biographical reading and research. The study of individuals as a way of building a historical picture is the longest and most difficult process in the writing of history. The more one investigates the different lives and motives of individuals, the more suspect become the generalizations For this reason the psychology of Fascist leaders is bound to look unsatisfactory.

When one turns to collective psychology the rewards are more immediate. This area of research deals not so much with the childhood and personality of individuals but with psychological phenomena which a whole group or society have in common. Group aggression, hero worship and subservience, or mass terror, mass insecurity and mass hatred, are subjects dealt with by collective psychology. As a field of inquiry it overlaps considerably with the realm of the sociologist and this chapter should be seen as merging into the next.

Fascism is clearly a natural subject for research in collective psychology. All Fascist movements placed emphasis on group action, on conformity, on mass loyalty to the leader and on individual submission to an ideology. This has led many observers to compare fascism with the great authoritarian religions of the world, which make similar demands on the individual. This analogy will be discussed in Chapter Eleven under the heading 'Cultural Approaches', but here it is important to note that fascism is not radically new in its collective and authoritarian structure. The psychologist is insistent in stressing that it appealed to very old and permanent aspects of the human mind.

Nevertheless fascism is a historical as well as a psychological event, so the questions about its collective life have to be posed in specific 20th-century terms. What then are the psychological explanations for such an outburst of group aggression, conformity and subservience between the wars?

Perhaps the most general theory comes from the works of C. G. Jung; a theory which was so misunderstood that Jung himself was called a Fascist by many of his critics. His own defence was not helped by the fact that the Nazi Reich hailed him as the true German psychologist as opposed to the 'degenerate' Freud. Most of Jung's works are involved with culture as well as psychological sickness and his view of Western man is a wide one: it sets him within his whole civilization and compares his behaviour and products with those of other civilizations in all parts of the world. He believed that all men were connected with each other by a collective unconscious in which dark, but often creative, forces were contained, linking the most civilized modern individual with the images of primitive society. As long as these forces could be acknowledged and put to imaginative and constructive use then man would be healthy, but once they were repressed and refused admission into the conscious life of the individual, they could become dangerous and might break out, bringing psychological sickness and destruction.

In the West, Jung believed, these primitive forces began to be severely repressed in the 18th and 19th centuries by the combination of rational thought, religious respectability and social orthodoxy. Man was urged to be sensible, sober and well-behaved: his politics and social thought ran along balanced, confident lines: his culture, particularly his art, was skilful and pleasant but rarely shocking, and his religion was solid and unexciting. This general respectability Jung called the 'persona' or mask of society, something man adopted to help him forget and repress the more challenging depths of his mind. To all outward appearances man was eminently stable and progressive.

Towards the end of the 19th century this persona began to crack. Philosophers such as Nietzsche called for new values and new men to replace the dead and irrelevant Christianity of the West; Europeans discovered the alluring primitive qualities of the Afro–Asian countries which they had conquered in the waves of imperialism, and the growing challenge of socialism unsettled the social security of the developed nations. Neither religion nor capitalism was capable any longer of preserving the old respectability. The pressure of the dark collective forces mounted until they swept into the defenceless mind of Western society, bringing astonishing acts of creation in modern art, but, more widely, powerful acts of destruction, as in the ideology and rule of fascism.

The psychology of fascism therefore, in Jung's terms, reveals the upsurge of the dark forces of mankind which had been unwisely repressed by earlier generations in Western Europe in the belief that repression meant civilization. On the contrary, Jung stated, only the recognition and controlled expression of these forces could bring lasting civilization. This is where he was misunderstood and called a Fascist. To unsubtle minds he appeared to be endorsing the aggressive side of fascism as a good in itself, but when his whole position is considered it is clear that he valued the collective unconscious only when it was controlled and directed by a humane and sensitive consciousness: his approval went not to Hitler but to Picasso.

More limited, but equally stimulating, is the explanation of Erich Fromm whose book, *Fear of Freedom*,[1] swiftly became the standard introduction to the collective psychology of Nazism. He saw the problem of man's freedom as a psychological one: how far does man want to be free? can he face the difficulties of freedom? is he prepared to act alone? will he value freedom when it is new, strange and uncomfortable? In short, does freedom breed as many fears as hopes? Writing in 1942, Fromm was intensely aware of the failures of democracy and freedom: fascism in general and Nazism in particular had declared democracy to be a fallacy: man could only be really free, it was said, through identification with the Fascist State. This was not just an idle claim: millions of men in both Italy and Germany appeared to find it a just one and willingly submitted to the rule of Hitler and Mussolini. How, asks Fromm, was this possible?

His answer is a clear one: modern democratic man was afraid of his freedom. He found himself, under democracy, in a society which was fragmented, broken up into groups which were isolated from each other and which had no safe traditional way of behaviour. He also found that his relationships were more impersonal and mechanical, and that he had to make difficult decisions about every aspect of life. Freedom thus brought insecurity and with it the wish to return to a more familiar pattern of life where the big decisions were made by others, and the individual was part of a traditional, collective society. Hitler, writes Fromm, was able to seize on this weakness and fear and build his party on the widespread public wish for security. He knew exactly what he was doing—in *Mein Kampf* he wrote:

> *Mass assemblies are necessary because, whilst attending them, the individual who feels on the point of joining a young movement and takes alarm if left to himself, receives his first impression of a larger community, and this has a strengthening and encouraging effect on most people. He*

[1] E. Fromm, *Fear of Freedom* (Routledge and Kegan Paul, 1942).

submits himself to the magic influences of what we call 'mass suggestion'. The desires, longings and indeed the strength of thousands is accumulated in the mind of each individual present. A man who enters such a meeting in doubt and hesitation leaves it inwardly fortified: he has become a member of a community.[1]

But there was more than just the feeling of security. Fromm suggests also that through the return to collective activity and mass movements the individual German felt more powerful and enjoyed in a sadistic way his country's dominance over other nations and his sense of racial superiority. Psychologically Nazism had much to offer those who wanted both security and sadistic power in place of the freedom they were unable to face. In return, it made its own demands, and here Fromm makes his most controversial point. As a price for its benefits the Nazi ideology demanded the total sacrifice of the individual. The masses were 'told again and again: the individual is nothing and does not count. The individual should accept this personal insignificance, dissolve himself in a higher power and then feel proud in participating in the strength and glory of this higher power.' Any individual, says Fromm, who submits to this sacrifice of himself must be masochistic and enjoy the destruction of his independence. The psychology of Nazism is thus based on a combination of masochism and sadism: 'There is a wish to submit to an overwhelmingly strong power, to annihilate the self, besides the wish to have power over helpless beings.'

Fromm's conclusion has been the starting point for others who also stress the question of freedom and security. For example, Gilbert in his studies of the Nazi leaders states that Nazism, like the dictatorship of Napoleon, was 'a reversion to authoritarian rule after a too drastic attempt to impose democracy on an authoritarian culture'. Germany's answer to the challenge of democratic freedom was to return to an earlier and more familiar way of life. Similarly, other modern dictatorships have shown regression of this sort: Russia developed its Stalinist tyranny after a brief attempt at democracy; China produced the régime of Mao Tse-tung after its equally brief period of

[1] A. Hitler, *My Struggle* (Hurst and Blackett, 1935), pp. 191-2.

revolutionary freedom; and Ghana submitted to Nkrumah after a few years of superficial British-style political freedom. All these dictatorships, together with Salazar's and Franco's, could be seen as reversions by the countries concerned to more deeply rooted systems. The facts are so striking that they almost amount to a valid psychological generalization.

It would not, however, apply generally to fascism. Italy had had over seventy years of developing democracy before Mussolini's rule, while French, Belgian and British fascisms could not easily be seen as the fear of freedom. In these three countries the established and secure way of life *was* democracy, so that fascism was more an *assertion* of freedom than a reversion to security. There is a great temptation to use psychological findings about Nazism for all Fascist movements and this must clearly be resisted. There is no clear sign that Mosleyites, or the men of Doriot's P.P.F., or the followers of Degrelle had deep-seated needs for an authoritarian régime or that they were masochistic in Fromm's sense. In fact many French Fascists, particularly the literary ones, saw fascism as a liberating force which freed the mind from dull conformity and traditional, over-secure patterns of thought. Fascism as a general European phenomenon would be quite misunderstood if it were seen merely as a product of psychological fear. Mussolini in his early Fascist years was constantly stressing the element of danger, excitement, experiment and restlessness in Italian fascism. Those who joined the *squadre* may well have gained the security of group activity, but they were also attracted by the very insecurity of risk and adventure. The same could be said of the members of the Spanish *Falange*.

The expressions 'fear of freedom' and 'the return to security' must therefore be used with caution in connection with the whole range of Fascist psychology. As explanations, they are most useful in answering the question 'Why did so many ordinary people support Hitler and Mussolini?' They offer a real insight into the behaviour of the masses, but when it comes to small minority groups of active, aggressive Fascists then other explanations will be needed to cater for the appeal of violence and adventure. Such explanations as exist belong more closely to sociology.

Social and Economic Approaches

1 SOCIAL

One way to approach the problem of Fascist aggression is through the question 'Which groups or classes stood to benefit by an aggressive ideology between the wars?' The answers will be tentative, since the sociology of fascism is little more developed than the psychology, but broad lines of explanation can be traced and various social needs discerned.

In the first place, many who had found excitement and satisfaction in the fighting of World War I were eager to continue a life of armed aggression. In some cases they were members of the regular army and could continue in military service during the peace; others, however, were volunteers or recruits who were disbanded in 1918 and sent back to non-existing civilian jobs, or to jobs and areas which lacked the energy and excitement of their war experiences. For four years violence and mass killing had been legalized in a state of inter-national war. Men had been trained to hate and destroy by statesmen and politicians who now asked them to forget the war and return peacefully to their homes. For those with nowhere in particular to go or with no one to return to, this demand was too great. They drifted into volunteer fighting units in different parts of Europe or into political bands which recaptured some of the atmosphere of war and violence.

Unemployed war veterans were thus a natural source of manpower for aspiring Fascist leaders. In Italy, Germany and France they were the most important group of adherents to the Fascist movements in their early days, and fascisms in all three countries studiously cultivated the appeal of uniforms, military formations and warlike discipline. Hitler and Mussolini resembled military generals more than old-style politicians and their success with war veterans encouraged their fantasies of greatness and historic calling. Their heroes were not great politicians like Walpole, Cavour, Guizot or Gladstone, but military leaders like Alexander, Caesar, Frederick the Great and Napoleon. One mistake which Hitler bitterly regretted was visiting Mussolini in 1934 dressed in a soft hat and raincoat when Mussolini appeared in military uniform wearing a dagger. It was a mistake he did not repeat.

A second and wider grouping which valued aggression was found among the youth of several countries who welcomed the opportunity for action and rebellion. Fascist youth movements were as important as Fascist armies and much attention was paid to them. Until the 20th century there had been few political movements based on a fundamentally youthful appeal. There are examples of student and youth participation in Russian anarchism, the Italian Risorgimento or Utopian socialism, but they were never a mass phenomenon. By World War I, however, the increase in educational facilities, the growth of towns and universities, a greater mobility due to car and bicycle, and a steady increase in leisure time made the youth of most European countries into a social and political force for the first time. Not surprisingly they were attracted by ideas and actions which claimed to be new, young and vital and which were regarded with suspicion by the older generation. Ideas of change and vitality were, as we have seen, profuse and compelling in pre-war Europe, and in many, like Futurism, the appeal to youth was couched in openly aggressive terms. So too was the propaganda of nationalism and imperialism. Young Europe was flattered and seduced by calls for a new spirit, a youthful vigour and a modern approach.

Almost all fascisms used and exploited this situation. In the case of José Antonio's *Falange* and Léon Degrelle's *Rex*, there would have been little without student ideals and enthusiasm which were turned aggressively against the failures of an older generation. The smaller French movement of the twenties, *Jeunesses Patriotes*, was even more conscious of this vigour and called for the Revolution of Youth. Most Fascist leaders were extremely young for the positions of power that they held, and in Italy and Germany the youth of the Fascist and Nazi parties were encouraged to act as educators of their parents.

In Germany there was already, before Hitler, a strongly aggressive Youth Movement which had become the mouthpiece of nationalism. It had started in 1901 as a hiking association for boys in a Berlin suburb and it was based on a love of the fatherland which transcended class divisions. It held mystical rituals of ancient Germanic origin and venerated the Eros principle as a means of deepening male friendships. Patriotism was a spiritual force and naturally the whole movement was closed to Jews and aliens. Most of the members came from a middle- or upperclass background and it owed something to the atmosphere of English public schools in the imperialist age.

The Hitler Youth, membership of which totalled nearly eight million young Germans by 1939, completely eclipsed this old nationalist movement whose élitism and effeteness it despised, but it drew on many of the same ideals, used many of its

The Hitler Youth at the Nuremberg rally in September 1936

methods and inspired a similar dedication to the German race and fatherland. It became even more anti-Semitic than its fore-runner, but this was in keeping with the rest of official Germany under the Nazi régime. Members of the Hitler Youth who recall their allegiance picture it as an inflated and politically minded Boy Scout movement which it was natural for any young boy to join. It also provided Hitler with a potential military force, and in the last years of the war, with the situation desperate, young boys of twelve and fourteen were sent to fight at the front. The Frenchmen who liberated Paris in August 1944 were surprised and slightly indignant to find that many of their German victims were barely of secondary school age. There was also in Hitler's Germany a League of German Girls which enrolled thousands of girls and instilled into them the same Nazi values and discipline, encouraging a hardness which effaced most feminine attributes except motherhood. The Reich needed its babies.

The Italian Fascist youth movement was not so highly developed as its Nazi equivalent, but it had started earlier and like most of Mussolini's régime it was a model for other fascisms to copy or surpass. The major party youth organization was called after a legendary boy hero, Balilla, who was said to have thrown a rock at Austrian policemen in the 18th century. The Nazis also had their youthful martyr, Horst Wessel, who was killed in a row with Communists in 1930. The Nazis said he was arguing about politics; the Communists said that the issue was about a prostitute. Whatever the truth, the 'Horst Wessel Song' became the Nazi Party anthem, its tune taken from a song of the Communist Party which in turn had borrowed it from a Salvation Army hymn.

In Italy the Balilla organization grew rapidly after 1927 when Mussolini secured the disintegration of the rival Catholic Boy Scout movement, but ten years later a new, all-inclusive youth group replaced it. The ideal Fascist, it proclaimed, 'tempers all enthusiasm with iron discipline . . . despises fear, loves the hard life and serves with faith, passion and happiness the Cause of Fascism'. It is an ideal which comes as near to being typically Fascist as anything in European fascism, and its appeal to the youth of inter-war Europe was a forceful one. In fact, the aspect of fascism which most impressed sympathetic but non-Fascist observers in Britain and France was this positive attitude to youth. The French writer, Montherlant, was one who found the youth of the French Republic spineless and decadent by comparison. It is probably true that one of the reasons for fascism's superiority over communism in many European countries was its skilful deployment of youth and youthful ideas. Communists did not sense or use the conflict of generations in the same way.

Thirdly, aggression and violence had something to offer the social outsiders and the uprooted. The critics of fascism made much of this factor: they accused Hitler, Mussolini, Doriot and Mosley in particular of using the scum of society, what Marx called the *Lumpenproletariat*, who were always ready to join any movement provided they were paid. Of the lesser Italian Fascist leaders Mack Smith wrote:

> *Most of them were unintelligent, grasping, jealous and incompetent, and jockeyed for place by telling tales against their rivals or else boosted each other's morale by organizing 'spontaneous' crowd demonstrations for one another.*[1]

No historian of French collaboration has resisted calling Darnand's *Milice* a movement of thugs and gangsters and Mosley's Black Shirts are normally given the same description. As for the S.S., they have become in Gerald Reitlinger's term, 'the alibi for the German nation': all the evils of the Nazi Reich have been accredited to them and modern Germans are taught to see them as sadists, criminals and murderers.

There is considerable truth in these accusations, though not all Fascist movements attracted the social underworld. Degrelle's *Rex* and the Spanish *Falange* did not depend on this kind of support, and the literary Fascists in France were highly critical of Darnand's men: they had a more élitist view of fascism which did not easily tolerate the less educated, less ideological aspects of the *Milice*. To a large extent Himmler was also an élitist, believing his S.S. to be the best quality of German manhood; but the applicants for membership were judged more by the blondness of their hair and the physique of their bodies than by their social and educational status. Thus, although the S.S.

[1] D. Mack Smith, *Italy: A Modern History* (University of Michigan, 1959). p. 392.

strutted through twenty years of German history as the ideal
Nazi types, they were often men of brute force with no affiliations
to any other part of society. The same is partially true of the first
active Fascists in Italy. The leaders of the *squadre* did not set out
to lure men away from existing parties and institutions, though
they did enrol a number of discontented ex-Communists; their
method was more to cater for those who had energy and
aggression but no organized outlet, and such people frequently
came straight from the streets.

To say that most fascisms attracted the socially maladjusted is
often a way of both condemning and dismissing them. When,
in 1964, A. J. P. Taylor reviewed Sir Ivone Kirkpatrick's study of
Mussolini, he called the Italian leader the 'First of the Rockers',
and continued:

> *Young rioters at Margate were called by the magistrates
> 'Sawdust Caesars'. The phrase was not original. Gilbert
> Seldes coined it for the study of Mussolini which he published
> in 1936.*
>
> *Mussolini and the Rockers have much in common: black
> shirts, love of speed and violent gesture, a persistent craze to
> race after nothing in particular. The Rockers settle down
> before they reach the end of their teens. Mussolini was a
> Rocker who never grew up.*[1]

These opening sentences, perceptive and humorous, set the
tone for a dismissal of Italian fascism. 'Actually,' Taylor concludes, 'there was nothing to fascism except rhetoric and castor
oil.' But such a judgment makes only a biting epitaph. If this
was the essence of fascism it becomes necessary to understand
why Italian society was so responsive. If Mussolini was a Rocker
and yet became leader of Italy, what does this tell us about
Italian politics? Similarly if the S.S. were thugs the question to
be asked is 'Why did Germany produce so many of them?'
Fascism clearly fulfilled an aggressive social need and the point
to emphasize here is that this need was widespread.

Beyond war veterans, youth movements and social outsiders,
lies the mass support for Hitler and Mussolini which does not fit

[1] *The Observer*, 14 June 1964.

into any of these categories. Among the millions who voted for the two dictators only a minority were actively involved in street violence or naked social aggression. The rest were able to satisfy aggressive needs in more respectable ways. Just as a state of international war legalizes the most extreme violence and makes it heroic and noble, so the two major movements of fascism legalized hatred and aggression by their nationalist and racialist propaganda. A respectable citizen of Rome or Berlin could share the arrogant nationalism of Mussolini or the fanatical anti-Semitism of Hitler without sacrificing his social position. He could support the *Duce* in his imperial conquest of Abyssinia or the Führer in the boycott of Jewish shops and still preserve the outward signs of normality and sociability. This state of affairs was not due merely to the successful propaganda of the two dictators. Both in Germany and in Italy nationalism was a respectable attitude well before the arrival of Mussolini and Hitler, and in Germany anti-Semitism was equally so. The two leaders built on existing aggression: they expanded and intensified it, but it was not their entire creation.

One has only to look at examples of anti-Semitism in imperial Germany to see how acceptable it was to large numbers of ordinary people. Over a period of several decades the Jew was dehumanized: he was seen by many as little more than an animal with no social or cultural rights. By 1890 most student fraternities at the leading universities had excluded Jews, and many schools were closed to them. Individuals like Theodor Fritsch, Eugen Dühring and, most famous, H. S. Chamberlain were widely influential with their well-argued, documented attacks on the Jewish race. Under the Weimar Republic the attitudes were little different: pictures, films, lectures and novels encouraged hatred and cruelty against the Jews, and the Nazis were only the most extreme of several political movements which used anti-Semitism to appeal to the average voter.

German racialism was therefore not the exclusive product of Nazism. Under Hitler it assumed primitive and barbaric proportions and it was executed with a horror and rigour which exceeded all previous movements, but to some extent Hitler was fulfilling long-standing social demands. Can these demands be explained? Why were so many Germans anti-Semitic?

Perhaps the first approach is to put German anti-Semitism into a European context. It was not the only country to have rooted racial prejudices. In Russia, the Jews had been savagely persecuted in the 19th century and many had fled from Russia and Central Europe into cosmopolitan centres such as Paris and Vienna, but in neither of these capitals were they free from attack. In France in the 1890s there was widespread antipathy to the Jews, who were seen as social parasites or traitors to the nation. During the Dreyfus Affair nationalism and anti-Semitism came together with ideas of regenerating France and liberating her from the Jewish menace, and although Jews were still accepted in high-class society there were many areas and social groups, particularly in the Catholic west and in the declining urban areas, where Jews were baited, stoned or boycotted. In Vienna, anti-Semitism was more closely integrated with politics, the eminent mayor Karl Lueger basing his Christian Social movement on a denunciation of the Jews. It was in Vienna that Hitler first noticed the strange dress of an Eastern European Jew, an incident he recalls in *Mein Kampf*:

> *Once when I was walking through the Inner City I suddenly came across a being in a long caftan with black sidelocks. My first thought was: is that a Jew? . . . I watched the man stealthily and cautiously, but the longer I stared at this strange countenance and studied it feature by feature, the more the question in a different form turned in my brain: is that a German?*[1]

Hitler's obsession with the Jews as aliens grew steadily from these Vienna days until his racialism became the central pillar of his fanatical politics. Once it was fully developed and Hitler firmly in power it found echoes in fascisms outside Germany. Mussolini, Mosley, Doriot and Bucard all adopted anti-Semitism in the 1930s and there were traces of it in the Spanish *Falange*. Out of all Western fascisms only the Belgian Rexists and the small group of Dutch National Socialists failed to stress the Jewish question in their political propaganda.

Thus Germany should not be seen as a complete exception within Europe, though the anti-Semitism of each different

[1] A. Hitler, *My Struggle* (Hurst and Blackett, 1935), pp. 30–1.

country should be given a separate analysis. In Germany's case the wide hostility to Jews has normally been ascribed to social insecurity among the middle and lower middle classes. The theory, which is well supported by social evidence, states that the groups most threatened by socialism or economic decline seized on the Jew as a scapegoat for their distress. They were encouraged to do so by three factors: firstly by the old Christian hostility to the Jew as the enemy of Christ and as the unscrupulous moneylender; secondly by the fact that Jewish finance and business were international and could easily be seen as a plot against the German nation; and thirdly by the social and cultural differences which the Jews themselves accentuated by their tight family circles, their Saturday sabbaths and their willingness to help fellow Jews in economic trouble.

Playing on these notes, a theme of anti-Semitism was composed with sufficient variations to fit the needs of many different social groups, from shopkeepers to smallholders, from unlucky investors to genuine victims of economic disaster. There was a

Nazi racialism. Separate park benches in Berlin for Aryans . . .

great deal of social and economic insecurity in Weimar Germany, with the year of riots and financial inflation in 1923, and the great depression, striking blackly at millions of homes, between 1929 and 1933. Anti-Semitism was undoubtedly an outlet which cost little and had quick results in the smashing of a Jewish shop or the arrest of a Jewish businessman. It looked as if things were happening even if the actual economic situation was not improving. Anti-Semitism was thus something of a false solution: it was a substitute for real change: it was a pseudo-revolution. Germany benefited little, if at all, from the persecution of the Jews or from the confiscation of their property, but those groups who desperately needed to recover security seized on anti-Semitism to protect themselves. They were clutching at air but it felt solid; one less Jew appeared to mean more in quantity and quality for themselves.

The Nazis knew that social and economic insecurity was the main cause of their phenomenal success in the years 1930 to 1933: Hitler frequently acknowledged his debt to the great

and for Jews

depression. But Nazi anti-Semitism also exploited religious, moral and conformist sentiments, as can be seen from a typical leaflet issued in September 1935:

Fellow German, do you know?

that the *Jew*

ravishes	your child
defiles	your wife
defiles	your sister
defiles	your sweetheart
murders	your parents
steals	your goods
insults	your honour
ridicules	your customs
ruins	your church
corrupts	your culture
contaminates	your race

that the *Jew*

slanders	you
cheats	you
robs	you
regards	you as cattle

It is almost impossible to give a sociological breakdown of people who responded to this kind of propaganda. It strikes on such a wide front that it could impress any social grouping.

This is even more true of German nationalism. The Nazis had no intention of basing their rule on any one section of society and their most intensive appeal was to a common factor in which all classes were involved—the 'German Spirit'. Workers as well as aristocrats had shown during World War I the width and strength of nationalist fervour and it was to this that Hitler's rhetoric and organization were aimed.

In Italy the sociology of nationalism was similar. Mussolini, like Hitler, understood that nationalism had permeated most of society. It was least respectable among the Communist and Socialist workers who treasured international ideals, as the

German Communists did also. In both countries, however, nationalism had a stronger drive than internationalism. It was impelled by the humiliation each nation felt in 1918, the Germans due to defeat and a harsh peace, the Italians due to frustrated war claims. Nationalism was an emotion which was less dependent on social insecurity than anti-Semitism was. It was the most common form of respectable aggression throughout Europe. There seemed little harm in waving the British, German or Italian flag at times of crisis and those who did so were not just the socially insecure. Nationalism in the 20th century has been as classless as Catholicism in the Middle Ages.

What emerges from all these points is that aggression has no single sociological explanation: it cannot be ascribed to any one class, group or emotion. Insecurity obviously explains a great deal but not everything. The Nazi and Italian Fascist youth movements were not motivated merely by insecurity, neither were the majority of nationalists. It would appear that aggression can stem from confidence as well as from fear, from stability as well as from instability. It tends to be more refined and respectable if it is not a case of desperate survival, but it can give very solid support to an extremist leader. One could say of Nazism, for example, that it depended on a small number of violent men but also on a large number of aggressive ones, and of these many were average, respectable people. To differing degrees the same may be true of most fascisms.

2 ECONOMIC

If psychology and sociology are as yet unable to offer a full explanation for the rise and success of fascism, can an economic approach provide something more final? Several writers in the thirties felt that it could, especially adherents to the Marxist–Leninist school of thought. A persuasive case was made out for the view that fascism was the last frantic effort of dying capitalism to retain its hold over society and the means of production. Attacked and weakened by socialism and the growing power of the proletariat, the capitalist class was said to have turned to the State and made a deal with the Fascist leaders: in return for political subservience they were to be assured of continuing economic mastery. Fascism therefore was an economic necessity if capitalism was to survive.

This theory, like so many compelling early theories about fascism, has sufficient support to make it interesting but insufficient breadth to make it a final explanation. In its favour stand all the examples of industrial and financial patronage bestowed on Nazism and the fact that Hitler, when in power, retained a capitalist economy. He perfected his anti-Communist propaganda and curbed the socialists within his party. As Führer he destroyed trade unions and ended all collective bargaining for higher wages and better conditions. To make Germany independent, he launched his economic programme for greater home production of almost every commodity. This was the policy of 'autarky' (complete national self-sufficiency): Germany was to be invulnerable, no international slump would affect her again. Finally, Hitler's armaments programme and war economy promised enormous profits for those industries which could fulfil his programme.

His success in the first few years was phenomenal by any standards. In September 1936 Hitler announced that his measures to step up production had reduced unemployment from six million to one million and he claimed that the class war had been resolved and the threat of communism removed. He was clearly in a strong position to appeal to the nationalism of the capitalist class and to their vested interests in order and strong government. During the years 1933–8 the German economy reached and surpassed the output and investment levels of 1928–9, the last year before the world depression, and the increase in productivity was by no means confined to armaments. Nazi Germany, while making intensive preparations for war, also created a prosperous civilian economy. It is now clear that the private sector was not sacrificed to the military until the war itself was under way.

Among the many who made spectacular profits under the Nazi régime the name of Alfred von Krupp has become a symbol of economic subservience. Krupp was the head of a vast munitions empire which had served the war aims of imperial Germany and had not been dissolved in 1918. Until 1933 he was suspicious, and even hostile, towards the flamboyant Nazi leader, but he quickly became convinced of Hitler's ability once the Nazi methods began to restore German prosperity. In 1930 Hitler had been asked what he would do with Krupp's if he came to power. He replied: 'Of course I should leave it alone. Do you think that I should be so mad as to destroy Germany's economy?' Krupp responded with the same deference. After the war he said to the Nuremberg judges: 'We at Krupp's merely wanted a system that would function well, that would give us the opportunity of producing without being disturbed. Politics is not our business.' The pact was mutually satisfying. Hitler was able to pursue his military ambitions: Krupp was able to expand his economic monopoly. Both men were absorbed in their own spheres and were totally unscrupulous, Krupp imitating his Führer's inhumanity by using slave labour in degrading conditions to increase his production.

Krupp had been convinced by the reality of Hitler's policies whereas a number of other capitalist leaders had responded even earlier to mere promises and propaganda. Between 1929 and 1933 Hitler enticed German industry by his nationalism and vigorous denunciation of the Bolshevik peril and all democratic failures under Weimar. The positive response of capital and industry developed as this propaganda began to bite into the national consciousness. At first it was the coal and steel producers of the Rhineland, threatened as they were by the Communist activities of their area, who actively encouraged the Nazi leader. Fritz Thyssen is the most notorious Nazi patron in this period. As chairman of the United Steelworks he had considerable money and influence at his disposal, and when he openly joined the Nazi Party in 1931 he brought Hitler into touch with most of the big leaders in industry. It is not known just how much money Thyssen paid to the Nazis but it was sufficient to justify the title of his memoirs: *I paid Hitler*. These reminiscences were published in 1941, two years after Thyssen had broken with Hitler and fled to Switzerland. The rupture between the industrialist and the Führer has been used to prove several different points, but seen in connection with Thyssen's earlier rejection of the Kaiser in 1918 it is less ambiguous. In September 1918, before the end of the war, he wrote a pamphlet accusing the Kaiser and his court of policies which could only end in industrial disaster and bankruptcy. In it he stated:

> *The Emperor and his family . . . in 1912 decided to embark
> on a great war of conquest. But to do this they had to get
> the commercial community to support them. They did this
> by holding out to them hopes of great personal gain as a
> result of the war. In the light of events that have taken place
> since August 1914 these promises now appear supremely
> ridiculous, but most of us at the time were led to believe that
> they would probably be realized.*[1]

This passage is echoed almost in detail by the foreword to his
memoirs in 1941:

> *Hitler deceived me, as he deceived the German people as a
> whole and all men of good will. It may perhaps be said—to
> me and to all Germans—that we should not have allowed
> ourselves to be deceived. For my part I accept the validity
> of this charge. I plead guilty. I was completely mistaken
> regarding Hitler and his party. I believed in his promises,
> in his loyalty, in his political genius . . . Hitler has deceived
> us all.*[2]

In both cases Thyssen supported power and autocracy,
believing it would bring national greatness and economic success.
He was an ardent nationalist though clearly a naïve politician:
he was apparently incapable of learning from experience. In the
end, however, his nationalist sense was a shrewd one and he
rightly judged the outcome of both the Kaiser's and the Führer's
obsession with war. He illustrates, as he himself says, the tragedy
of modern Germany: its inability to understand its own history
until it was too late.

But does he illustrate the decline of capitalism into fascism?
The same question could also be asked of Dr. Hjalmar Schacht.
Known as Hitler's financial wizard, Schacht had been the
eminent financier who had stabilized German currency after
the disastrous inflation of 1923. As president of the *Reichsbank*

---

[1] *The Thyssen Pamphlet* (1918).
[2] F. Thyssen, *I paid Hitler*, trans. C. Saerchinger (Hodder and Stoughton, 1941), p. 19.

he attempted to put the German economy on a sound financial
basis and opposed all policies which threatened to produce
another inflationary crisis. He believed that reparation payments
to the Allies and the American short-term loans to German
industry were both working against the national interest, and
when he was unable to stop either he resigned in 1929. Four
years later Hitler recalled him and he was entrusted with the
ministry of economics. For three years the economy was pliant
in Schacht's hands: he bent and twisted it to fit Hitler's policies,
and persuaded both Germany and Europe of the durability of
Hitler's régime. By 1937, however, he was aware that not even
his inventive methods could prevent catastrophic inflation if
Hitler's war economy increased. He resigned his posts, and
control of German economics fell more and more to Hitler and
Göring. Nazism was confident that war would solve all problems,
but Schacht as an economist was sceptical. Like Thyssen he
foresaw disaster for Germany, though unlike Thyssen he did not
make a final break with the Nazi Reich.

These two cases prove little except that Krupp's total
abdication to Nazi demands was not followed by all leading
German capitalists, but they do demand that the general
economic picture of Nazism should be drawn with caution.
Capitalism prospered but was not given a completely free rein.
The wage and price structure, marketing and labour relations
were controlled, or at least scrutinized, by the Minister of
Economics. Under the minister was an advisory body called the
National Economic Chamber in which subservience to Nazism
was the main qualification. Every member took the following
pledge:

> *I bind myself as follower to The Leader and National
> Chancellor with unalterable faith. In fulfilment of the
> National Socialist will, I will dedicate all my power to the
> upbuilding of the Third Reich and I will direct all my
> thoughts and energies so that in my own activities and those
> of my colleagues and through all the functions and authorities
> entrusted to me, only the highest aims will be pursued, the
> work of The Leader promoted and an enduring and true
> people's community assured.*

The pledge is a reminder that in Nazi Germany political ends were supreme. However much a capitalist economy benefited from Nazi policy, it was in the end directed by a non-economic ideology. The Nazi economy was not the climax of *laissez-faire* capitalism, rather a combination of free enterprise and rigid doctrinaire control. The confiscation of capitalist concerns run by Jews is itself an indication that Nazism was not basically a concerted capitalist enterprise. Hitler was scarcely interested in economics—his policies had their roots in political and cultural realities—but he provided order and stability, and to these qualities capitalism responded.

For similar reasons the régime of Mussolini had attracted business confidence and support in the early twenties. The first Fascist groups to appear in the cities of Italy were as revolutionary as the Socialists, but in the state of semi-civil war between 1920 and 1922, Mussolini turned his followers into anti-Socialists, strike-breakers and custodians of private property. As such they were useful allies of capitalist interests, and an alliance of fascism and capitalism was gradually built up, overcoming the initial hostility of the Commercial Bank, Mussolini's most powerful capitalist opponent. In many ways the alliance is surprising, since Italian fascism was partly based on a rejection of old-style capitalism and on the introduction of a new organic economy, the Corporate State.

Was corporatism ever more than a pious hope? This depends, naturally, on what was intended by corporatism, and this is where ambiguity starts. The corporate ideal proclaimed the abolition of strife between worker and employer and the end of capitalist exploitation. All units of each industry would be united in a corporation in which manager and foreman, owner and benchhand would be fairly represented, and in which all would work together for the national good. Private interests and union principles would be transcended in this new organism, and the public would benefit by increased production and industrial harmony. This ideal was rooted in various 19th-century theories which had criticized the capitalist world for fragmenting society and breaking it into conflicting units. Many Christian Socialists had held this view and had tried to restructure small parts of the economy in order to heal these divisions. In Britain

Ludlow and F. D. Maurice, in France La Tour du Pin and Léon Harmel, and in Germany Bishop Ketteler, had all held a basically corporate view, but had only limited success against the all-pervading orthodoxy of capitalist economy.

Italian fascism, followed later by all other fascisms, took over this old ideal and gave it a new dimension. To corporatism they added the concept of the all-powerful State; corporations would work for the good of the Fascist State and would be the agents of State policy and national advancement. Thus the new economy would not be capitalist or Socialist; it would not be totally free or totally restricted: it would be organic and nationalist. The end product would be the Corporate State in which the corporations would unite in a chamber and replace the old parliament and then administer the country's economy in accordance with Fascist principles. The Italian Labour Charter of 1927 expressed the general aim with clarity:

> *1 The Italian nation is an organic whole, having life, purposes and means of action superior in power and duration to those of the individuals, single or associated, of which it is composed. It is a moral, political and economic unity which is realized integrally in the Fascist State.*

> *2 . . . The process of production, from the national point of view is a single whole: its aims are united and identified with the wellbeing of the producers and the promotion of national power.*

The theory of national economy had much to recommend it, and the corporate ideal was seen by many throughout Europe as humane and progressive, but when it came to practical application, the ambiguity latent in the Fascist theory was forcefully exposed. If the corporations represent the unity of workers and employers throughout national life, what is the State? Surely the two should be synonymous? But in Italy it was quickly apparent that the State was Mussolini and the Fascist Party, and that policy and administration came from an autocratic centre and not from the organic unity of all producers. Corporations, then, in Fascist Italy became a theoretical showpiece but a practical illusion. In July 1926 a

Ministry of Corporations was set up, but without corporations. Shortly afterwards the first corporation, that of the stage, came into precarious existence. In 1930 the National Council of Corporations was set up and in 1933 Mussolini declared: 'Today we can affirm that the capitalist method of production is out of date.' A year later, twenty-two corporations were established with Mussolini as general president, and finally in 1939 a Chamber of *Fasci* and Corporations did replace the old parliamentary system. Throughout this whole development, however, Mussolini retained State control in his own hands, and made enough concessions to big industries and business to nullify the creeping socialism of the corporations. Economic power remained with the employers, with whom the Fascist Party had made an agreement in 1925. Known as the Vidoni Pact, this established a working arrangement between party and industry, based on a suppression of strikes and a dissolution of all factory workers' committees which were not specifically Fascist.

The Italian Corporate State was therefore a mixture of party control and capitalist economy. Mussolini summed it up in a frank statement: 'We control the political forces, we control the moral forces, we control the economic forces, thus we are in the midst of the corporate Fascist State.' As with Germany, it is arguable whether this situation was entirely to the capitalists' liking. As the party's control, or 'supervision' as it was called, increased, industries were submitted to price regulations and their productivity dictated by the current demands of Fascist policy. Thus, after the Abyssinian victory, Mussolini proclaimed a war economy and a policy of autarky. Industrial expansion was regimented and home products were so heavily protected that costs rapidly increased to dangerous inflationary levels. Neither control nor autarky was in the interest of all capitalists, commerce suffering particularly from restrictions on imports. To this extent Italian fascism fulfilled some of its anti-capitalist propaganda, although for most capitalist concerns the merits of the régime outweighed its disadvantages. It certainly seemed preferable to the socialism or communism which hovered as the European alternative.

With reference to the fascisms which did not achieve power and were thus prevented from establishing their own economic

system, the theory that capitalism was the parent of fascism is
far less defensible. In particular, Degrelle's *Rex* and José
Antonio's *Falange* stand out as aggressively anti-capitalist. One
of the slogans of *Rex* ran:

> *Against inhuman hyper-capitalism!*
> *Against profiteering politicians!*
> *For Bread and Dignity!*
> *Workers of all classes unite!*

Degrelle stood firmly against the Belgian Establishment,
whether political, religious or economic, and his ideal of
corporatism was a moral unity of all Belgians who had suffered
from the corruption and exploitation of the ruling groups in
Belgian society. He received no backing from the body of
industrial and financial interests. He did, however, draw support
from declining small capitalists, as has almost every non-Socialist
movement of protest in 20th-century politics. Marx's *petite
bourgeoisie*, the class that is most afraid of slipping into poverty
and most ambitious to climb the social and economic ladder, is
represented in *Rex* as in other fascisms, but the attitudes of this
class are not consistent nor do they explain the width of Fascist
appeal. They are a major element in the making of the Fascist
synthesis, but they should not be used either in Belgian or
other national histories as scapegoats for the complex Fascist
phenomenon.

In Spain José Antonio could easily have become the agent of
Spanish capitalism, which was seriously threatened by the wave
of syndicalism and anarchism in all big towns. He was to some
extent financed by gifts from this source, but his ideology and
the character of his movement remained until his death opposed
to capitalist control of the economy. Like the Italian Fascists,
the *Falange* had an impressive economic ideal, the 'establishment
of a complete system of national syndicates, embracing employers
and employees, to organize, co-ordinate and represent all of
Spain's economic activity'. This did not amount to an attack on
private property but would entail the 'nationalization of credit
facilities by the State to eliminate capitalist usury'. After the
Jefe's death and the submission of the *Falange* to Franco's
authoritarian control, this revolutionary economic programme

became as illusory as Mussolini's. In Franco's régime, as in Salazar's in Portugal, there is a façade of corporate ideals, but behind it State-supervised capitalism is the reality of the economy. It is a long way from the early Falangist declarations. Mosley's party in Britain deliberately emphasized the National Socialist side of fascism in order to separate itself both from the British Labour Party and from Conservative capitalism. To the question 'What is the difference between fascism and capitalism, since both admit the system of private enterprise?' Mosley replied:

> *In brief definition, capitalism is the system by which capital uses the Nation for its own purposes. Fascism is the system by which the Nation uses capital for its own purposes. Private enterprise is permitted and encouraged so long as it coincides with the national interests. Private enterprise is not permitted when it conflicts with the national interests. Under Fascism private enterprise may serve but not exploit. This is secured by the Corporative System which lays down the limits within which industry may operate and those limits are the welfare of the Nation.*[1]

It is almost identical to the Italian ideal and in France the first small Fascist movement, *Le Faisceau*, made similar statements, criticizing capitalism yet not breaking entirely from private property. The later French Fascists, particularly Déat and Doriot, coming as they did from left-wing movements, were also anti-capitalist, though under the German occupation they modified their hostility to fit the Nazi attitudes.

In summary, it would seem that the view of European fascism as the last stand of capitalism is at best a half truth. In theory, the most general Fascist economy was intended to take the form of the Corporate State, and this was by no means an ideal solution for capitalists: in practice, fascism, especially in Italy and Germany, did not attain the corporate goal. Under Mussolini and Hitler the capitalist class was given security and protection against the socialism of the trade unions, but this security was bought at the price of freedom—a sacrifice which was in the end, as Thyssen saw, against the long-term interests

[1] Sir O. Mosley, *Fascism. 100 Questions Asked and Answered* (B.U.F., 1936), No. 35.

of the capitalist economy. Fascism turned against all independence, and unrestricted private enterprise was one among
the many casualties. This fact, however, did not prevent leading
capitalists within both Italy and Germany from underwriting
the structure and excesses of the régimes. Without this support
the dictators could hardly have survived, nor could the present
régimes of Franco and Salazar look so permanent.

The entire validity of an economic interpretation of fascism
was challenged in 1939 by Peter Drucker, a Viennese who came
to England in 1933 and joined an international banking house as
an economist. In this position he was thrown constantly against
the nationalist economy of Nazi Germany and became a shrewd
observer of Nazi society and ideology. By the end of the thirties
he was convinced that fascism in general and Nazism in particular
was in no way an economic movement. His book, *The End of
Economic Man*, put forward his case with insight and pungency.
In a chapter headed 'Fascist non-economic society' he states:

> It becomes clear, in the first place, that it is pointless to ask
> which class put fascism into power. No single class can have
> put fascism into power. That a gang of ruthless industrialists
> backed Hitler and Mussolini is as far from, and as near to,
> the truth as that the great toiling masses backed them. Both
> were necessarily supported by a minority of all classes . . .
>
> Secondly, it is a moot question whether totalitarianism is
> capitalist or socialist. It is neither. Having found both
> invalid, fascism seeks a society beyond socialism and capitalism
> that is not based upon economic considerations.[1]

To what then did fascism appeal? Drucker develops his thesis
by claiming that fascism is fundamentally a revolt against the
view of man as an economic unit, a view which both capitalism
and socialism held in common. Instead fascism turns from
Economic Man to Heroic Man and appeals to man's non-
economic values—values of heroism, self-sacrifice, discipline
and comradeship. To those who had no place in the economic
hierarchy, it offered, not higher wages or economic promotion,
but an active development of the personality. This can be seen,
Drucker maintains, in the leisure-time activities sponsored by

[1] P. Drucker, *The End of Economic Man* (Heinemann, 1939), pp. 123–4.

both Nazism and Italian fascism. In Germany workers were encouraged to join the movement of *Kraft durch Freude* (Strength through Joy) and in Italy the *Dopo Lavoro* (After Work). Both movements brought sport, camping, hikes and team spirit within the experience of the factory or farm worker. Gradually these movements became more obligatory and were used as police methods of controlling potential opponents to the régimes, but their object was clearly to provide non-economic returns for the working man's labour. Similarly the two dictatorships offered the capitalist classes the non-economic values of nationalism and cultural or racial supremacy. Heroic Man was the ideal throughout.

This thesis was more than a flash of intuition: it was an astonishing feat of objectivity at a period when stereotyped economic explanations were the norm. It was regarded with suspicion because it was too understanding and sounded like a product of fascism itself. Not that Drucker concluded without drawing a moral: in the last chapter he stated that the democracies must fight fascism with their own non-economic values —the values of Free and Equal Man. Drucker's theory is a powerful contribution both to the controversies of the time and to the interpretations of history, but it has its limitations. There is no convincing sign in modern European history that we have reached the end of Economic Man: economic values continue to predominate with only a minority opposing them. Nor can we be sure that the millions who followed Hitler and Mussolini clearly distinguished between Economic and Heroic Man: did the stormtrooper, for example, value order and strength more highly than his regular pay and daily meal? Both dictators came to power in periods of economic chaos and both offered economic incentives as well as non-economic values. The ideals of corporatism and national socialism were themselves inseparable from the economic problems of inter-war Europe.

The lasting contribution of Drucker is his stress on the quality of the Fascist appeal: it did transcend class and economic barriers and it did emphasize the non-economic values of both individuals and society. It is this unique quality which distinguishes it from the class-conscious, economically centred ideologies of capitalism and socialism. None of the main Fascist leaders, except Mosley, was an economic expert, and in most doctrines of fascism, economics appears more as a by-product than as the substructure of all other thought. Fascism, if it did not herald the end of Economic Man, certainly suggested an alternative. There was much talk, especially among Fascist intellectuals such as Giovanni Gentile in Italy or Drieu La Rochelle in France, of Fascist Man as the ideal type in a new Europe. The qualities ascribed to this man certainly did not indicate economic preoccupations: he was built more on cultural lines, and one extension of Drucker's thesis is to approach fascism as a radically new cultural movement. What are the grounds for this approach? Are its claims too vague and too large?

CHAPTER TWELVE

Cultural Approaches

In *Thus Spake Zarathustra*, Nietzsche's prophetic work
addressed to the Europe of his day, his spokesman Zarathustra
meets an old saint who has left his holy hut to look for roots
in the forest:

> *'And what does the saint do in the forest?' asked
> Zarathustra.*
>
> *The saint answered 'I make songs and sing them, and
> when I make songs I laugh, weep, and mutter: thus I praise
> God.*
>
> *'With singing, weeping and muttering I praise the God
> who is my God. But what do you bring us as a gift?'*
>
> *When Zarathustra heard these words he saluted the saint
> and said 'What should I have to give you! But let me go
> quickly, that I may take nothing from you!' And thus they
> parted from one another, the old man and Zarathustra,
> laughing as two boys laugh.*
>
> *But when Zarathustra was alone, he spoke thus to his
> heart: 'Could it be possible! This old saint has not yet heard
> in his forest that God is dead!'* [1]

The saint is seen to be out of touch with his times. The world
which Nietzsche portrays at the end of the 19th century is one
which has destroyed God, the Church and traditional Christian
ethics. A divine absolute is no longer capable of holding society
together: man must therefore look to himself. Zarathustra goes
on to proclaim that man must overcome and surpass himself:
the era of the 'superman' is at hand.

[1] F. Nietzsche, *Thus Spake Zarathustra*, trans. R. J. Hollingdale (Penguin,
1961), p. 41.

Throughout this work the language is religious, the atmosphere that of biblical prophecy, while the poetic utterances of Zarathustra are close to mysticism. If God is really dead, surely these religious overtones should not persist? The non-religious language of science and rationalism would be more appropriate. Does it seem, therefore, that Nietzsche wants a new absolute, new rituals and new beliefs to fill the void left by God's death? Is he one of the many 19th-century thinkers in search of a secular religion?

Many commentators on Nietzsche answer these questions in the affirmative and thus make him into the great spokesman of his age, a man who knew that the concept of the Christian God was no longer valid but who could not escape from religious ideas and religious atmosphere. The psychologist C. G. Jung was one who saw Nietzsche in this way and developed from this point a whole interpretation of modern man, one aspect of which has been presented in 'Psychological Approaches' (Chapter Ten). He himself felt strongly that the old God was dead but knew that man could not accept a universe or even a Europe without some sort of religious purpose. Modern man was therefore, according to Jung, in search of a soul: he was looking for an adequate replacement for God, something that would give meaning and insight, inspiration and ideals, as well as answers to the difficult problems of life. During this search strange gods were found, some in the form of old values like art, others in the form of new, disturbing and dynamic powers like fascism and communism. In each case certain men were raising the new gods to the height of the old Christian divinity and paying to them the same devotion and homage.

Was fascism really a substitute religion of this kind? Did it emerge as a candidate for the vacant throne of God? Was it an attempt to produce a new culture, replacing the long tradition of Western, Christian thought? These are some of the questions which arise when a cultural approach to fascism is made. But before they can be examined one persistent ghost should be laid. Whatever the final estimation of Fascist life and culture, it was *not* the realization of Nietzschean ideas. Among the many things Nietzsche hated was anti-Semitism, worship of the State, and all subservience. He rebelled against Bismarck's German Reich, preferring to live in Switzerland or France, and he used some of his most vitriolic language against Prussianism. When Hitler was later called 'the Nietzschean superman', grave injustice was done to the subtlety of Nietzsche's concept. His superman was to be an individual who had overcome the weakness, destructiveness and nihilism in his own being and had reached a higher level of human sensitivity and creative power. He was not to be a product of advanced evolution—Nietzsche was strongly opposed to any Darwinian interpretation of his work—nor was it clear whether he would be a political leader of any kind. Judging from both Nietzsche's writings and his life, one could speculate that Hitler would have filled him with nothing but contempt and disgust. There may be superficial similarities in the language and ideas of Nietzsche and those of fascism, but there is no genuine causal connection. The Nazis, who proclaimed Nietzsche as a forerunner, were forced to suppress many of his works and to quote him in disjointed and misleading passages.

Nietzsche, therefore, is mentioned here not as a cause of fascism but as a thinker who described in brilliant, if ambiguous, terms the cultural condition of modern Europe. He may, or may not, have been wrong about the death of God, but he expressed an attitude which was permeating most of European thought. His diagnosis was not an eccentric one.

A cultural approach to fascism could thus begin at this point. In the 20th century, men have been searching for new values, not just new laws, better conditions or higher wages, but cultural values on which to base a whole view of man and society. Peter Drucker, as quoted in the last chapter, felt in 1939 that fascism was providing just such a revaluation.[1] It was presenting the world with a vision of 'man as hero' to replace the outworn picture of 'man as economic unit'. Going back to Fascist sources, one finds that Mussolini frequently used the phrase '*l'uomo nuovo, il Fascista*' (the new man, the Fascist) and that in most Fascist statements the language is prophetic, looking to a future in which man will be transformed. 'Fascism', said Mussolini in a famous definitive phrase, 'is not only a party, it is a régime; it is not only a régime but a faith; it is not only a faith but a religion.' There is certainly some justification for exploring these grandiose claims.

[1] See pp. 217–18.

The dominating Nazi signs
of swastika and eagle

One finds initially that all
fascisms resemble a religion in
their use of symbols, myths and
rituals. The symbols of the Nazi
swastika, the Italian *fasces* or
the British flash and circle, to
mention only three, were used
to give direction and solidarity
to the movements. Without symbols a mass movement will lose
its orientation, since the symbol
acts as a substitute leader and
ideology. Hitler could not be
everywhere at once commanding
allegiance, nor could the Nazi
ideology be constantly under
men's eyes, but the swastika
could symbolize everything Nazi in all places at all times. Like
the Star of David or the Catholic crucifix it inspired loyalty and
devotion and was employed consciously by the Nazis to rival
its religious counterparts. The swastika was often reduced to a
jagged cross to suggest a relationship with Christianity which
was of propaganda value. Degrelle also used the cross long after
his movement, *Rex*, had ceased to be a purely Catholic one.

In the early stages of Nazism, Hitler took a personal interest
in the actual design of the symbols. He himself sketched out the
eagle armband of the S.A. after discovering in an anti-Semitic
book that the eagle was the Aryan among birds. The swastika
was not his invention, however. It was already very popular
with students in Germany after World War I and was worn by
soldiers who had enlisted for the fight against Bolshevism. In
adopting it, the Nazis claimed that the swastika was an ancient
Teutonic or Nordic symbol. This is doubtful, even though, as a
symbol of the sun, it has been found in several ancient civilizations.

The Italian claim on the old Roman *fasces* is, by comparison, less pretentious. Mussolini saw himself as the leader of the Third Rome which Mazzini had prophesied in the mid-19th century. With the second Rome, that of the Popes, he came to terms in the Lateran Treaty of 1929, and from the first Rome, that of the Emperors, he took as much as his régime could assimilate. There was to be no doubt which of these three Romes was to be the greatest: the *fasces* were intended to proclaim the authority of the past and the greatness of the present.

Uniforms were another natural source of symbolism, consciously parallel to religious practice. The black, brown or green shirts, the jackboots and belts, gave to the Fascists the appearance of a special order set apart from society like monks or holy men. Periods of training and rituals of initiation were developed and emphasis put on obedience and discipline. Marcel Déat, the French Fascist and collaborator, described his movement as an Order, imposing a strict rule of life on its members whom he described in religious terms as 'regulars'. The mark of these regulars was to be the distinctive uniform. It was a highly symbolic act when Doriot, Déat's fellow Fascist, first donned a Nazi uniform during the war. This uniform had been highly prized since the 1920s: when Nazis were forbidden by certain state authorities to wear their black shirts the men appeared in the streets with their chests bare but with the black ties knotted round their necks. On or off, the shirts were a potent symbol.

The colours themselves were significant symbols. 'Black', said Mosley, 'best expresses the iron determination of fascism in the conquest of red anarchy.' But this distinction between black and red was not so blatantly made in Germany. From the early days of the Nazi movement the colour red figured in armbands and flags: in some areas and on some occasions red seemed the predominant colour, mystifying the public and rivalling the Communist symbols. Many workers drifted into Nazi meetings under the illusion that the red banners and posters outside indicated a genuine commitment to socialism.

Accent on colour, uniform and sign, and the distribution of these throughout society, had the dual effect of encouraging supporters and intimidating the opposition. The mass production of Nazi leaflets headed with the swastika and the appearance of

the sign on street walls and underground passages throughout
Germany gave the impression well before Hitler's accession to
power that the country was overrun by Nazism. In fact the Nazis
never gained a national majority in any free election: the symbols
suggested a power and universality which was false, but many
Germans paid more attention to the swastikas than the voting
figures. In Italy Mussolini came to power without such a highly
developed system of mass persuasion, but once established he
multiplied party posters quoting his speeches, brandishing the
fasces and announcing 'The *Duce* is always right', as a ubiquitous
reminder that fascism was in control. Familiar advertising and
propaganda brings a sense of security like well-known biblical
passages on a church hoarding or shrines at crossroads. Both
Hitler and Mussolini knew how to manipulate public opinion
by symbolic gestures.

The use of myths as well as symbols was most significant
among the Nazis, who employed them as cultural factors in
almost every aspect of the Reich. They turned to myths of the
past—the sagas of the German *Volk* as rediscovered by the
German Romantics from Herder to Wagner; to myths of past
and present—the Jewish 'plot' and the supremacy of the Aryan
race; and to myths of the future—the creation of a New Order
in Europe. All these myths inspired a sense of German superiority
and Nazi leadership. Hitler and his colleagues were the Teutonic
heroes reborn, and Germany was seen as determined by its
history to be the agent of a new and greater European civilization. Nazi art portrayed Hitler as an ancient knight in shining
armour bearing the standard of Aryan culture, and 'Aryan man'
was the subject of all forms of scholarship and expression from
treatise to sculpture. The myths were never clearly defined: it
was never clear whether Nordic features, for example, were
different from those of the ancient Greeks, nor whether Germanic
culture originated in the Rhineland or in the lands of the
North. Similarly the myth of the future, the New Order,
was as vague as the Christian Kingdom of God on earth, but
was powerful for that very reason: individual Nazis and
other Fascists outside Germany made the New Order stand
for their own particular utopias. Hitler himself had his own
vision which he expressed in his attempt to destroy all European

Jews, gypsies and other 'racial inferiors'. His utopia was to be
a pure civilization with the German as the model of all humanity.
It was not the same New Order that excited the French Fascists
·with their hopes of a confederated Fascist Europe, but it was
nevertheless a utopian vision which activated Hitler's own
thought and policy. This is exactly the kind of myth which
Georges Sorel had advocated for a revolutionary movement,
whether religious or secular.[1]

Although Hitler claimed that he had never read it, his racial
myths seem to owe much to a book by Alfred Rosenberg, the
self-appointed philosopher of the Nazi movement. Called *Der
Mythus des 20 Jahrhunderts* ('The Myth of the 20th Century')
the book stated that the Nordic race and the German State had
the great task of rescuing the world from its recent degenerate
history which was symbolized, in Rosenberg's view, by such
weaknesses as the French Revolution, Marxism and Christianity.
By emphasizing the identity of soul and race, the German could
rise above inferior nations and fulfil the mission of Nordic, Aryan
man. The race-soul was the highest value and thus had a kind
of mythical character. 'This is the task of our century,' he wrote,
'to create out of a new myth of life a new type of man.'
Rosenberg became the deputy leader of the Nazis while Hitler
was in prison after the failed Munich *Putsch* of 1923, and his
ideas were diffused throughout the party. His anti-Christianity
caused a little concern among a few Nazis, but in general his
myth of the German race and its mission in modern Europe
was to become the basis of Nazi ideology. Together with the
personal obsessions of Hitler and other leaders it was a powerful
act of cultural aggression.

The myths of the Third Rome and Fascist Man were the
Italian equivalent of Nazi utopias. These future idylls were
widely proclaimed in the period of Mussolini's imperial
conquests: Italy was seen as the bringer of Mediterranean
culture to the primitive darkness of Africa and a missionary
zeal was stimulated in the troops who moved into Abyssinia.
This cultural arrogance shows the debt of Italian fascism to the
nationalism of d'Annunzio and Corradini, and to Mazzini well
before them. In the 1900s d'Annunzio had lyricized the
Mediterranean sea as the symbol of Italian greatness, and in

[1] See Chapter One, pp. 32–3.

his brief régime in Fiume had instituted the worship of Italian music and poetry as a political duty. D'Annunzio had read and admired Nietzsche but showed no more respect for his total philosophy than the Nazis. He seized on the idea of the super-man and argued that such a man would be a southerner of dark complexion. Mussolini approved of this definition and cultivated his own myth of *Il Duce*. Not content with having his portrait on posters all over Italy, he ordered a vast carving of his face to be made in stone and positioned in the desert where the Italian armies had conquered. With the dimensions but none of the ambiguity of the Sphinx, this Imperial bust stood as a symbol of Fascist culture, large, brash and unsubtle, but not devoid of power.

Other fascisms were poorer in myths than the two leading movements. Doriot saw himself, and was seen by his followers, as a saviour figure who could achieve for France what Hitler had for Germany, and both José Antonio and Léon Degrelle were the objects of hero worship which raised them above the common man. To some extent the *Falange*'s vision of the Spanish *Patria* was a myth. The statement that 'The *Patria* is a transcendant synthesis . . .' evokes a more than political vision. It was an evocation of the spiritual unity of Spain which had never existed but which was set out as the object of Falangist belief. Where the *Falange* differed from Italian fascism and German Nazism, however, was in its refusal to join, or its failure to assimilate, the more traditional forms of nationalism. Where Mussolini and Hitler took over the conservative nationalism of pre-1914, José Antonio tried to keep his movement distinct from reactionary Carlism and conservative militarism. It was these latter varieties of Spanish nationalism which appealed most fervently to the glory and traditions of medieval Spain: the *Falange*'s roots in the Spanish past were thus more shallow. The Falangist *Patria* had none of the mythical potency of the German *Volk*. Even weaker were the abstractions of Mosley and Degrelle: the British Empire of Mosley's Black Shirts and the purified Belgium of *Rex* had only a limited cultural appeal.

Together, symbols and myths formed the basis of ritual. D'Annunzio in Fiume had appropriated the dialogue between priest and congregation which forms the corporative act of

Christian worship and had turned it into an emotional ritual in the service of nationalism. Mussolini continued the tradition, appealing to the crowds with the question 'Who is the ruler of Italy?' and receiving the mass reply '*Il Duce! Il Duce!*' In Germany the '*Heil Hitler!*' and '*Sieg Heil!*' of Nazi demonstrations gave a staccato fury to the rituals of obedience. Massed in their thousands with outstretched arms and framed by the huge swastika banners, the Nazis gave to the Nuremberg and Berlin rallies a terrifying primitive violence. Their shouts of allegiance, their rhythmic marching step and the final singing of the 'Horst Wessel Song' were all agents of mass intoxication and conversion. The end product was belief, and from belief stemmed unquestioning action. These rallies, centring on the figure and voice of Hitler, were the national climax of a Nazi ritualism which penetrated through all the separate institutions and movements. The Hitler Youth, for example, shouted its own protestations of belief in regimented meetings—'You are nothing; your nation is everything' and 'Common good before private gain'—slogans which stimulated the spiritual sense of self-sacrifice and moral development.

The similarity of these rituals to traditional religious worship is underlined by the Fascist perversion of the Catholic Mass in Italy. In 1938 the combined Fascist Youth, meeting at a camp in Rome, held a Mass led by the camp's chaplain and the party secretary. It began with the singing of '*Giovinezza*', the Fascist Youth song, and an invocation to the Divine Being to bring success to Mussolini's imperial policy. When the Host was elevated fifteen thousand youths raised their bayonets and pointed them in aggressive dedication to the sky. The service then concluded with a prayer to the *Duce* and another Fascist anthem. In 1919 d'Annunzio had prayed to the 'God of Italy' to guide his conquest of Fiume: in the terms of Fascist ritual Mussolini was close to becoming that god.

Idolization of the leader is not only common to all fascisms but also to autocratic communism and other dictatorships. Stalin was as much the self-declared heir to the fallen Christian god as was Mussolini or Hitler: an Uzbek poem to Stalin begins with the words 'O thou who broughtest man to birth', an expression which goes beyond even the Nazi catechisms of

belief. Leader idolatry should not therefore be taken as conclusive
proof that fascism was a substitute religion, but when joined
to the stress on symbol and myth the parallel is already a
tempting one.

It gains further strength when Fascist education is considered.
Throughout the 19th century the churches of Christian Europe
fought a losing battle against the educational reforms of anti-
clerical or secular governments. The religious case was argued on
the grounds that education was a spiritual, as well as intellectual,
experience and for that reason the churches should have regular
access to the minds of the young. In reply the reformers proclaimed the freedom of education from all ideological bias,
though frequently such claims masked the anti-clerical prejudice
of the reforms. Fascism, true to its synthesis, adopted both the
position of the churches and that of the anti-clericals, and forged
an educational system which was not traditionally religious but
was openly and assertively ideological.

When Hitler came to power, German schools were already
dominated by nationalist thinking and ideas of the *Volk*.
Many of the student fraternities had been closed to the
Jews, and G. L. Mosse, the historian of *völkisch* thought
and Nazi culture, has claimed that schoolteachers were just as
important as capitalist support in the triumph of Nazism.[1] Many
of the current textbooks were critical of Weimar Germany and
directed the reader back to the glory and heroism of earlier
periods, and Germany's defeat in World War I was regarded with
deep humiliation which bred recrimination and aggression. The
Nazis had no difficulty in winning the bulk of the student
movements even before Hitler was Chancellor.

The Führer, therefore, was not revolutionary when he
increased the nationalist and anti-Semitic prejudice of German
education. Teachers were co-ordinated in a National Socialist
Teachers' League and party pressure was exerted at all levels.
The result was a shallow and fanatical syllabus of German
self-glorification, anti-Semitism and intellectual subservience.
Hitler himself had no interest in the free-ranging intellect and
saw education merely as a polemical instrument. He founded
Ordensburgen (Order Castles) to train a Nazi élite and expressed
his aim in uncompromising words:

[1] G. L. Mosse, *The Crisis of German Ideology* (Weidenfeld and Nicolson, 1966),
Chapter 8.

*The weak must be chiselled away. In my Order Castles young
people will grow up who will frighten the world. I want a
violent, arrogant, unafraid, cruel youth who must be able
to suffer pain. Nothing weak or tender must be left in them.
Their eyes must bespeak once again the free, magnificent
beast of prey. I want my young people strong and beautiful.
I shall train them in all kinds of athletics, for I want youth
that are athletic—that is first and foremost. Thus will I
erase a thousand years of human domestication. Thus will
I face the pure and noble raw material. Thus I can create
the new. I do not want an intellectual education.*[1]

This spirit soon pervaded the pedagogic journals, and the more
scholarly schools were forced to adapt to the organic ideal of
the Hitler Youth. The frontiers between different disciplines
became blurred as they fell under the universal influence of Nazi
ideology. History, literature and science could all be used to
buttress the achievements of Nazism and as tools to expose the
'Jewish conspiracy'. In 1934 an official journal presented a model
history course lasting forty weeks, covering the salvation of
Germany by the Nazi Party from the degradation of Weimar. It
was set out in four columns: Number of Weeks, Subject,
Relation to the Jews, and Reading Material. Typical entries read:

Weeks	Subject	Relation to the Jews	Reading Material
25–28	Adolf Hitler National Socialism	Judah's Foe!	*Mein Kampf*
33–36	National Socialism at grips with crime and the underworld	Jewish instigators of murder The Jewish press	Horst Wessel
37–40	Germany's Youth at the helm! The Victory of Faith	The last fight against Judah	The Reich Party Congress

The 'Victory of Faith' was as significant in an educational
syllabus as the swastika on a party banner. Nazism was to be
seen as more than a political triumph: the young were to be
moulded by the spiritual values with which Nazism had

[1] Quoted in H. Vogt, *The Burden of Guilt*, trans. H. Strauss (O.U.P., 1965),
p. 163.

conquered the soul of Germany. Education under Hitler shows strong affinities with more extreme religious indoctrination. In both cases the way to knowledge was directed by belief.

Mussolini's Italy paralleled the Nazi Order Castles with Party Leadership Schools which demanded three qualifications for entry: political passion, organizational ability and athletic prowess. They came into being in 1934 and took the form of evening classes so that youth already employed could participate. Here the 'Fascist Man' was to be produced on a diet of Fascist doctrine, Fascist party history, Fascist organization, Fascist economics and the contemporary Italian problems of transport, colonial policy and military growth. These schools appeared to thrive, since in 1939 they were given a headquarters in Rome called the National Centre of Political Preparation for Youth: the writings of Mussolini figured prominently in the curriculum.

The rest of Italian education was more free from sectarian Fascist ideology than the schools in Nazi Germany. The Catholic Church was left in nominal charge of much of the elementary

Members of the Hitler Youth burning Jewish and Marxist books in Salzburg, April 1938

teaching but intellectual opposition to the régime was made virtually impossible by inspections and oversight by local party officials. In addition, the pressure on children to join one of the party youth organizations, and the training received in these movements, fed back into the school situation: children themselves became the agents of Fascist orthodoxy and were used to expose their teachers. The same was even more true of Germany: half-Jewish schoolteachers were arrested, often due to the zeal of Jew-hunting pupils whose real education was at the hands of the Hitler Youth.

In Germany therefore, and to a lesser extent in Italy, education was seen as an integral part of an ideological system. In Italy the totalitarian control was never a full reality, and other systems, such as the Catholic world view, continued to influence the young, but in Germany the attempt to create an entirely new cultural pattern shows the extent to which Nazism rivalled the religions of the past. 'One is either a German or a Christian,' said Hitler to Hermann Rauschning. 'You cannot be both.' The racial character was thus elevated to the cultural status of a religion. 'German' became a word signifying a distinct culture, separated from the rest of European civilization.

This is particularly apparent in the Nazi attitude to art. In the 1920s the small Nazi Party showed an early hostility to German artists who painted in one of the many modern styles, whether in abstract forms like Paul Klee or in Expressionist colour and line like Nolde and Kokoschka. Despite the fact that Nazism, like other fascisms, drew on the explosive and energetic ideas of the early 20th century, it could never accept these ideas when applied to painting and sculpture. In this, Nazism showed itself to be conventional and unadventurous. It shared the general public hostility and incomprehension which labelled modern art as immoral, distorted and worthless. Hitler had his own reasons, in his failure as a painter, for making these superficial judgments, but there was more to it than personal insecurity. Nazi ideology was aimed at the broad mass of the people and an attack on modern art was an easy way of gaining public sympathy at the expense of a few artists. In Dessau, in 1932, the City Council, dominated by Nazis, forced the famous Bauhaus School of Art to move to Berlin where it was finally closed once Hitler came to power. The Bauhaus had already had to move in 1925 from Weimar where the public had been intolerant, and the Nazis fully understood the force of this hostility. In using it at Dessau for their own ends, they showed to the art world their open antagonism to current artistic values. The great masters of the Bauhaus, including Klee, Kandinsky, Gropius, Feininger and Moholy-Nagy, became the first victims of the Nazi culture: their products and paintings were gradually confiscated and held up to ridicule and the artists themselves left Germany to maintain their freedom.

The persecution grew steadily once the Nazi régime was established. The North German primitive Expressionist, Emil Nolde, although a member of the Nazi Party, was told he must alter his style, and the Gestapo was sent to stop another Expressionist, Schmidt-Rottluff, from painting altogether. Goebbels as Minister of Propaganda presided over a Reich culture chamber to which all artists had to be affiliated if they wanted to paint. Art criticism was replaced by 'meditations on art' which amounted to mere descriptions of the subject matter, and the concept of 'German' art became the criterion of value. By this definition all art which Nazism disliked or mistrusted was called un-German; this included most of the great works by modern German artists which remained inside the Reich after 1933. To persuade the Germans that such paintings were fundamentally alien to their culture, Hitler and Goebbels organized a public pillory of the confiscated works. They were hung under insulting criticisms and slogans in a giant exhibition called 'Degenerate Art' in 1937. Nudes by Kokoschka, for example, were labelled with the question 'Do German girls really look like this?' and appeal was made to traditional religious sensibility by exhibiting a tortured crucifixion by Nolde as an attack on true German religion.

Ridicule was only a negative weapon: there had to be a positive 'German' art to rival and correct the 'degenerate' trend. Another exhibition was therefore held at the same time showing the ideals of Nazism portrayed in naturalistic paintings of heroic youths, peasants, and marching groups of Nazi workers, soldiers and stormtroopers. Artists such as Elk Eber, Adolf Ziegler and Johannes Beutner contributed variations on the Aryan figure, and there were a number of chaste nudes and peasant girls stripped to the waist in idyllic working conditions. 'We are not prudes,' said Goebbels, and indeed the painting of male and female nudes was encouraged to demonstrate anatomical interest in healthy Aryan bodies. The prevalence of the male nude was a direct reference to classical Greek art and the most noted Nazi sculptor, Arno Becker, who had trained in France under Rodin, produced vast heads and figures with stereotyped classical features.

Throughout this particular exhibition of 1937, and others of an identical nature mounted in the House of German Art in Munich, the emphasis was the same. The art was forged in the crucible of Nazi ideology and was directly polemical. It could only be assessed in terms of the symbols, myths and beliefs of Nazi culture. Its aesthetics were unimportant and the individuality of the artists insignificant. The 'German' art of the Nazi Reich was functional in that it served a system of belief: it was used as ritualistic décor.

Such a conclusion could be further illustrated by reference to the sheer size and classical dimensions of Nazi architecture with its accent on monumentality. The new, parading culture saw itself reflected in the gigantic columns of the Nuremberg

Examples of Nazi art. 1. Adolf Ziegler's *The Judgment of Paris*

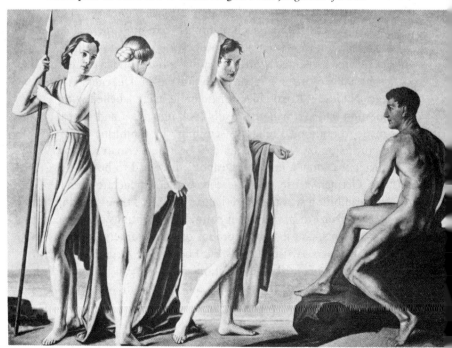

stadium: only one individual, the Führer, was allowed to dominate his environment. But there was no cult of the object for its own sake. When the film director Otto Zielke made *Der Stahltier* ('The Steel Animal') to commemorate the hundredth anniversary of German railways, Goebbels banned the film for its abstract treatment of rails, engines, points, signals and other hard-edged objects of the railway world. Goebbels had wanted an explicit statement of German greatness, not a poem to the beauty of iron and steel.

When details of cultural life under the Third Reich are added together, the evidence of totalitarian control becomes overwhelming. Nazism was constructing an entire culture to match and expound its national and racial ideology. Its art and architecture raised monuments to its own glory and thereby intensified belief in its own truths. Systematic religions have done exactly this, and at periods of dogmatism there have been close religious parallels to the cultural persecution of the Nazis. In its symbols, myths, rituals, education and culture Nazism looks convincingly like a substitute religion.

Italian fascism comes near to this position, but its greater

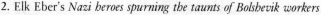

2. Elk Eber's *Nazi heroes spurning the taunts of Bolshevik workers*

cultural tolerance marks a distinct departure from Nazi Germany. Due to Mussolini's sympathy with Italian Futurism there was an initial readiness to tolerate the developments in modern art and literature. It was not a full support, and in the thirties Mussolini attempted to develop a separate Fascist style of art and architecture. The word 'style' figures prominently in Italian Fascist writings and speeches and was applied to every aspect of life, suggesting force, exuberance, discipline, strength and youth. When applied to culture it could undervalue sensitive personal expression like the paintings of Marino Marini, but could applaud strong formal designs like those of the great architect Pier Luigi Nervi, many of whose pioneer concrete constructions were built during the Fascist régime. In the Italian Academy created by Mussolini to develop Fascist culture, a prominent member was Marinetti, the old Futurist leader. Marinetti, once the vitriolic enemy of all art institutions, had become sober and established, but traces of his former dynamic personality remained: in 1937 he attacked the art of Nazi Germany as being merely static and photographic. By comparison, art in Fascist Italy was adventurous, though the number of writers and painters who left the country for political reasons impoverished the cultural scene. There was no 20th-century renaissance under Mussolini, whatever the *Duce* proclaimed, but neither was there aesthetic sterility.

Outside Italy and Germany the Fascist influence on art and literature was too diffuse to allow many conclusions. It would seem that the cult of youthful activism was the aspect of fascism which had most influence, an aspect which Mussolini made central to his Italian doctrine, concluding, 'Thus the Fascist accepts life and loves it . . .' D'Annunzio had made the same affirmation: 'Life is beautiful. It is worthy to be lived magnificently and severely'; and in the literature of French fascism this positive value is reasserted in the writings, for example, of Drieu La Rochelle, before he became suicidal, and of Alphonse de Chateaubriant, who claimed that fascism was a 'revolution inside man'. Fernandez, another Fascist sympathizer and an adherent of Doriot's P.P.F., claimed that he preferred fascism to communism since 'I love trains that are just about to leave'. This excitement for the new and mobile was shared in Britain by Wyndham Lewis, the author and painter, whose ideas

resembled those of the Futurist Marinetti, while approval for the
force and power of European fascism came from the American
poet Ezra Pound. But neither these literary exponents of fascism,
nor isolated individuals elsewhere, point to a distinctively Fascist
culture. One has to return to the two dictatorships, and in
particular to Germany, for such a phenomenon.

If Nazism almost constituted a new religion, one would expect
it to have persecuted the adherents of older religions such as
Judaism and Christianity. In the first case its fanatical anti-
Semitism needs no further comment, and in the second there is
ample evidence of its hostility to both Protestantism and Catholicism as soon as either showed independence of thought. It is true
that Hitler was prepared to punctuate his speeches with Christian
allusions and to appeal when necessary to the providence of God.
There was also a commitment to 'Positive Christianity' in the Nazi
Party programme, while the 1933 Concordat with the Vatican
was a showpiece to impress the Catholic regions of Europe.
Nevertheless, Hitler remained basically contemptuous of what
he called the 'Jewish Christ-creed with its effeminate pity-ethics'
and contrasted it with 'a strong heroic belief of God in Nature,
God in our own people, in our destiny, in our blood'. Those
Protestants and Catholics who could acquiesce in this nationalist
perversion of their belief remained free to practise their religion
under the Nazi régime; but those who restated their Christianity
in terms critical of Nazi race-worship were arrested, tortured and
killed. In terms of figures of those persecuted for their beliefs,
Nazism was a climax of the extreme anti-clericalism which had
been present in Western European history since the collapse of
an all-Christian society.

This anti-clericalism was shared by José Antonio, Jacques
Doriot and many of the Italian Fascists, and even by Degrelle,
who became critical of the Catholic hierarchy when he ceased to
be a fervent Catholic himself. Nazism alone, however, had the
power and conviction to stand as an antithesis to Christian belief
and ethics, though it did so with a shrewd eye to propaganda;
many Christians who supported Nazism were unaware of any
inconsistency in their attitudes. The Catholic politician Franz
von Papen, who negotiated the Concordat in 1933, denounced
Hitler's brutality as immoral, but did not break with Nazism,

and only saw its paganism in retrospect when Hitler was dead and Germany in ruins. He was typical of thousands, both Protestant and Catholic, who approved of the orderly society which Nazism had created, who responded to the quasi-spiritual values of Nazi doctrine and who ignored the fate of those Christians who criticized the régime. Nazism, however fundamental its opposition to Christian theology and ethics, never alienated the entire Christian population as it did the Jewish community. Its policy towards Christians was an ambivalent one of tolerance and persecution, and a total clash between its own beliefs and those of Christianity was avoided.

Any answer to the question 'Was fascism a secular religion?' must take this ambivalence into account. Even in Nazi Germany, where Fascist totalitarianism was most developed, the new culture was not an entire break from the old. In Italy the elements of continuity were still more pronounced, and in other fascisms, although there were seeds of a secular religion, they were denied the opportunity to become an effective system. The cultural historian might therefore conclude that fascism certainly contended for the vacant throne of God, that in Nazism it produced a creed and practice which closely resembled a religion, but that, in general, fascism was too diffuse and divided to give to 20th-century man more than a glimpse of a new faith. The glimpse itself was in many cases a conversion experience, and the devotees of Fascist doctrines rivalled the most fanatical followers of any other religion in their conviction and allegiance. Along with its symbols and rituals fascism had its own saints and martyrs. Whether they or their cult penetrated Western culture to any depth is an open question. They appeared to be rejected in World War II, but there has been no shortage of movements and régimes to preserve their image. Where the values persist, Fascist conviction equal to religious fervour can still be found. The myth of Fascist Man remains.

CHAPTER THIRTEEN

Towards a Definition

In Rome on 27 October 1930, Mussolini declared:

Today I affirm that the idea, doctrine and spirit of fascism are universal. It is Italian in its particular institution but it is universal in spirit; nor could it be otherwise, for spirit is universal by its very nature. It is therefore possible to foresee a Fascist Europe which will model its institutions on Fascist doctrine and practice, a Europe which will solve in the Fascist way the problems of the modern state of the 20th century.[1]

Here is Mussolini the internationalist, proclaiming a universal faith on the eighth anniversary of the march on Rome. But in the same speech Mussolini the nationalist is also on display:

By the year 1950 Italy will be the only country of young people in Europe while the rest of Europe will be wrinkled and decrepit. People will come from over the frontier to see the phenomenon of this blooming spring of the Italian people.[2]

The inconsistency is glaring, but it is found throughout Italian fascism and in most other Fascist movements of Western Europe. It can stand as a final example of all the paradoxes of which fascism was composed and which make an adequate definition elusive. Any definition would need to respect the particular origins, obsessions and ambitions of the national movements and yet hint at the general cultural revolution which so many Fascists envisaged. Fascism could be described as a combination of radical nationalism, revolutionary action, authoritarian rule and

[1] Quoted in G. Seldes, *Sawdust Caesar* (Arthur Barker, 1936), p. 387.
[2] *Ibid.*, p. 386.

aggressive, violent ideals. This would go some way towards a summary, but the limitations of such a definition are all too apparent.

It could be argued that the best way to define fascism is not in a positive but in a negative way, by reference to its opposites, but this too presents difficulties. At one time its opposite was naturally assumed to be communism, since fascism was said to be on the extreme Right of politics and communism on the extreme Left. This appeared self-evident when the traditional semi-circle of political parties was drawn, i.e.:

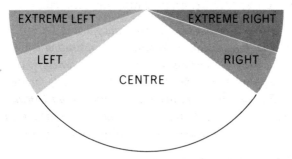

Such a diagram served the political scene of the 19th century when socialism was on the extreme Left and autocratic conservatism on the extreme Right, but in the 20th century a new diagram is needed in the form of a circle, i.e.:

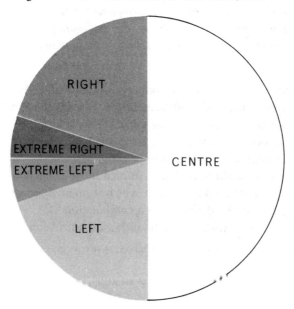

This circular image does greater justice to the realities of 20th-century politics by recognizing that extreme Left and extreme Right, communism and fascism, converge at many points and are in some cases indistinguishable. Doriot, for example, moved with ease from French communism to his Fascist P.P.F. without changing his attitudes or methods, and most of the conclusions on Nazi culture in the last chapter could be applied to Stalinism. The circle, however, does not minimize the differences which kept the two systems apart. Travelling the longest route round the circle, it is a very long way indeed from extreme Left to extreme Right. Thus communism and fascism are as distinct in some respects as they are similar in others.

This was most clearly apparent in the Spanish Civil War. If one looked at methods, the Communists were as violent, as authoritarian and as tightly organized as the Fascists; they were both supported by dictators, Stalin on the one hand and Hitler and Mussolini on the other, and they were both as intolerant of any deviation from the party line. They were next to each other on the circle. But if one looked at their history and their ideology the two had little in common: the Communists stood in the Marxist tradition and aimed at proletarian revolution, while the Fascists had their national values and a vision of an organic society. They were quite distinct.

Fascism therefore will only be partly defined by its opposition to communism. It is perhaps more profitable to look for its political opposites across the circle in the centre, where one finds progressive conservatism, liberalism and radical individualism. It is at least historically true that in the countries where these political attitudes were most entrenched—Britain, France and Belgium—neither fascism nor communism came to power.

A different approach towards a definition lies through the study of personality. Is there a Fascist type of person? Professor Eysenck, the psychologist of behaviour, is one authority who approaches politics in this way. In his book *Sense and Nonsense in Psychology* he gives a number of questions which reveal one's personality in relation to public and political issues such as anti-Semitism, flogging, birth control and nationalization. Out of this test a Fascist type emerges as tough-minded, very aggressive, fairly conservative, fairly rigid and fairly intolerant.

The aggression, in particular, is stressed by Eysenck. Only forty-three Fascists were involved in his survey so the findings are, at best, tentative, but on an aggression rating Fascists frequently scored an average of 24 and 30 as compared with Communists who scored an average of 16, and those with politics of the centre who averaged 11.[1] Research along this line is urgently needed, as Eysenck states: it is crippled with difficulties, since people with extreme views tend to react with hostility to psychological surveys. The value of the approach, however, lies in its conviction that politics is not just a question of economic or social conditioning but also of personality structure. Since the Fascists themselves claimed to produce a 'new man' who would be recognized, above all, by his personality, this approach points in a promising direction.

Finally there is the claim that history needs no definitions: the facts speak for themselves. However unsatisfactory in theory, this claim appears to remove many of the difficulties. To the question 'What was fascism?' the answers crowd on each other in shattering intensity: Mussolini justifying the murder of Matteotti; Degrelle hypnotizing his audience with attacks on Belgian politicians; a British Black Shirt smashing a Jewish shop window in London's East End; a Falangist repaying murder for murder in Madrid; opposition silenced in Germany; Darnand's *Milice* torturing Resisters in Occupied France; smoke rising from the bodies of Jews, slaughtered in a hell which man had devised. These facts certainly speak, but what of the dangers of selectivity? Could other facts be selected to show fascism in a more favourable light? The real difficulties of interpretation and historical understanding remain. The polemicist alone will claim there is no problem: but the polemicist produces no insight into history, only a projection of himself. This lesson, at least, fascism has taught us.

---

[1] H. J. Eysenck, *Sense and Nonsense in Psychology* (Penguin, 1957) p 300.

FURTHER READING

General Histories and Comparisons

E. WEBER: *Varieties of Fascism* (Van Nostrand, 1964)
Succinct and perceptive introduction to all the Fascist
movements of Europe, followed by selected documents.

E. NOLTE: *Three Faces of Fascism* (Weidenfeld and Nicolson, 1965)
A comparative study of *Action française*, Italian fascism and
German Nazism. Full of insight.

Journal of Contemporary History, vol. i, 1965: *International
    Fascism* (Weidenfeld and Nicolson, 1965)
Among the essays are two badly needed ones on Doriot and
José Antonio.

H. ROGGER and E. WEBER (eds.): *The European Right*
    (Weidenfeld and Nicolson, 1965)
Wider than fascism, providing useful perspectives. One of the
very few sources on Léon Degrelle.

S. J. WOOLF (ed.): *European Fascism* also *The Nature of Fascism*
    (both Weidenfeld and Nicolson, 1968)
These two collections of essays and discussions have greatly
advanced the understanding of the various national movements
and the collective phenomenon of fascism.

Special Approaches

P. F. DRUCKER: *The End of Economic Man* (Heinemann, 1939)
An early but remarkably understanding portrayal of Nazism
in terms of its ideological appeal.

E. FROMM: *Fear of Freedom* (Routledge and Kegan Paul, 1942)

Z. BARBU: *Democracy and Dictatorship*
    (Routledge and Kegan Paul, 1956)
Both books contain psychological studies of Nazism in terms
of insecurity. They should be read together since the latter has
some shrewd criticisms of the former.

G. M. GILBERT: *The Psychology of Dictatorship*
    (Ronald Press, New York, 1950)
Intimate accounts of the psychodynamics of Nazi leaders, as
discovered before the Nuremberg Trials.

H. ARENDT: *The Burden of our Time* (Secker and Warburg, 1951)

N. COHN: *Warrant for Genocide* (Eyre and Spottiswoode, 1967)
Arendt makes a bold and imaginative attempt to survey the phenomenon of totalitarianism, with particular interest in anti-Semitism. Cohn reconstructs with brilliance the history of the influential anti-Semitic fraud *The Protocols of the Learned Elders of Zion.*

Italian Fascism

1 Immediate cultural background to the early years of Italian fascism can be found in:

A. RHODES: *The Poet as Superman: D'Annunzio*
(Weidenfeld and Nicolson, 1959)

J. JOLL: *Intellectuals in Politics* (Weidenfeld and Nicolson, 1960)
Contains an essay on Marinetti and Futurism.

2 Basic statements from *Il Duce*:

B. MUSSOLINI: *My Autobiography*, trans. by R. W. Child
(Hurst and Blackett, 1936)

B. MUSSOLINI: *The Political and Social Doctrine of Fascism*
(Hogarth, 1932)

3 General histories and biographies:

C. SETON-WATSON: *Italy from Liberalism to Fascism*
(Methuen, 1967)
Excellent political background.

D. MACK SMITH: *Italy: A Modern History*
(University of Michigan, 1959)
Contains a colourful, biting chapter on the theory and practice of fascism.

I. KIRKPATRICK: *Mussolini: Study of a Demagogue* (Odhams, 1964)

L. FERMI: *Mussolini* (University of Chicago Press, 1961)
Two biographies which complement each other, but neither is definitive.

D. L. GERMINO: *The Italian Fascist Party in Power*
(University of Minnesota Press, 1950)
An analysis with excellent moments, but sadly over-selective.

F. CHABOD: *A History of Italian Fascism*
(Weidenfeld and Nicolson, 1963)

4 Particular studies:

E. WISKEMANN: *The Rome–Berlin Axis* (O.U.P., 1949)
Vital for the foreign policy of both dictators.

F. W. DEAKIN: *The Brutal Friendship: Mussolini, Hitler and the Fall of Italian Fascism* (Weidenfeld and Nicolson, 1962)
Full, scholarly account of the final years; excellent narrative and analysis, with extended documentary quotation.

German Nazism

1 Cultural and political roots:

G. L. MOSSE: *The Crisis of German Ideology* (Weidenfeld and Nicolson, 1966)
A detailed revelation of the continuity of German nationalism, *völkisch* culture and racialism from mid-19th century to Hitler.

F. STERN: *The Politics of Cultural Despair* (University of California Press, 1961)
The theme is the rise of a modern Germanic ideology in politics and culture—an excellent study.

K. VON KLEMPERER: *Germany's New Conservatism* (O.U.P., 1957)
The charismatic ideals of a generation of dynamic thinkers, 1900–30, whose precise influence on Nazism is still controversial.

W. Z. LAQUEUR: *Young Germany: A History of the German Youth Movement* (Routledge and Kegan Paul, 1962)

R. G. L. WAITE: *Vanguard of Nazism. The Free Corps Movement in Postwar Germany 1918–1923* (Harvard U.P., 1952)
Together these create a vivid picture of youthful activism and radical reaction in pre-Nazi Germany.

2 Hitler on Hitler:

A. HITLER: *Mein Kampf* (various translations after 1933)

N. BAYNES (ed.): *The Speeches of Adolf Hitler*, 2 vols. (O.U.P., 1942)

Hitler: Table Talk 1941–1944, trans. by N. Cameron and R. H. Stevens (Weidenfeld and Nicolson, 1953)

H. RAUSCHNING: *Hitler Speaks* (Butterworth, 1939)

3 General histories and biographies:

A. BULLOCK: *Hitler: A Study in Tyranny* (Odhams, 1952)
The first, and still the outstanding, interpretation.

J. JETZINGER: *Hitler's Youth*, trans. by L. Wilson
(Hutchinson, 1958)

H. R. TREVOR-ROPER: *The Last Days of Hitler* (Macmillan, 1947)
A dramatic historical reconstruction.

F. NEUMANN: *Behemoth: The Structure and Practice of National
Socialism* (Gollancz, 1942)

H. RAUSCHNING: *Germany's Revolution of Destruction*, trans. by
E. W. Dickes (Heinemann, 1939)
Two contemporary analyses, both with intermittent insights
of startling clarity.

4 Particular studies:

W. S. ALLEN: *The Nazi Seizure of Power*
(Eyre and Spottiswoode, 1966)
A local study of great importance.

Z. A. B. ZEMAN: *Nazi Propaganda* (O.U.P., 1964)
The growth of mass persuasion, with many fascinating details.

J. WHEELER-BENNETT: *The Nemesis of Power: The German Army
in Politics 1918–45* (Macmillan, 1953)
Compulsive reading, with the plot of 1944 staged as a tragedy.

G. REITLINGER: *The S.S.: Alibi of a Nation* (Heinemann, 1956)
Power, organization and brutality fully exposed.

G. LEWY: *The Catholic Church and Nazi Germany*
(Weidenfeld and Nicolson, 1964)
A well-argued case, though tending towards polemic.

G. L. MOSSE: *Nazi Culture* (W. H. Allen, 1966)
A wide-ranging edition of sources to illustrate all aspects of
life under the Third Reich.

D. SCHOENBAUM: *Hitler's Social Revolution: Class and Status in
Nazi Germany* (Weidenfeld and Nicolson, 1967)

A. SCHWEITZER: *Big Business in the Third Reich*
(Eyre and Spottiswoode, 1964)

B. H. KLEIN: *Germany's Economic Preparation for War*
(Harvard U.P., 1959)
Puts Germany's war economy into perspective.

France

E. NOLTE (see page 243) treats *Action française* as an integral part of 20th-century fascism. For a more cautious approach see the excellent study:
E. WEBER: *Action française* (Stanford U.P., 1962)

There is very little in English on the rise of Doriot and other French Fascists in the inter-war years, though one treatment uses the international situation as a linking theme to compare the various aspects of French right-wing politics:
C. MICAUD: *The French Right and Nazi Germany 1933–1939*
(Duke U.P., 1943)

On the Vichy régime and collaboration see two good histories:
P. FARMER: *Vichy: Political Dilemma* (O.U.P., 1955)
R. ARON: *The Vichy Régime*, trans. by H. Hare (Putnam, 1958)

For a survey of Fascist groups during the war, see the relevant chapters in the very readable history:
A. WERTH: *France 1940–55*
(Holt, Rinehart and Winston, New York, 1956)

Britain

The best way into Mosley and the B.U.F. is through the source work of doctrine:
O. MOSLEY: *The Greater Britain* (B.U.F., London, 1932)

Mosley's autobiography, although necessarily subjective in approach, is well worth reading, both for his account of the political background of the B.U.F. and for his character sketches of the various personalities (Mussolini included) with whom he came in contact during his career:
O. MOSLEY: *My Life* (Nelson, 1968)

Serious studies of the movement are limited to one early journalistic account and a recent history which is colourful and objective:
J. DRENNAN: *B.U.F.: Oswald Mosley and British Fascism*
(Murray, 1934)

C. CROSS: *The Fascists in Britain* (Barrie and Rockliff, 1961)

Spain

R. CARR: *Spain 1808–1939* (O.U.P., 1966)

G. BRENAN: *The Spanish Labyrinth* (Cambridge U.P., 1943)
Both are essential for an understanding of the nature of
Spanish politics before and during the Civil War.

H. THOMAS: *The Spanish Civil War*
(Eyre and Spottiswoode, 1961)
The information contained is impressive and the powerful
evocation of bitterness, dedication and ruthlessness is skilfully
controlled.

S. G. PAYNE: *Falange* (Stanford U.P., 1962)
It follows the fortunes of José Antonio and his movement with
careful, well-documented analysis. A very useful book.

Belgium

For this country reference should be made to the chapter by Jean
Stengers in *The European Right* and to his bibliography which
follows. There is as yet no English history of *Rex*.

APPENDIX—CHRONOLOGICAL BACKGROUND

1914	1–4 Aug.	War breaks out between Germany and Austria-Hungary on the one hand and Russia, France and Britain on the other.
1915	23 May	Italy enters the war against Austria-Hungary.
1917	8–14 Mar.	(Old Style, 23 Feb. to 1 Mar.) Overthrow of the Tsar in the 'February Revolution' in Russia.
	6 Apr.	United States enters war against Germany.
	7 Nov.	(Old Style, 26 Oct.) Bolshevik victory in the 'October Revolution' in Russia.
	5 Dec.	Bolshevik régime makes peace with Germany at Brest-Litovsk.
1918	16 Jul.	Execution of Tsar Nicholas II.
	Jul.–Oct.	Decisive Allied victories against Germany and Austria-Hungary.
	3 Nov.	Armistice signed with Austria-Hungary.
	9 Nov.	Revolution in Berlin. Kaiser Wilhelm II abdicates.
	11 Nov.	Armistice with Germany.
1919	5–11 Jan.	Unsuccessful Communist (Spartacist) revolution in Berlin.
	23 Jan.	Socialist (S.P.D.) victory in German elections.
	Feb.–Mar.	Mussolini forms his *Fasci del Combattimento*.
	22 Jun.	German National Assembly at Weimar unwillingly authorizes signing of Peace Treaty.
	28 Jun.	Peace of Versailles signed.
	31 Jul.	The Weimar republican constitution adopted in Germany.
	12 Sept.	Gabriele d'Annunzio leads Italian volunteers on the port of Fiume.
1920	10 Jan.	The League of Nations comes into being.
	26–9 Jul.	Hitler becomes leader of the German National Socialist Workers' Party.
1921	Feb.–Mar.	Widespread clashes between Communists and Fascists in Italy.
	14 May	Twenty-nine Fascists returned in Italian general election.
1922	16 Apr.	Germany and Russia re-open diplomatic and trade relations in the Treaty of Rapallo.
	24 Jun.	Walter Rathenau, German Foreign Minister, murdered by young German Nationalists.
	Aug.	Intensive clashes between Italian Fascists and left-wing parties.
	28 Oct.	Mussolini's 'march on Rome'.

	30 Oct.	Mussolini forms a Fascist government.
1923	11 Jan.	German failure to pay the reparations demanded by the Treaty of Versailles leads to coercive measures by French and Belgian troops, who occupy the Ruhr.
	19 Jan.	German government counters by proclaiming passive resistance. German economy slumps.
	Aug.	Widespread strikes and riots in Germany as the value of the mark collapses.
	14 Sept.	Miguel Primo de Rivera becomes dictator of Spain.
	26 Sept.	Germany abandons passive resistance.
	Oct.	Value of German mark falls to 10,000 million to the pound sterling.
	8–9 Nov.	Hitler's unsuccessful *Putsch* at Munich.
1924	21 Jan.	Lenin dies.
	9 Mar.	Mussolini's government annexes Fiume.
	1 Apr.	Hitler sentenced to five years' imprisonment (*but released on 20 Dec.*).
	Jun.	Murder of Italian opposition deputy, Giacomo Matteotti.
	16 Aug.	The Dawes Plan lays down quantity of reparations to be paid by Germany, but no time limit given.
	18 Aug.	French troops begin withdrawal from the Ruhr.
1925	3 Jan.	Mussolini assumes personal responsibility for murder of Matteotti and commits fascism to political dictatorship.
	25 Apr.	Paul von Hindenburg elected President of Germany.
	5–16 Oct.	Locarno Conference guarantees frontiers of Western Europe.
1926	3–12 May	General Strike in Britain.
1928	27 Apr.	Oliveira Salazar becomes Minister of Finance in Portugal, and assumes wide emergency powers.
	27 Aug.	Kellogg–Briand Pact outlawing war signed in Paris by sixty-five nations.
1929	6 Feb.	Germany accepts Kellogg–Briand Pact.
	11 Feb.	Lateran Treaty between Mussolini and the Pope ends long Church–State feud in Italy and sets up independent Vatican State.
	7 Jun.	The Young Plan lays down annual German reparations to be paid until 1988.
	6 Aug.	German government accepts Young Plan, and occupying Allied forces agree to leave the Rhineland by 30 June 1930.
	31 Oct.	Beginning of Great Depression. United States suspends loans to Europe following financial crash on Wall Street stock exchange.

	22 Dec.	Referendum in Germany upholds the Young Plan despite intensive opposition from Nazis and Nationalists.
1930	28 Jan.	Primo de Rivera's dictatorship ends in Spain.
	17 Jun.	American government signs the Smoot–Hawley high tariff act which begins European tariff war.
	14 Sept.	In response to worsening economic situation, Nazis win 107 seats and Communists 77 in German elections.
1931	Feb.	Sir Oswald Mosley leaves the British Labour Party and founds the New Party.
	14 Apr.	After Spanish Republican rising, King Alfonso escapes from Spain.
	11 May	Bankruptcy of Credit-Anstalt Bank in Austria points to economic collapse in Central Europe.
	Jun.	Papal encyclical *Non abbiamo bisogno* denounces Mussolini's interference with Catholic freedom.
	Jul.–Aug.	Closure and bankruptcy of German banks.
	25 Aug.	MacDonald forms a National government in Britain to deal with the economic crisis.
	18 Sept.	Japan invades Northern China (Manchuria).
	11 Oct.	Hitler forms alliance with Nationalist leader Hugenberg.
1932	7 Jan.	German government declares its inability to resume reparation payments.
	13 Mar.	In German Presidential elections Hindenburg gains 18 million and Hitler 11 million votes (Thälmann, Communist, 5 million). Insufficient majority.
	10 Apr.	In second vote Hindenburg re-elected President by 19 million votes against Hitler's 13 million (Communist, 3 million).
	5 Jul.	Salazar elected Premier of Portugal.
	31 Jul.	In German Reichstag elections Nazis become largest party with 230 seats.
	?	Sir Oswald Mosley founds British Union of Fascists (*exact date not known*).
1933	Jan.	Strikes and riots in Spain by anarchists and syndicalists.
	30 Jan.	Hitler appointed Chancellor of Germany.
	27 Feb.	Reichstag Fire used by Nazis as an excuse to suspend civil liberties.
	23 Mar.	The Reichstag passes an Enabling Act to allow Hitler to rule by dictatorial powers.
	1 Apr.	Anti-Semitic campaign opens in Germany with national boycott of Jewish businesses.
	2 May	Suppression of German Trade Unions.

14 Jul.	All political parties, except Nazis, suppressed in Germany.
20 Jul.	Hitler makes a Concordat with the Papacy announcing freedom of Catholic organizations in Germany.
?	José Antonio Primo de Rivera forms the Fascist *Falange* (*exact date not known*).

1934	6 Feb.	Right-wing riots in Paris suggest a Fascist threat to the Republic.
	12–13 Feb.	French workers reply by a general strike.
	30 Jun.	Hitler liquidates S.A. leaders and other rivals in the Röhm Purge.
	25 Jul.	Austrian Premier, Dollfuss, murdered in unsuccessful Nazi *coup*. Mussolini supports Austrian independence.
	2 Aug.	Paul von Hindenburg dies.
	19 Aug.	Hitler approved by German plebiscite as Führer of Germany.
	Dec.	Stalin begins his purge of old rivals.

1935	13 Jan.	The Saar, under international authority since end of World War I, votes to be re-incorporated into Germany.
	16 Mar.	Hitler repudiates disarmament clauses of Versailles.
	11–14 Apr.	Britain, France and Italy agree at Stresa to a common front to retain Germany and maintain Austrian independence.
	18 Jun.	Britain appears to undermine Stresa agreement by a naval agreement with Germany.
	27 Jun.	A peace ballot in Britain shows strong support for the ideals of collective security.
	15 Sept.	The Nuremberg Laws legalize persecution of German Jews.
	2 Oct.	Italy invades Abyssinia.
	19 Oct.	League of Nations imposes sanctions on Mussolini.
	9 Dec.	Public outcry against the Hoare–Laval Pact which favoured Italy in a settlement of the Abyssinian question. Both Foreign Ministers later resign.

1936	16 Feb.	In Spanish elections the left-wing Popular Front wins a majority over Centre and Right.
	7 Mar.	Germany occupies the demilitarized area of the Rhineland.
	3 May	In French elections the left-wing Popular Front wins a majority over all other parties.
	9 May	Italy formally annexes Abyssinia.
	24 May	The Fascist Party *Rex* led by Léon Degrelle wins twenty-one seats in Belgian elections.
	Jun.	The French Popular Front government under Léon Blum dissolves the Fascist leagues.

	11 Jul.	Austro–German convention acknowledges Austria's independence.
	18 Jul.	Spanish Civil War begins with army revolt against the Republic.
	9 Sept.	London conference on non-intervention in Spain.
	1 Oct.	General Franco becomes leader of the Spanish insurgents.
	1 Nov.	Rome–Berlin axis announced by Hitler and Mussolini.
	18 Nov.	Germany and Italy recognize General Franco as head of Spain.
	20 Nov.	José Antonio Primo de Rivera shot by the Spanish Republican government.
	10 Dec.	Edward VIII abdicates in Britain after constitutional crisis.
	?	Jacques Doriot forms the *Parti Populaire Français*, which becomes the leading French Fascist movement (*exact date not known*).

1937	14 Mar.	Papal encyclical *Mit Brennender Sorge* denounces German persecution of Catholics and the worship of State and race.
	18 Mar.	Papal encyclical *Divini Redemptoris* denounces atheistic communism.
	27 Apr.	Spanish town of Guernica destroyed by German and Nationalist aircraft.
	28 May	Neville Chamberlain becomes Prime Minister of Britain.
	23 Jun.	Germany and Italy withdraw from the non-intervention committee on Spain.
	13 Oct.	Germany guarantees the inviolability of Belgium.
	6 Nov.	Italy, Germany and Japan form a front against communism (Anti-Comintern Pact).
	Nov.	Continued unrest among Germans in the Sudeten area of Czechoslovakia threatens Central European peace.
	11 Dec.	Italy withdraws from the League in protest at its sanctions policy over Abyssinia.

1938	11 Mar.	German troops enter Austria after Mussolini has agreed not to interfere.
	13 Mar.	Austria declared part of the German Reich.
	16 Apr.	Britain recognizes Italian sovereignty over Abyssinia.
	23 Apr.	Sudeten Germans demand full autonomy.
	15 Sept. 27 Sept.	Neville Chamberlain flies to meet Hitler over the Sudeten problem.
	29 Sept.	The Munich Conference transfers the Sudetenland to Germany. The remaining Czech frontiers are guaranteed.
	1–10 Oct.	German troops occupy the Sudetenland.

| | 10 Nov. | Anti-Semitic legislation introduced into Italy. |
| | Dec. | Franco begins final offensive in Catalonia. |

1939	26 Jan.	Franco, aided by Italians, takes Barcelona.
	27 Feb.	Britain and France recognize Franco's government.
	15 Mar.	Hitler breaks the Munich Agreement by invading the rest of Czechoslovakia and occupying Prague.
	28 Mar.	Madrid surrenders to Franco. Spanish Civil War ends.
	31 Mar.	Britain and France make secret pledge to support Poland in the event of German aggression.
	22 May	Hitler and Mussolini agree to a ten-year political and military alliance ('Pact of Steel').
	23 Aug.	Russia signs a non-aggression treaty with Germany (Nazi–Soviet Pact).
	26–31 Aug.	Attempts by Britain and France to secure agreement with Hitler over Danzig and Poland fail.
	1 Sept.	Germany invades Poland.
	3 Sept.	Britain and France declare war on Germany.
	17 Sept.	Russia invades Poland from the east.
	28 Sept.	Germans reach Warsaw.
	30 Nov.	Russia invades Finland.

1940	9 Apr.	Germany invades Norway and Denmark.
	7 May	Neville Chamberlain resigns: Churchill forms a coalition government.
	10 May	Germany invades Holland, Luxembourg and Belgium.
	14 May	German army breaks through the French defences.
	28 May	Belgium capitulates.
	29 May	British forces retreat to Dunkirk and are evacuated (by 3 Jun.).
	10 Jun.	Italy declares war on France and Britain.
	14 Jun.	Germans enter Paris.
	15 Jun.	United States refuses France's appeal for aid.
	16 Jun.	Marshal Pétain becomes head of the French government with responsibility to make peace with Germans.
	18 Jun.	General Charles de Gaulle broadcasts an appeal from London to all Frenchmen to continue the war.
	22 Jun.	France signs an armistice with Germany by which France is divided into an occupied and an unoccupied (Vichy) zone.
	3 Jul.	British navy sinks part of the French fleet to prevent its falling into German hands.
	5 Jul.	Vichy government breaks off relations with Britain.
	Aug. and Sept.	Battle of Britain fought in the air over south-east England. German invasion plans thwarted.
	Oct.	Mussolini attacks Greece.

	Dec.	British Eighth Army opens offensive in North Africa against Italians.

1941	31 Mar.	German counter-offensive opens in North Africa.
	Apr.	Germany invades Yugoslavia and Greece.
	22 Jun.	Germany invades Russia. Communists throughout Europe join underground resistance against German occupying forces.
	3 Sept.	Germans advance to outskirts of Leningrad.
	25 Oct.	First German offensive against Moscow repulsed.
	7 Dec.	Japan bombs Pearl Harbour, Hawaii and British Malaya.
	8 Dec.	Britain and the United States declare war against Japan.
	11 Dec.	United States declares war on Germany and Italy.

1942	1 Feb.	Vidkun Quisling becomes Premier of Norway in a puppet government under Nazi control. Subsequent puppet régimes elsewhere known as 'Quisling governments'.
	15 Feb.	Singapore surrenders to Japanese, who then advance into Burma and threaten India.
	31 May	S.S. leader Heydrich assassinated by Czech patriots, provoking fierce reprisals.
	13 Sept.	Full German attack on Stalingrad opens.
	Nov.	German commander Rommel defeated by the Allies in North Africa.
	Nov.	Germans occupy the whole of France. Vichy government under Pétain and Laval remains as puppet régime.
	Nov.	Russians launch counter-attack on the German army at Stalingrad (*German army defeated Jan. 1943*).

1943	Feb.–May	Heavy R.A.F. raids on Berlin and other German cities.
	20 Apr.	S.S. troops massacre Polish Jews in the Warsaw Ghetto.
	12 May	German army in Tunisia surrenders.
	4 Jun.	French Committee of National Liberation formed in Algiers, first under Generals Giraud and de Gaulle, later under de Gaulle alone.
	10 Jul.	Allies land in Sicily.
	26 Jul.	Mussolini falls from power by vote in Fascist Grand Council.
	3 Sept.	Allies cross to the Italian mainland.
	13 Oct.	New Italian government under Marshal Badoglio transfers Italy's support from Germany to the Allies.

	28 Nov.	Churchill, Stalin and Roosevelt meet at Teheran to discuss the overthrow of Germany.
1944	21 May	Allies break through German lines in Italy.
	4 Jun.	Allies enter Rome.
	6 Jun.	D-Day landings in Normandy, preceded by heavy bombing of the Normandy coast.
	13 Jun.	First German flying bomb drops on London.
	20 Jul.	The army plot to assassinate Hitler fails. Savage retaliation by Hitler.
	1 Aug.	Warsaw rising against Germans begins as Russians advance into Poland.
	15 Aug.	British land in Southern France.
	Aug.	Liberation of Paris by Parisians in advance of Allied troops.
	25 Aug.	De Gaulle enters Paris in triumph.
	29 Sept.	Russians invade Yugoslavia, driving the Germans back.
	Oct.	Russians advance into Hungary.
	16 Dec.	Last German offensive on the Western front begins ('Battle of the Bulge').
1945	4–11 Feb.	Churchill, Stalin and Roosevelt confer at Yalta to plan details of Germany's surrender.
	15 Feb.	Allied troops reach the Rhine.
	20 Apr.	Russians reach Berlin.
	28 Apr.	Mussolini captured and killed by Italian partisans.
	30 Apr.	Hitler kills himself and Eva Braun in the Berlin bunker.
	2 May	Berlin surrenders to the Russians.
	7 May	General Jodl makes final unconditional surrender of Germany.
	5 Jun.	Allied Control Council divides Germany into four occupied zones: British, American, Russian and French.
	17 Jul.	Opening of conference at Potsdam to settle the occupation and future of Germany (*ended 2 Aug.*).
	6 Aug. ⎱ 9 Aug. ⎰	United States drops atomic bombs on Hiroshima and Nagasaki in Japan.
	14 Aug.	Japan surrenders. End of World War II.
	20 Nov.	Trial of Nazi war criminals opens at Nuremberg.

INDEX

Italic figures refer to illustrations